11 Nov'ε

The United States and Latin America

The American Assembly
Columbia University
December 1959

Final Edition

Background papers
and the Final Report
of the Sixteenth
American Assembly,
Arden House,
Harriman Campus of
Columbia University,
Harriman, New York
October 15-18, 1959

Preface

The essays in this book were designed and written under the editorial supervision of Herbert L. Matthews not only to provide background for the participants in the Sixteenth American Assembly at Arden House, October 15-18, 1959, but also to aid discussion of United States relations with Latin America at subsequent regional, state and municipal Assembly sessions and to help inform the general reader.

The aim is a clear presentation of both facts and ideas to increase public understanding of Latin America. The Assembly as a non-partisan, educational institution itself neither endorses nor takes any stand on views advanced in this volume; and among the individual authors there is not necessarily unanimity of opinion.

The conclusions and recommendations for national policy, presented in the Final Report of the Sixteenth American Assembly beginning on p. 209, are the results of the independent deliberations at Arden House.

The entire Sixteenth American Assembly program is supported by a grant from the Ford Foundation for which I express warm gratitude on behalf of the Assembly Trustees.

THE AMERICAN ASSEMBLY
Henry M. Wriston
President

Contents

Introduction:

Understanding Latin America   1
Herbert L. Matthews, *Editor*

1. Toward an appreciation of Latin America   5
Frank Tannenbaum

LAND AND PEOPLE   9

THE LIMITS OF THE CONQUEST   15

RELIGION   24

THE HACIENDA   29

EDUCATION   38

LEADERSHIP   45

2. Political change in Latin America   59
K. H. Silvert

POLITICAL LIKENESSES AND DIVERSITIES   61

POLITICAL VALUES AND TYPES OF POLITIES   63

THE USES OF FORCE   68

PARTIES AND PRESSURE GROUPS   72

SOME INTERNATIONAL ECHOES OF INTERNAL POLITICS   79

3. The role of the press and communications   81
Edward W. Barrett and Penn T. Kimball

WHY PROPER COVERAGE MEANS SO MUCH   83

AMERICAN KNOWLEDGE OF LATIN AMERICA   87

OBSTACLES TO BETTER COVERAGE   93

A SPOT CHECK OF LATIN AMERICAN NEWS   98

NOTEWORTHY EFFORTS TO IMPROVE COVERAGE   103

CONCLUSIONS   111

4. The economic picture   115
Reynold E. Carlson

INTRODUCTION   115

DIVERSITIES AND GROWTH RATES   117

LATIN AMERICAN TRADE AND THE UNITED STATES   123

INFLATION   126

THE ROLE OF FOREIGN CAPITAL   130

OFFICIAL CAPITAL   134

5. Diplomatic relations   143
Herbert L. Matthews

THE MONROE DOCTRINE   144

THE ERA OF IMPERIALISM   147

IMPERIALISM FADES AWAY   152

THE DOCTRINE OF NONINTERVENTION   154

PAN-AMERICANISM AND THE UNITED STATES   157

THE COLD WAR IN THE HEMISPHERE   161

ECONOMIC POLICIES   168

THE MEANING OF THE NIXON TRIP   175

PRESENT AND FUTURE   185

A note on recognition policy:

Latin American governments and the United States   195
Charles G. Fenwick

Final report of the Sixteenth American Assembly   209

Participants in the Sixteenth American Assembly   215

The American Assembly   219

OUTLINE MAP
OF THE
AMERICANS

Seattle

C A N A D A

Statute Miles
0

U N I T E D

Ottawa

Chicago

s Angeles

S T A T E S

New York

Washington

N o r t h

A t l a n t i c

O c e a n

BERMUDA

Gulf of
Mexico

MEXICO

Mexico City

Havana

BAHAMAS

CUBA

HAITI

DOMINICAN REPUBLIC

BR.
HOND.

Belize

Port-au-Prince

PUERTO RICO

HONDURAS

JAMAICA

San
Juan

Ciudad
Trujillo

GUATEMALA

Tegucigalpa

WEST
INDIES

Guatemala

Caribbean Sea

San Salvador

NICARAGUA

EL SALVADOR

Managua

Caracas

San José

Panama

BR. GUIANA

Georgetown

COSTA RICA

VENEZUELA

SURINAM

Paramaribo

PANAMA

FR. GUIANA

Cayenne

Bogota

COLOMBIA

EQUATOR

EQUATOR

GALAPAGOS IS.

Quito

ECUADOR

Belém

PERU

B R A Z I L

S o u t h

Lima

P a c i f i c

La Paz

BOLIVIA

Brasilia
o(Future capital)

PARAGUAY

Rio de Janei

O c e a n

Antofagasta

Asuncion

S o u t h

A
R
G
E
N
T
I
N
A

URUGUAY

Santiago

Montevideo

A t l a n t

CHILE

Buenos
Aires

O c e a n

FALKLAND
ISLANDS

Introduction:

Understanding Latin America

HERBERT L. MATTHEWS   *Editor*

No excuses are necessary for making a study of United States relations with Latin America. The importance of the region to us is only equalled, except for specialists, by our ignorance of it. It has been Latin America which impinged on our consciousness by such events as the Nixon trip, the revolutions in Venezuela and Cuba, and the unrest in the Caribbean.

Here is a world at our doorstep on which, to a considerable degree, we depend for our existence as a world power. If we were deprived of the raw materials of the area or its markets, our economy and security would be gravely—perhaps vitally—affected. It is an area where no hostile power can be allowed to gain a foothold for, strategically, this is our "soft underbelly." We cannot win the cold war in Latin America, but we can lose it there. Neutralism or an intense Yankeephobia could hurt us badly. A day will come when the Russians will make their bid for Latin America.

In terms of United States trade and investment, Canada and Latin America outweigh the whole rest of the world put together. Yet our foreign policy interests, expressed in the cold war, are directed far more to Europe

HERBERT L. MATTHEWS has been on the Editorial Board of *The New York Times* since 1949. Before that he was war correspondent and foreign correspondent in Europe, Africa and Asia for *The Times* for nineteen years. In the last ten years Mr. Matthews has specialized in Latin American affairs for *The Times* as editor and on occasion as correspondent. He won the Maria Moors Cabot Award in 1956. He is the author of the following books: *Eyewitness in Abyssinia, Two Wars and More to Come, The Fruits of Fascism, The Education of a Correspondent, Assignment to Austerity* (co-author with Mrs. Matthews), and *The Yoke and the Arrows.*

and Asia. So we see the paradox of a financial and economic axis running north and south, and a political and military axis running east and west.

The case of Cuba provides the best possible evidence of the job of education that must be done. Cuba is not Iceland. It is an island just off our coast with which we have been linked geographically, historically, economically and through personal contacts since the beginnings of our nation. Yet when on January 1, 1959, the dictatorship of General Fulgencio Batista was overthrown, when Fidel Castro triumphed, when in succeeding months he and his young followers set in motion the drastic social revolution for which they fought, North Americans were astonished.

The great majority of our spokesmen in the mass communication media, upon which the American public depends for information, did not know what happened or why it happened and could not interpret the event except in terms of the cold war and our emotions and attitudes toward communism. In the business world and in some branches of the United States government and armed services, the reaction of the Cuban revolution showed a similar lack of understanding. The legitimate bases for dismay and protest were weakened by misconceptions and wrong information. Such criticism had a destructive effect on Cuban-United States relations and only served to strengthen the Castro regime internally and to make the revolution more drastic.

The question of whether one approved or disapproved of the Cuban revolution is not the issue. Everyone is entitled to an opinion of this highly controversial event. What is being argued here is that the Cuban revolution presented the United States with one of the most critical and delicate diplomatic problems of modern times in the Latin American field. It is an issue which is going to affect our hemispheric policies profoundly, and probably for years to come. It must be worked out on a basis of knowledge, understanding and—one hopes—sympathy for the aspirations behind it.

These factors have generally been lacking, and, most of all, knowledge. In different but less acute ways, because the problems are not so immediate or provocative, the whole Latin American scene has suffered from a North American failure to know and to understand.

Cuba is just one example. Americans would be no better able to explain the Bolivian revolution or even, in many cases, to say where Bolivia is on the map. The experiences of Vice President Richard M. Nixon on his trip to South America in April and May, 1958, came as a tremendous shock to American opinion, which thereupon was urged to comfort itself by blaming everything on the Communists.

There is no need to belabor these points. An awareness has grown among us in these last few years that we have neglected or know little or nothing of an area of the world which is of supreme importance to us. The revolutions, the decline of the military dictators, the tidal wave of political changes of a democratic nature, the insistent demands for social justice, the efforts to industrialize and raise standards of living, the population explosion—these and other powerful forces are in motion. We must expect political instability, social ferment and extreme sensitivity. We must try to understand.

This will not be easy. A group of papers and a series of Assemblies are not going to provide all the knowledge and understanding we require. Latin America is a region of twenty countries as different from each other as France, Italy and Spain, and at different stages of political, economic and social progress.

Yet there is such a thing as "Latin America." It has its common denominators. The aim of these papers is simply to bring them out, to provide a basis for understanding so that the problems of United States relations with Latin America can be tackled with intelligence and realism.

It is hoped that in the end the reader will have some idea of what Latin America is like—its physical make-up, its people and their ways of life, its political movements, its economy. Because of the prevailing lack of knowledge of the area in the United States, a pioneer study of the handling of Latin American news by United States newspapers has been made. There is also an account and discussion of our diplomatic relations with Latin America which is necessarily controversial and provocative, for it is a field where interpretation and opinions are open to dispute. Finally, because of the special role that the recognition of new governments has played in Latin American relations, there is a study of this subject by a noted authority.

The attempt—perhaps overly ambitious—is to give a comprehensive picture in miniature of Latin America as seen from the United States. It cannot, of course, be really complete and the points of view cannot be those of all United States students of Latin American affairs. In a work of this sort one seeks to bring out what is important. These papers are an invitation to discussion as well as a contribution to knowledge.

The relations between the United States and Latin America are, naturally, a continuing process. The past has shaped the present, and we, today, are shaping the future. We can do so with more hope if we have some degree of knowledge and understanding. These truisms contain the simple concepts that lie behind the series of papers here offered for discussion at the Sixteenth American Assembly and elsewhere.

3

1. Toward an appreciation of Latin America

FRANK TANNENBAUM

Don Federico de Onís, for so many years the leading influence in Hispanic studies in the United States, likes to say that he can always recognize an American in Paris but cannot tell whether he comes from New York or Buenos Aires, from Chicago or Caracas. There is something about his bearing—the way he holds his head, his swinging arms and long strides, the innocence and optimism reflected in every gesture—which marks him as a child of the New World. This is one way of saying that Americans, North and South, are in some measure interchangeable, that their history has moulded them in a similar if not identical crucible. For the familiar list of differences between the United States and Latin America is only partially true and denies the imprint of their experience on this side of the Atlantic. The conquest and settlement of America have moulded a recognizable folk. Four centuries of a common heritage have given all of us

FRANK TANNENBAUM, Professor of Latin American History at Columbia University, has over the years worked and lectured in Latin America and by one means or another (on mule or afoot, for example) has traveled the entire region. Dr. Tannenbaum has been a newspaper correspondent in Mexico, and member of Latin American or North American governmental or private commissions, survey teams, and associations. For years the Seminar on Latin American Affairs which he conducts has attracted many of the distinguished people of Latin America. He has written numerous books and articles on various phases of life in that area.

"something" recognizable as American rather than European. It is discernible in our prose and poetry, in our politics, in our attitude toward the outside world, in our popular heroes, folk tales, the stories we tell our children and in the moral issues that trouble the grown-up.

That "something" comes from the universal American experience with the Indian, the Negro, the open spaces and wide horizons, the peculiar use of the horse (the cowboy, the *gaucho,* the *llanero,* the *charro* are brothers under the skin); the American experience with ranching—driving cattle a thousand miles as is still done in Brazil, for instance. Among all of our people there persists the tradition of a culture uprooted in the old world and replanted in the new: the mixture of races from many parts of the globe, the continuing flow of immigrants and their rapid conversion into something different from what they were, the evidence of social and physical mobility, the pride and self-cofidence born of a world easily moulded. It derives from the common American belief in progress, from the notion that government belongs to the people, that it is a human and malleable instrument that yields to pressure and is open to change by political "revolt" at the ballot-box or by a "revolution," from the rebellions by which all of the nations in this hemisphere achieved their independence, from the fact that all of our great national heroes are "rebels" against a king in the Old World. Our Americanism is evidenced by a belief in democracy even in areas where the *caudillo* and the political "boss" are continuing and sometimes sinister figures; it is evidenced by the fact that most of our political upheavals have been in the name of democracy.

These many influences that we have all shared in their different degrees and varying forms have given the people on this side of the Atlantic a view of the world and a sense of meaning about the ways of man with nature and his fellows, a psychological and spiritual heritage deeper than the obvious differences that separate them. It extends even to our sense of isolation from the rest of the world, the feeling of separation from Europe and Asia. It is no accident that an inter-American system, now the oldest international organization, has survived for over half a century.

All these identities deeply based in our common history have given us our cultural similarities and a large measure of what the anthropologist would call a "similar character structure." But the differences are also marked and frequently commented upon. Despite our common origin in Europe, the conquerors and settlers in Central and South America have had a different history from those of the United States. They have had a harder route to travel from the day they established their first colony to their present position of sovereign nations.

For one thing, the West Indies, Central and South America have proved less propitious to human habitation than the United States. Taken as a whole, Latin America is more isolated from the rest of the world, more tropical, more mountainous and has proportionately less good farming land. South America, more than twice the size of the United States with Alaska thrown in, faces Africa rather than Europe and lies at a greater distance from China, India, the Middle East and Europe than does the United States. Until the opening of the Panama Canal, a ship would have to go around Cape Horn to reach the ports of Valparaiso in Chile or Callao in Peru. And until the airplane became an easy means of travel, business men and diplomats going from Lima, Quito or Bogotá to Europe would travel via New York. Through the centuries, South America and Central America as well lay outside the normal trade routes, and it is still almost impossible to go from Panama to the East Coast of South America by ship.

South America stretches 4,500 miles in length and about 3,000 miles in width. The west coast is blocked off from the rest of the continent by a mountain range that, paralleling the ocean, runs without a break from Venezuela to the very tip of Chile, or the entire 4,500 miles. This mountain chain is like a wall between three and four miles in height.

The passes are few; except for the extreme south they are high, most of them 14,000 or over. A pass in the Andes is a narrow winding rift in the edging along some mountain stream rushing down from the heights. The mule trail, railroad and more recent automobile road must all crowd the same steep, narrow and circuitous slit, eroded through the centuries, and compete for a footing against the towering ledge. It is worth emphasizing this point—and anyone who has gone by automobile from Lima to Cerro de Pasco or Tingo María will appreciate its significance. These are not trade routes for extensive and heavy traffic; they are skilled and ingenious engineering performances. They are not, except in a limited sense, means of communication between the west coast of South America and the other side of the mountains; they are certainly not commercial routes between the Pacific and the Atlantic—and are not likely to be.

In the Andes themselves, human life tends to be grouped in large and small pockets, valleys tucked away somewhere betwen 8,000 and 14,000 feet above sea level and overhung by surrounding peaks. This is the case of Quito, Bogotá, La Paz, Cuzco, and even the less high Caracas, which lies a stone's throw from the coast. These are some of the larger cities. And this is the case with the smaller towns and villages in the Andes. They are each separately a little isolated pocket where men have congregated because there is shelter and warmth provided by the surrounding mountains, and moisture enough to nourish animal and plant life. On the whole, the Andes have insufficient rain, and in many places agriculture depends upon irrigation.

On the other side of the Andes going from the Pacific, once across the divide one looks down into the Amazonian basin many thousands of feet below and runs into unceasing rain. This rain forest, *la montaña* as it is called, stretches along the Amazonian headwater from Colombia to Boli-

7

via. The slope of the mountain is practically uninhabited. Closer to the river where the land flattens out and the rains abate, sparsely settled Indian communities are to be found. Farther south along the Eastern Andes in Santa Cruz de la Sierra, and still farther in the Pilcomayo River basin, rain conditions change materially and groupings of human beings are more frequent.

East of *la montaña* and below it is the Amazonian basin, estimated at 2,000,000 square miles, about as large as the United States. The hamlet of Napo in Ecuador, some 2,600 miles from the Atlantic, stands only 1,600 feet above sea level, and Manaus, 1,000 miles from the mouth of the Amazon, is only 100 feet above sea level. The river falls at about one-eighth of an inch per mile for the last 500 miles of its course to the sea. The river itself is longer than the distance between New York and Liverpool and at least one of its great tributaries, the Mamoré-Madeira, is about 3,000 miles in length, and six others are over 1,000 miles. Here is a vast river system, with an estimated 30,000 to 40,000 miles of navigable waters, that lies but little above sea level and is subject to rains so heavy and floods of such frequency that the organic matter in the soil has been bleached away. Agriculturally it is not a productive area.

It might be added that South America has in addition three other river systems, which, if not as great as the Amazon, are formidable by any standards: the Rio de la Plata that empties into the Atlantic at Buenos Aires, the Orinoco that divides Venezuela in two, and the Rio Magdalena, for centuries the main route from the coast to Bogotá.

As we reach the east coast of South America we find a steep mountain range rising 10,000 feet, with an average height of about 4,000 feet. This escarpment is close to the sea and runs for some 1,700 miles from north to south, almost the entire length of Brazil. Between the Andes on the West, the Brazilian range on the East and the Amazonian rivers and forest on the North, the interior of South America is difficult to penetrate, to cross, or to abide in. The Amazonian forests, stretching endlessly along the rivers and covering the Western mountains, are more difficult to traverse than the Sahara Desert. Only the rivers give access to the interior and so far they have not induced extensive internal settlement.

In southern Brazil we enter a temperate climate, and as we reach Argentina we are in treeless pampa, flat, rich in good soils, with adequate rains and an almost ideal climate. These good lands, however, are comparatively limited, become drier as one goes West and South, and long before one reaches the foothills of the Andes have to be irrigated for agriculture. The continent narrows sharply below the province of Buenos Aires, and Patagonia has to date, like the Amazon basin, remained for most of mankind an unknown world. One need but add as a generalization that if we take the Equatorial zone as 60 degrees—30 degrees north and 30 south—then most of South America is in the Equatorial Zone and

8

most of North America is out of it. South America is like Africa, North America like Europe. Only about 8 per cent of Europe has a mean annual temperature of between 60° and 70° Fahrenheit while 66 per cent of South America has over 70° and 20 per cent over 80° Fahrenheit. The high temperature is compounded by the heavy rains. The Amazonian basin and Central Brazil have between 70 and 80 inches of rain a year. The La Plata area has adequate rain and temperatures that fall below 70°. Southern Chile is rainy and cool, and the coast between Panama and Ecuador is hot, humid and wet, having one of the heaviest annual rainfalls on the globe. Mexico and Central America, like South America, are relatively cool in the mountains, with ideal temperatures but hot and wet on the coast except for northwestern Mexico, which is more like California and Arizona.

Land and people

This rather long description of South America seems essential if one is to understand the political, economic and social conditions in Latin America. What this teaches is that Latin America is isolated from the world and isolated internally. Before the airplane it was easier to go to the United States from Lima or Rio de Janeiro than to go overland from the capital of Peru to the capital of Brazil. The interior of South America is empty. Whatever the figure means, it is asserted that in the Amazonian basin— an area of 2,000,000 square miles—there is about one person or less per square mile and most of these live in the scattered small towns. In fact one half of the continent has only one person per square mile. The vast majority of the 130,000,000 people in South America live within 200 miles of the coast. All of the really big cities lie at the edge of the Pacific or Atlantic Oceans—Montevideo, Buenos Aires, São Paulo, Rio de Janeiro, Caracas, Lima, Callao, Guayaquil, Valparaiso and Santiago. Bogotá, Quito and La Paz, though away from the coast, are relatively speaking coastal cities. The great urban centers face out toward the sea and not toward the interior. There is no St. Louis, Chicago, Minneapolis, Denver and Salt Lake City in the center of South America. In all of the Amazonian basin there is only Belem with 230,000; Manaus, 1,000 miles up the River, with 100,000 people; and another 1,000 miles farther up and serving as the commercial center for the upper Amazon is Iquitos, with about 42,000.

Latin America as a whole has a population of about 185,000,000 people scattered over 7,769,247 square miles, with about 23 persons per square mile as against 57 in the United States. Significantly, only 4 per cent of the area of South America is in tillage or under tree crops as against 24 per cent in the United States. Nearly 50 per cent of Latin

9

American lands are in forest; nearly 30 per cent are unused or unusable, and the rest in pasture and other uses. In some ways South America represents what the United States would have been if its people had not crossed the Appalachian Mountains. This can best be illustrated by some figures. In Brazil 89 per cent of the population and an even higher percentage of the railroads and area under cultivation are in the coastal area. In Argentina one-third of the population is in greater Buenos Aires and is increasing relative to the rest of the nation. Montevideo has more than half of Uruguay's population. It is almost a universal rule in Latin American countries that the vast majority of the population occupies a fraction of the area.

The isolation of the provincial town

The impact of mountain, desert and jungle on the history, politics and social organization has been profound. Almost nowhere in Latin America does one meet with human occupancy that covers the countryside and fills in the space between the towns; quite the contrary. Latin America consists of cities, towns and villages, with no human habitation in between. This is true almost everywhere. Buenos Aires, Quito, Lima, Caracas, are large cities surrounded by a human vacuum. This is true of Cuzco and Arequipa, of Cuenca and Ibara, of Zacatecas and Chihuahua, and of the thousands of smaller towns and villages. The mountains on the Pacific side of Central and South America, and the broken character of the Mexican *altiplano* have all served the same end—to isolate the community, large or small, and shut it off from the nation.

The large city is impressive and dominating. In Mexico, for example, there are over 100,000 little villages. The vast majority do not have more than 400 inhabitants. 99 per cent of all the towns have fewer than 2,000 people. This is a universal phenomenon.

Brazil and Ecuador differ to the extent that each has two large metropolitan centers, and Colombia has nine cities of relatively equal size. Beyond that, we have thousands of provincial capitals, pueblos, villages, large or small, equally isolated from the rest, surrounded by high, almost impassable mountains, cut off from the nation. It has always been that way.

The typical community is a little town of a few houses grouped about a square, with a church, a municipal building, a jail, a few poorly stocked stores. The rest is probably unpaved streets, houses with doors closed and no windows facing the street, a courtyard where the life of the family goes on, where the few animals are kept and where flowers may be grown. The house, isolated from the community, is shut in on itself. So is the town: it is peaceful, quiet, self-conscious and proud. Its contacts with the outside world are limited; it buys little and sells little. The capital of the state or of the nation is a long way off; there is no reason for going

10

there. Most of the things needed are locally produced. The houses are built of local materials, the shoes and clothing locally made, and even now perhaps they are fashioned from hide tanned and cloth woven locally. In the main, the food is locally grown. If it is a large town of, say 5,000 people it will have a local band. It may have a 4-page weekly newspaper. The big paper from the capital may be received by a few more sophisticated people. The important institutions will be the town government, the school, and most important of all, the church. These are the places where the town as a whole gathers.

But the community we have just described is relatively large. Most inhabited places are much smaller, perhaps under 400. Of the nation and its politics this little village knows little—the police, the administrator appointed by the center, the echoes of the occasional political campaign. And this little village, or larger community, even the provincial capital lives in a world a thousand miles away from the big city where the President is located. It is almost as if we were dealing with two different universes.

The capital city has millions of people—Mexico, 2.5 million for the city proper and 4.5 million for the metropolitan district; Buenos Aires at 5.6 million for the metropolitan district; the municipality of Rio de Janeiro with about 3,000,000; Lima, over 1,000,000. But the difference is not merely in size, though that is important. The case of Lima, the capital of Peru with its million people, is typical. It is not only the largest city, it is, one might say, the nation. It dominates all other towns. The next largest city is Arequipa with a little over a hundred thousand, followed by Trujillo with fifty thousand, Cuzco with another 50,000 and then Huancayo with 40,000. It is worth putting them all down for the lesson they teach: Icá—29,000, Piura—27,000, Cajemarca, where Atahualpa was strangled by Pizarro—21,000, Puno—21,000, the recently expanded Chiclayo—45,000, and the Amazonian city of Iquitos—about 42,000. That is all in a population of some 10,000,000 people. The capital is larger than all of the other cities combined.

If one takes out Brazil, Colombia and Ecuador, this is the case all over Latin America. And to leave the capital is to leave the center of power, wealth, education and the sophistication of the modern world. The gap between Lima and Cuzco, Trujillo or Cajamarca is very wide. But the contrast between Lima and the thousands of little isolated towns hidden in mountain crevices and cut off from contact with the outside world is so great that Lima, in fact, lives in a distinct universe. We are dealing with one of the basic dilemmas in Latin America. The little town of 100 or 200 families is the typical community. That is where the people live, not only in Peru but in all Latin America. If one excepts Argentina, and Uruguay, 50 to 70 per cent or more of the people live in villages. And this little village in Peru has almost nothing that identifies it with

11

the modern world. If "nothing" is too strong a word, it has little—very little. It has no Spanish, for the people speak Quechua; it has no newspaper for the people are illiterate; it has no books; it may have no school. The people are barefooted or wear homemade sandals; they sleep on the floor; they carry their burdens on their own backs; they have no modern tools; they have few animals. They have retained many of their ancient family customs, such as trial marriage. They may work their land in common if they have any land. In look, manner, attitude and belief, they are not part of the same world as Lima.

The proverbial wisdom of the peasant and the sophisticated knowledge of the elite operate on two different planes, and it is difficult for them to meet. But this is true not only in Peru; it is true in Brazil, in Colombia, in Guatemala, especially perhaps in Guatemala. For in Guatemala the incomprehension, if not the outright hostility, of the *ladino* (mestizo) toward the Indian and his colorful dress and stubborn unyielding ways is very marked indeed.

Regionalism

There is, however, another side to this story. Isolation has given strength to regionalism, a pride in the locality and its ways. Arequipa is "the mother of revolutions." Presidents of Venezuela come from "Táchira." Sucre is the "real" capital of Bolivia. "Cuzco" is the "heart" of Peru. The region has been the source of vitality, and the Latin American nations, it can be said, have been governed not by political parties, but by regions, regional families and regional *caudillos.* A political change has often meant merely that the people from one region have displaced those of another, that the Venezuelan *llanero* has been substituted by the people from the *sierra,* that Rio Grande do Sul has replaced São Paulo, that Guayaquil rather than Quito is ruling Ecuador.

Regionalism is not only political. It is often social, racial, linguistic and economic. In Brazil, Bahía has many elements of a distinctive culture different from that of Rio Grande do Sul. Almost every part of Brazil is conscious of such differences. The language is filled with local words, meanings and accents. In Mexico, the people of Yucatan, Tabasco, Sonora are equally proud of their own ways and scornful of the rest. The important influence has been the region. And this is understandable enough. A place like Arequipa has been isolated from Lima throughout the centuries. Overland, it took about a month, as there were no roads and the mule paths were not made for speed or for a large army; and by sea, after spending three days to get to Mollendo (before the railroads) it would depend upon the good fortune of a boat going north. In Brazil it was easier to go from Belem, at the mouth of the Amazon, to Europe than to Rio de Janeiro. Before airmail it required a minimum of forty days for a letter to Rio de Janeiro from Porto Velho on the upper Madeira River. The distances between Santa Cruz and La Paz in Bolivia are so great and, with the bad roads, so difficult, that there has long been a current of separatism in Santa Cruz.

From the other side of *la montaña* it seems natural to believe that the outlet is down the rivers to the Atlantic rather than through the jungle and difficult trails over the Andes to the Pacific. Really heavy traffic from the Pacific side until only a few years ago, and perhaps even now in spite of the new roads, had to round Cape Horn or go through the Panama Canal to reach either Iquitos or Santa Cruz. And these are merely extreme examples of what is a daily occurrence.

These regions are not merely physical but in many instances linguistic, racial and often economic as well, so that the center, i.e. the world where the capital is located, is really a different and perhaps a hostile world, where the leaders of the locality have been killed and exiled, where manners, attitudes and ways are so strange as to seem foreign. If one remembers this, then the significance of regionalism becomes clear.

These are different universes and difficult to contain within a single political frame, and difficult to forge a nation out of or to develop a party system in—or even a common ideal. *Caciquismo*—local bossism bent on looking after its own, with all of the possible variations for local tyranny and injustice—has this virtue, that it is local. The people can identify with it against the center and follow the local leadership against the national government just because it belongs to the locality, and the local leader, no matter how repugnant or terrible he may look to the "civilized," sophisticated and educated in Mexico City, Bogotá, Caracas or Lima, has the support of the locality. I am speaking of the past, not the distant years of long ago, but of the days before the airplane and radio communication, when the center was much farther away and much less well informed, and when the locality and its leadership were not only a political but a military threat, and socially felt "superior" to the center and its leaders. But this is not very long ago, and when the regions get their tempers up—as illustrated by Colombia in recent years and to some extent still evident—the natural difficulties can still make the region confident and the center fearful and uncertain. All of this merely points to greater instability on the part of the national government than would appear even under the best of conditions.

One could, of course, speak of Texas, California, the South and New England as illustrative of the point—except that one does not see Texas marching on Washington to place a Texan hero in the presidential chair, either before or after an election. And that is what has happened a thousand times in Latin America. The national energy and turbulence have come from the locality, the group, the region, the state—and this region was often both political, economic, social, and geographic. This, how-

13

ever, is still only part of the story of the meaning of internal isolation. We must not see Mexico, Peru or Guatemala, as a large capital, with a number of smaller but comparable cities. It is very much more accurate to see Mexico as a country of over a hundred thousand neighborhoods, i.e. *pueblos, caseríos, ranchos,* etc., with an average of fewer than 400 people, with more than 50,000 hamlets having fewer than that, and to recognize that each of these little pueblos is a self-contained world, separated, if not cut off, from the rest by a thousand elements that isolate them from each other.

I remember on a market day standing in the doorway of a grocery store in one of the larger towns of Chiapas as the Indians were coming into market carrying their burdens on their backs, and the owner of the store remarked as each one passed, "Tlajobal," "Chamula," "Matananguero." "How do you know?" I asked. "Oh, by their hats." That was true. Each one that passed had a different hat. He wore the hat of his community; all the people in the village wore the same kind of hat. All the Indian women in the villages of Guatemala wear a waist specially colored and designed and with a special cut. No such waist is worn by any other woman of any other village, and wherever a woman may be, she is known by her waist as belonging to a certain village.

But most of all, the individual living in one of these communities belongs to a society and is related through an extended family which will include almost every member of the community. For not only are the families large and have intermarried with each other generation after generation, but the system of *compadrazgo* (godfather, godmother relationship) will effectively have tied people together in such a way that in smaller communities (and most of them are small) the individual is part of a beehive where the community acts, feels and thinks as a group. As one man explained the difference between his and a neighboring village, "Say the children, say the women, say the men, says the whole village." The *pueblo* belongs to the individual and he to it.

These villagers have not migrated to other villages, because they would be strangers; they have neither house nor land, neither family nor friends, and they would find the customs different. In fact, they might not be allowed to stay. I have heard reports of cases within the last years of villages in Guatemala, Colombia and Bolivia where strangers were encouraged to leave before nightfall. The rural community (and in most of the countries under consideration, over 50 per cent of the population lives in little communities) may outnumber the larger cities by a hundred to one. The world we are talking about lacks integration, and not just politically. And this picture of separation, regionalism and localism to be complete has to include the fact that the hacienda, which occupies so large a place in the Latin American scene, is almost completely autochthonous. It not

14

only keeps, if it can, its people from moving from one place to another, but its people stay out of the local and regional market, for the hacienda has its own store, and sometimes its own coinage.

It must be evident to the reader that the centrifugal forces are more active than the centripetal. The capital city with its centralization notwithstanding, the making of a nation has proved more difficult than the proclamation of nationalism as a credo and a policy. This is even true in Argentina.

The limits of the conquest

If isolation is one of the keys to an understanding of Latin America, the character of the Spanish conquest is another. The emphasis is upon conquest rather than colonization or settlement. If by conquest we mean total submission to a conqueror, it was never fully accomplished. In Northern Mexico, the war against the Apaches went on into the late nineteenth century; so too the war against Indians in Argentina; and in Chile the Araucanians were not united with the Republic until the middle eighties of the last century. But even today there are numerous Indian groups in the high mountains such as the Huichol, or the Lacandón in the jungle in Mexico, or the Indians on the Upper Magdalena River in Colombia, that are continuously warring against the white man exploring the area for oil, the Auca Indians in Ecuador who recently murdered three white missionaries on the Napo River, the Brazilian Indians who attacked the parties stretching telegraph lines through the interior of the country, and other small groups too numerous to mention who are beyond the reach of the nation.

The point to remember is that conquest did not mean effective occupancy everywhere, and that Spanish colonial government and society had an unincorporated frontier which not even the Jesuit or Franciscan missionaries were always successful in penetrating. Here is an area where Spanish influence is minimal, where neither the Spanish language nor the Spanish nor modern republican government have established themselves. This is also the case with the Church, though the Church has penetrated further than other European institutions brought over by the conqueror.

But more important to the history and development of Latin America has been the failure of the ideal of the Spanish crown to convert the Indian in America to a good European on the Spanish model. The conquest was neither settlement, nor colonization, nor effective occupancy except as military outposts, as gatherers of tribute, as managers of mines, as owners of plantations, as government officials, or as a Church hierarchy. The failure to colonize is understandable, and Spanish achievement is of heroic proportions.

15

The Indian

The difficulty of terrain was much greater than in the United States. But that was of lesser importance than the presence of millions of human beings already on the land. The surprise of the European at the variety of peoples and cultures and their incredible, almost enchanted forms, as if they were of another world, as if they were especially moulded to serve the devil, as many of the Spaniards believed, could not have been greater than the surprise of the Indians. For to the Indians these were creatures come from Heaven—gods possessed of magical powers. Between these two races no effective means of understanding, no moral basis of accommodation, was found by the Spaniard, or by his Latin American successors. These races met as billiard balls do: they met but did not penetrate. The one exception was the Catholic missions. It was only there that the Indian prospered and multiplied. Everywhere else he was troubled by disease, mistreatment, and most of all perhaps by the strange ways and expectancies of his conquerors. The missions had relatively a marginal role in the total enterprise and an unhappy ending.

For the rest of the story of the relations between the Spaniard, better perhaps between the European, and the Indian has been one of incessant attrition. The Indian proved stubborn and unyielding, and Spanish colonial policies in some measure insulated the Indian from the disintegrating influences of the conquistador and his heirs.

The complicated history of colonial legislation and administration cannot be considered here. Sufficient for the purpose in hand is to say that wherever the Indian managed to retain his land and his own community, he remained an Indian, keeping his language, his customs, his family organization, his religious rituals even if he became a Catholic, using the same tools, working the land much the same way as before the conquest, eating the same food and living in the same kind of house. The Spanish influence was important enough. It deprived the Indian of his leadership, of his learned men, of his old idols and old priests, of his men of science, of his government, of his faith in himself as a man. It imposed on him tribute, services and demands for labor which proved damaging and led to a decline of the Indian population during the colonial period. Letters from the viceroys of Peru are filled with the repeated prognostications that the Indian *"se está acabando,"* is disappearing.

But in those places where he lived in his own community, if he survived at all, he remained an Indian in his ways and attitudes. In some degree, but less so, the Indians incorporated into a hacienda, and retaining some form of community organization and collective responsibilities, also survived as Indians. Only where the natives were drawn into the urban centers, into mining towns, into cities as servants and individual workers, or where they learned European skills, did they cease to be

16

Indians. The Spanish conquest found in the Indian population a barrier which it never fully overcame. A cultural community is more resilient than a forest. The American pioneer could fell his trees and clear his lands, because on the whole the country was empty. In Latin America all of the seemingly occupiable land was already filled, and the people on it continued to till it as they had before, for a European master, or to pay him tribute, but continued Indians in all of their language and ways. They would not learn to be good Europeans, not even if they were beaten or had their ears cut off. They obeyed their new masters because they had no choice. They did his services, but closed in on themselves and became silent, with bowed heads, with no claims on anyone—except, if possible, to be left alone. The result was a nation within a nation, a culture within a culture, two people living in proximity but belonging to two different universes.

A contemporary Ecuadorian historian describes what happened to the Indian in the following words: "The psychological resistance of the Indian to the Spaniard was and remains to this day in his repugnance to the assimilation of the white man's civilization, one of the most extraordinary phenomena in human history. This resistance has lasted for ages . . . and has the frightening implication of collective suicide." (Pareja)

This is not the entire story. There were, as there always are, notable exceptions. But the Spanish conquest did not change the Indian into a good European on the Spanish model nor has he become a good Latin American. Anyone who will take the trouble can see this today easily in Guatemala. The Indian in Chichicastenango, or in San Miguel Acatlan, is not a white man, does not want to be one, and disciplines those of his members who are too friendly or try to ape white men. The few white men govern and collect taxes and exploit the Indians as they can. But there is no friendship between them, no understanding, and in spite of proximity, in spite of the fact that both the Indian and the *ladino* (white man) have taken over from each other certain cultural traits, like the tortilla on one side and the European chicken or sheep on the other, they are not intermingling socially; they are not intermarrying, and the process of amalgamation between the two races has in Indian areas probably declined. And the Indian is in all probability increasing more rapidly than the more urbanized population.

What we have are two nations and two cultures and here, as in Peru, Ecuador and Bolivia, the Indian is in the majority—regardless of what the official statistics say. The statistics, to repeat Luis Alberto Sánchez, are poetry. And this problem of the Indian in varying degrees is well nigh universal. It was eliminated in Argentina in 1879 by what can only be described as extermination under a military campaign by General Julio A. Roca. In Uruguay and Costa Rica it is practically non-existent. But in

17

most of the continental countries there are smaller or larger groups that do not identify with the ruling elements of the nation.

When one asks for an explanation of the difficulties in any one of the Andean countries, or in Central America and Mexico, one of the answers is that they are not homogeneous nations. No one knows how many Indians there are in Latin America. Figures have been given that vary between 14 and 30 million. It depends upon the definition of who is an Indian. If an Indian who learns to say a few words in Spanish is no longer counted an Indian, you get one result. If race rather than language is used, then you get another. The point to remember is that the population in Latin America has doubled in the last thirty years, and the Indian population has also doubled. We can now see that racially the conquest has left the modern countries a heritage which they have found difficult to deal with.

In failing to integrate the Indian, Spain also failed to make the Spanish tongue the universal medium of communication. It was a very great achievement to have spread the Castillian tongue over so vast an area and to have made it possible for the people in Chile to feel at home in the language spoken in Mexico. But this achievement again has fallen short of its ideal aim. The Indian does not speak Spanish, or if he has picked up some Spanish words, he does not use them at home. The women usually know less of the white man's language than do the men; and the farther we get away from the big city, the provincial capital, the county seat, the less is Spanish the language of the people. In Mexico according to the 1950 census 30 per cent of the people were Indian who spoke a hundred languages, if one can take the census figures at their face value.

We really have no adequate picture of the effective reach of Spanish and therefore no real understanding of the political, social and cultural difficulties that face these nations. Our preoccupation with the big city and its many ramifications has blinded North and South Americans to the complexity of the culture south of the United States.

That culture is not only Latin but also American. And American means Indian—and Indian means non-European not only in race and language but in a thousand other things as well. That the Latin will ultimately absorb the American has been taken for granted from the beginning, which is more than four centuries ago. And so it may prove in the end, but the end is a long way off, and history has shown itself capable of many an unexpected turn.

The mestizo

This brings us to the mestizo. The mestizo, the child of a European father and an Indian mother, is the most important by-product of the Spanish conquest. For this child of Europe and America has taken over

18

the leadership of Latin America. The president of the country, the member of the Cabinet, the general of the army, the artist like Diego Rivera, the novelist like Ciro Alegría, or Machado de Assis, the politician, business man, university professor, is likely to be a mestizo.

While Argentina, Uruguay and Central Chile are classified as white, the dominant European immigration in these countries is of the middle of the nineteenth century or later. Until then the population was predominantly mestizo, and the mixed strain has not entirely disappeared. And as one goes from Buenos Aires to Tucumán, Salta and Jujuy, the Indian strain becomes more and more evident. Taking Latin America as a whole, where the Indian has disappeared or declined in numbers, the mestizo, the negro and mulatto have taken his place. It is, I think, a safe generalization that the mestizo is the dominant influence in Latin America. This is a remarkable achievement. For the mestizo is a new race, nonexistent at the time of the discovery and looked upon with suspicion and hostility throughout the three centuries of colonial rule. The colonial governments, the Spaniards and the criollos treated the mestizo as an inferior human being, described him as undependable, as possessing the bad characteristics of the Spaniard and Indian, as lazy, vagabond, unstable and untrustworthy. And in fact more than one Latin American sociologist, as for instance Bunge, in the early part of this century ascribed Latin America's political and social shortcomings to the racial hybrid and saw little hope for the future. They repeated the estimate of the Spanish viceroys who deplored the presence of the mestizo as a disturbing element, as difficult to discipline.

Whatever the objective merits of this judgment, the fact remains that this being who came into the world (usually outside the marriage bond, though in the days of the conquest there were some notable cases of marriage between conquistadors and Incaic "Princesses" in Peru), who was abandoned by his father and raised by his mother, was neither Indian nor Spaniard. He grew up in a world of unstable values, where his mother and father lived in different cultures, had different standards, different notions of good and right, and different basic loyalties. He had no tradition, no invariable rules, no place in the community comparable with his ambitions. For here he differed from the Indian who wished only to be left alone in his little village; the mestizo aspired to the role of his father, the European, the criollo. The wars of independence gave him his first opportunity to play a role on the public stage and gave him a footing on the social and economic ladder. (An exception must be made for Brazil, where the Bandeirantes played an important role in the development of the country.) The mestizo was the soldier, the corporal and sergeant, the subordinate official. It was only after the wars of independence, whose chief leaders were criollos, that the mestizo began to rise from petty official to colonel and general.

19

The turbulence and the civil wars that tore Latin America apart for a century provided him with the opportunity to assert his leadership. A glance at the figures who played the dominant political roles before 1850 and after the mid-century is revealing. The mestizo had established his dominance in government and politics, had risen in social status, had repudiated his Indian heritage and taken over criollo and European ways and had done it all by the skin of his teeth. The turbulence, the instability, are in one sense the evidence and the means of the change that was taking place in this child of two races which never came to understand or appreciate each other. The mestizo in time replaced both races in the exercise of political power, in wealth and in the practice of the civilizing arts. Where he reached for status and worldly goods, he did so largely at the expense of the Indian and at the price of increasing the gap that separates the two groups. The so-called liberal revolutions in Mexico, Guatemala, Ecuador and generally throughout the area, which ended in the defeat of the criollo oligarchy that had survived the independence and that stripped the Church of its lands, endowed the mestizo with worldly goods.

He became the master of the Indian and the owner of land. He acquired land taken from the Church, and now as general, governor, cacique, president, he married into the older oligarchy and replaced it as the dominant figure, not only in politics but in rural wealth as well. The liberal revolutions in the mid-century and later, as the one in Guatemala in 1871, tended to give the Indian equality before the law but it did not change his social status or increase his economic opportunities, and as in Mexico it weakened his ability to defend his communal lands against the expanding hacienda. Nor did these changes bring the Indian and mestizo closer together. In fact, it increased the distance between them, and the mestizo took over the prejudice of the criollo against the Indian as an inferior being. So that now, as one American anthropologist has said of a certain part of Guatemala, it is "completely improbable" for a marriage between an Indian and a mestizo to take place. And this statement for a particular community in Guatemala can be generalized for the Indian areas as a whole. The Indian, to achieve social status among mestizos, must first shed his language, his clothes, his ways, his occupation, his family and his community—a difficult venture at best.

The negro

The negro, like the Indian and mestizo, has a special place and a unique role in the Latin American complex, and is one of the essential keys to an understanding of the area. Of the 12,000,000 or more negroes transported by slave traders to the Western Hemisphere in the 350 years between 1500 and 1850, a large proportion went to what are now the

20

Latin American nations. In greater or lesser numbers they were to be found in every part of the area from Chile to Cuba. Next to Haiti, the largest proportion probably went to Brazil, though Cuba was a close second. There are certain general features of negro occupancy in Latin America which have influenced both the economic as well as the social development of Latin America. For one thing, the slave filled in those areas where the Indian disappeared shortly after European arrival, or was so intractable that negro labor was used instead. As a general rule the negro did not play an important role in those parts of Latin America where the Indian survived in large numbers, and that was usually in areas of sedentary agriculture. The negro survived and prospered best in tropical parts of America, and these were largely coastal lowlands. The negro was mainly used in the cultivation of sugar, cacao and other crops that do well in warm moist climates.

The negroes were purchased as *individuals* by European masters and were therefore closer to and more dependent on the white man. In fact, they were present in the early Spanish expeditions and, though slaves, were in some ways treated as superior to the Indian and were used occasionally as foremen or overseers where negro and Indian labor were found together. Unlike the Indian, who proved extremely recalcitrant, the negro was malleable and culturally receptive. He acquired European language, religion, dress, food and habits with surprising speed, and has in those countries where he is numerically important become a significant influence in the economic, political, and notably in the cultural life of the countries he resides in. He has, as the Indian has not, become culturally a European; and in Brazil, Cuba, Venezuela and Panama, important in literature, music, art, and architecture. Notably so has this been the case in Brazil where some of the greatest figures in the arts, music and literature have been mulattos and negroes.

The Indian had no natural and trusted spokesman and interpreter acceptable to the larger community, whereas the negro had many of them. The negro felt at home in some subtle sense even while he was a slave—as the reading of the literature will reveal. The Indian has never felt at home with the white man and does not do so today. But there are other historical influences which help explain the accommodation of the negro within the Latin American community in a way that has not happened among us.

The negro slave brought into the Iberian peninsula as early as 1442 fitted into a society where slavery was still in existence. As a result of the many centuries of warfare with the Moors, if not for other reasons, it had remained a traditional feature of the Spanish society to accept slavery as normal, while it had long since died out in Western Europe. At the time the negro was brought to Spain, there were Moorish slaves, Jewish slaves and Spaniards as slaves. Prisoners taken in battle could be held for ransom or could he held as slaves, and the laws allowed other reasons for slavery. The important point is that there was a slave law, an elaborate code embodied as part of the *Siete Partidas* going back to Alfonso the Wise (1252-1284) which endowed the slave with a legal personality, with duties and with rights. The slave was known to the law as a human being; he could marry; he could buy his freedom; he could change his master if he found one to purchase him; he could under certain conditions testify in court even against his master. And if a slave became a priest, he had to give his master one slave, but if he became a bishop, he had to give him two slaves.

The negro brought over from Africa became the beneficiary of this body of law. He was not merely a slave, a chattel under West Indian and American colonial codes, but also a human being with rights enforceable in the king's court. The negro under Iberian conditions was also converted to the Catholic faith and the master had to see to it that he came to church. While the Catholic doctrine did not oppose slavery as such, it asserted that master and slave were equal in the sight of God; that what mattered was the moral and religious character of man and that the master must treat his slaves as moral beings, as brothers in Christ. It also emphasized the merits of manumission. The negroes in the Spanish and Portuguese colonies were the inheritors of this legal and religious tradition. It is not suggested that slavery was not cruel; that in Brazil, Cuba, Venezuela or Peru abominable and inhuman acts were not committed against negro slaves; that they were not chained and beaten. But cruelty was against the law, and unusual punishment could be brought before the court by a recognized legal protector of the slave, and the killing of a slave was treated as murder. The entire atmosphere was different, and manumission was so frequent that there were often more freed negroes than there were slaves.

The fact that the slave had both a legal personality and a moral status made manumission natural, and the abolition of slavery no great shock. The question of the slave's fitness for freedom never arose, and the freed negro was a free man, not a freedman. He was legally the equal of all other free men. And when slavery was abolished in Brazil the crowd in the galleries threw flowers upon the members of the Congress, and the people danced all night in the streets of Rio de Janeiro. The question of segregation, so agonizing and so disturbing in our own South, could never have arisen anywhere in Latin America—neither with the negro nor with the Indian. And this tradition in Latin America makes it most difficult for them to understand our problem or our way of dealing with it.

Racial prejudice

This does not mean there is no racial prejudice in Latin America. It exists against both the Indian and the negro, but it is a prejudice which has

22

no sanction in the law. It is social and economic and cultural. It is determined more by social status than by a sense that people of color are inferior in nature—though this feeling exists particularly about the Indian. But any Indian, and any mulatto, if he can escape from his poverty, if he can acquire the graces, the language, the manners, the dress, the schooling and the associations that will admit him into the best society, will have no insuperable difficulties socially, especially if he is wealthy, and will, if he has it in him, be elected to Congress, be a member of the cabinet or become president of the country. The fact that he is an Indian or a mulatto will not bar him—and there are numerous instances of mulattoes and a few of Indians who have risen to the highest or to very high posts politically. In that sense there is no race prejudice. The case is different for the pure black man—in some countries at least, Peru for instance, or Ecuador, or Colombia, or Venezuela—or perhaps even Cuba, and even in Brazil, the pure black man has not, perhaps could not, rise to the highest political post, or really be accepted by the "best" social set. That is the difference between Latin American racial conditions and our own.

There is something else that needs adding. The opportunities for wealth, education, professional advancement as doctors or lawyers, and for active politics (outside of the South) is very much greater among us in the United States than in Latin America. True enough, this advancement economically and professionally takes place mostly, though by no means entirely, within the colored community. But the way to opportunity is not closed—neither in the arts, nor in the professions, nor in education, nor in opportunities to distinction. The road is narrow and steep—but there is a road. In contrast, in Latin America the road does not exist. This is too strong a way to put it. Perhaps it would be more accurate to say that the door is shut but not locked. The gap between the "lower" classes, between not only the Indian and the negro poor, but between just the poor, just the illiterate, just the children of the little rural hut that I saw in Cundinamarca and the elite in Bogotá, or between the Hauasipongo on a hacienda in Ecuador and the traveled sophisticated literary people in Quito, is so wide that it is almost unbridgeable. That is in part because the countries are poor, the wealthy families fewer and the poor more numerous.

But I think there is something else and that is the hierarchical structure (the aristocratic tradition, the basic authoritarian character of the society, the essentially caste-like form of the way people are grouped and identified, and the paternal concept that the poor must always be poor, that the servant must always remain a servant) has set a division in the culture between the "upper" and the "lower" that is very great indeed. Never in the history of the United States has there been such a distance, such a seemingly impossible distance, between our poorest farmer or immigrant and the wealthiest and most self-conscious of our aristocracy—if that word

23

has any real meaning in our culture. This difference I am noting is obviously not racial, not biological, not the color of skin, nor origin—but it is perhaps even more effective as a dividing line, and perhaps more permanent. It is an ingrained part of the total scheme of things.

But we are fooling ourselves—and Latin Americans who speak as if this were not the case are also fooling themselves—if we or they think that what we call democracy is a thing of formal law and constitutional enactment. It has as a background a feeling of equality, or perhaps egalitarianism, "where a man is a man for all that," where no man rides a high horse, and is not expected to ride one. At this point American and Latin American society stand wide apart. And the difference socially at this level of discourse between the basic conditions of social equality and opportunity in the United States and Latin America are broad and deep—and not really changeable for a long time to come.

We can at this point turn from race to religion as another key to the culture we are trying to understand.

Religion

The American Indian at the time of the discovery was a profoundly religious and mystical human being. A great part of his daily existence was bound up in religious rites, in propitiating his many gods, in finding grace, justification and peace. Every act had its religious significance, every wind, every change in the color of the moon, every appearance of the unexpected had its religious portent. In the highly developed cultures such as the Aztec and the Inca, a large priesthood served to interpret the will of the gods, and a profound mystic philosophy and a questioning of the essence of human existence informed and disciplined their attitude toward life and death.

The Spanish conquest was insensible to the spiritual and moral values that ruled the lives of the American Indians. The conquistador, whatever his virtues of courage and fealty, was no philosopher, no mystic; and he was obtuse—in most cases—to the values inherent in this strange world he found himself in.

The greatest shock to the American Indian civilization was the complete denial of its existence by the soldiers of Spain, a denial manifest in indifference or in brutal destruction of ancient gods, their objects of worship and their temples; pulling the gold off the walls in the Temple to the Sun in Cuzco was merely one of a thousand instances of an irreverence for the spirit of a culture that centered in its religion. And in destroying the religious temples and the religious leaders the soul of Indian civilization was also destroyed. Its values, its beliefs, its pattern of existence and its great art and artists were scattered by the wind that blew across the ocean.

24

What was left of the Indian as a human being with a belief in God and the burden of the sudden tragedy that had overtaken his world, found refuge in the Christian Church. That is the true meaning of the conversion of millions of Indians in so short a time. The Catholic Church saved what meaning there was left to existence, after all had been taken from him by men he could not understand and whose motives were completely incomprehensible to him. And in the Church the Indian could rebuild a faith in the forces that govern the world, that bring day and night, sunshine and rain, life and death. And the Church wisely built where the old temples were, and the saints in the Church gave the Indian full scope for his attachment to a particular mystery, a special symbol, a unique identity with the forces that lay beyond human reach and were all powerful. The Church did something in addition. It in some way brought the conqueror and the conquered into the same Church. It gave the Indian identity with the European, a sense that they were both mortal, and gave the conquistador a conscience that he was dealing with human beings who had souls and who were inside his Church and children of the same God as himself. It required a papal bull to make that point for the conquistador. For the strangeness of American culture, the ways of the Indians, the bitterness of the conquest, and the belief in the devil working his evil designs through strange beings made it easy to deny to the Indian his claim to human fellowship.

The Church was the Indian's salvation here and now by giving him a place where he could feel free in spirit, and where he could reweave the threads that had always bound him to the world beyond his immediate senses—and that service the Church has continued to perform for the Indian through the centuries that have changed both the original zeal of the early friars and raised problems and difficulties of a political and social nature. But these are secondary to the great spiritual role in the life of the Indian, that of giving a meaning to existence in a world ruled by men who have remained strange and incomprehensible.

It is useful in trying to unravel the mysteries of Latin American culture to remember that during the colonial period the Church ruled while the State governed. While the State in its paternal preoccupation was meddling with the public and material aspects of life, the Church ruled the most intimate and personal needs and preoccupations of the individual, from the cradle to the grave and beyond. The Church in the large city, small town, village, and even on the pathway over the mountains was ever present, for there would be a cross or small chapel at every difficult passage, at the top of every hill one climbed. The Church was everywhere—even when the priest was absent. But so it had been before the conquest and before the white man. Every mountain, every stream, every strange and marvelous thing (and to the unpretentious, the humble and the pious, simple things are marvelous and strange) had its own *huaco* (shrine, holy place) and

25

continued to have it in the new faith by identification with a favorite and miraculous saint.

The Church was everywhere and with every individual all of his life and filled all of his days. The day began with early morning mass and ended with an Ave Maria, and every occasion, every sorrow, every joy, every holiday had its own special religious symbolism to be acted out in church. During the colonial period the Church was also the school, the university, the hospital, the home of the aged, the sick and the abandoned. It served the individual and the community in many ways. In the absence of newspapers, libraries, museums, theaters, the religious exercise and ritualism in the churches, the orders, the monasteries and the convents filled the role of giving the individual his place in an enchanted and meaningful world. And everything that happened from a bull fight to the arrival of a new Viceroy, an earthquake, or the King's birthday always required public manifestation, processions, prayers, masses and sermons in which the Church was active, perhaps the chief actor in the drama, or better, the chief embodiment of the symbolism that endowed every activity with meaning. It surrounded life at all turns and all times. The church or cathedral bell dominated the community, and daily life was disciplined and ordered to its sound.

In cities like Lima, Quito, Mexico, the church buildings, the monasteries dominated all buildings, and the profession of priest or membership in an order, belonging to a monastery or convent, was a high calling and a privilege. The few diaries that have come down from the colonial period reveal preoccupation with the ever present Church. The daily record is filled with religious processions, with the celebration of the saint's day in this or that monastery, church, convent, or ward, with gossip, scandal and even riot, because of the great popular interest in the election of a prior or prioress in monastery and convent.

The independence movement brought so many difficulties to the Church that it has not to this day fully recovered from them. For one thing the hierarchy being largely Spanish were less friendly to the independence movement than the lower clergy. And as a result the American churches were to considerable extent without bishops during and for a period after the conflict was over. And during the conflict the Papacy sided with Spain against the independence because of the pressure of the powerful Spanish Embassy in Rome. After all, Spain had been the great Defender of the Faith since the Reformation. The ideas of the French Revolution which were not unknown or unspoken in Latin America made the claims of Spanish sovereignty also seem on the side of justice, morality and faith.

The resulting rift between the American leadership and Rome was aggravated by the claim of the new governments to the rights of the patronage which had been exercised by the Spanish Crown and by the insistence of the Church that the patronage had been personal with the king and that now when the king was gone from America the Church was free. This question remains in fact unsettled and variously compromised in different countries.

But more serious perhaps than the above was the struggle that emerged between Church and State when the new governments attempted to pattern themselves on French and American constitutional precepts. It became evident, and quickly, that trouble lay ahead for the Church from the modern State with its claim to the control of education, to the equal enforcement of the same law against all citizens; with its opposition to corporate privileges, i.e., *fueros,* in a special law enforceable in ecclesiastical courts; and with its opposition to exemption from taxation of the Church for its properties. In fact, the revolutionary lawyers trained in the Roman law and imbued with French anti-clericalism on one side, and the priests traditionally identified with the corporate Church and its claims on the individual on the other, found it most difficult to abide in the same world. The quarrel between the anti-clerical lawyer steeped in concepts of absolute sovereignty and the priest, who looked upon all matters that might touch the soul and affect human salvation as the special responsibility of the Church, ended in a conflict often bitter and bloody. And the lawyer won the battle. The Church in most countries lost its land, its wealth, its monopoly over education, its censorship over the literature and the press, over the hospitals, over public charity, over the universities, over marriage (for civil marriage became legal), over the registration of birth, over the burial grounds and over the right to exclude other faiths from the country. It came out of the struggle much poorer, much less influential, and in most places on the defensive against continuing threats to its remaining power.

A hundred years of conflict have gradually attenuated the bitterness, and the Church has recovered a measure of the prestige it had lost by taking sides in recent years against the dictatorship in Argentina, Colombia, Venezuela and less openly in Cuba. It has also taken a definite position on behalf of land reform and has slowly come to voice the social doctrines expressed in the *Rerum Novarum* of Pope Leo XIII. In some measure the Church's political position is therefore better than it has been since independence. It is more independent of the State and perhaps closer to the social movement sweeping Latin America than it was a few years ago. But these changes vis-a-vis the State and public policy have had little to do with the role of the Church as a religious institution. The people have remained Catholic, and the Latin-American anti-clerical often dies in the faith, is married in church and his children are baptized as if he had never fallen under the influence of French philosophers or the more recent Marxists.

The role of the Church in Latin America is therefore very different from what it is in the United States. There is personal or family identity with the favorite saint which to this day has a quality of intimacy. The city, the

27

town, has its patron or patroness: Santa Rosa in Lima, the Virgin of Guadalupe in Mexico, etc. Every parish in turn has a saint of its own: St. Francis, St. Dominic, St. John. All guilds—the goldsmiths, the seamen, the carpenters—used to have their own saints with their own *corfradía* inside the church, their own chapel in their corner. Every large hacienda had, and mostly still has, a chapel or sometimes a church—which occasionally connects with the main house, so that one goes from one part of the house to the other by passing through the chapel. And this chapel has its own saint that in some intimate way belongs to the family. He is the family patron who looks after its members and protects them. His name is invoked on every occasion. He has a familiar presence in family affairs as if he were a living member of it—and the children are baptized and married inside this family chapel and in the presence of the family patron. And in this chapel the members of the family used to be buried. The patron of the plantation is the patron of the plantation community, and the entire life of the plantation community is lived and in some measure ordered by the sound of the chapel bell. This is true of the smaller towns, the smaller cities and to some extent of the larger ones.

Not so much as a hundred years ago, travelers tell of the cathedral bells in Quito ringing for vespers and the entire city becoming quiet, the people kneeling down in the streets, taking off their hats and saying their prayers. But in essence it is still true—more of the women than of the men, of the unsophisticated, the poor, the illiterate (much more for these than the others), and it is true for the country folk and for the Indians very much indeed.

This personal sense of intimacy with the mysteries is seen in the family in another way. Each member old or young has a patron saint. The big occasion is not the birthday but the saint's day after whom the child was named—St. Francis, St. John, St. Peter, St. Katherine—depending on the name one received when baptized. The day is like Christmas. It begins with going to mass with one's friends, all in their best dresses. There are presents, music, visits. It lasts all day and sometimes with dancing late into the night. As the families are large, there are numerous occasions for such festivities, for each member of the family; for each of the grandparents, the parents, the children, and the grandchildren has his own particular patron saint who when his day arrives is celebrated in a similar fashion. Then there are the numerous first, second, third and fourth cousins, the aunts and uncles, the school friends, the companions and associates in business or the professions and last but not least, the "compadre"—the godfathers and godchildren—and these may literally run into the dozens. The life of the family and of the individual is greatly and continuously involved with the Church.

This is the most continuing influence in the life of the individual, especially as one gets away from the large urban center. It begins at birth and

28

terminates only in the burial ground. One must not exaggerate the implications of this relationship of the individual, the family and the community to the Church. But one need be careful not to underestimate it. It gives life a certain quality and adds something to the meaning of daily activities which is lacking in our community—for going to church is not just a Sunday affair—it is a part of daily life. And the priest and the bishop are present on every important occasion—personal, family or community. There are few gatherings of intellectuals where some member of a religious order does not take an active part. And there are certainly few public affairs where the members of the Church are not active participants. This participation is uneven and varies with the community, but there is added colorfulness and solemnity. And a certain emphasis upon eternal verities in even the least religious occasions is added by the presence of Franciscan or Dominican brothers, or when the Bishop of Ibara takes part in a conference on history and illustrates a point in popular folklore by playing the song on a piano.

The hacienda

The hacienda plays a special role in Latin America. It would be no exaggeration to say that the hacienda, or as it is known in Brazil, the *fazenda,* set the tone and determined the quality of Latin American culture during the nineteenth and early part of the twentieth century, until the first world war and in some instances (as in Ecuador, Chile and Peru, and in spite of appearances in Argentina and other areas) until the present. This is not an argument for unitary causation. There are also the Spanish tradition, the presence of the Indian and the negro, the broad influence of the Church and the impact of the larger world to consider. But we are dealing with an area where in most places over one half of the population is rural, and until very recently the rural proportion was much larger. We are also dealing with an area where the typical holding is in large units. The United Nations estimated in 1951 that 1½ per cent of the total land holdings in lots of over 15,000 acres are equal to half the agricultural land. Some of these are very extensive indeed. There were plantations in Mexico of a million acres, and there are similar units in Brazil and in other countries. And one family may have a number of agricultural units of large acreage scattered over the country.

It is not the size of the hacienda that is in question, but its organization. Before entering into a discussion of the hacienda as such, it is useful to note that at least in the Andean countries and in Central America and Mexico we are dealing with two distinctive agricultural systems: the hacienda and the village community. In Guatemala, for instance, the hacienda will have the valley, the slopes and rolling hills, the best agri-

29

cultural lands, while the Indian villages will occupy the steep mountains, the inaccessible areas and the poor soil. This was true in Mexico; it is true in Ecuador and in Peru. In fact, the hacienda has the best agricultural lands, and the Indian or mestizo villages the poorest. The village may be communal, following an older Indian tradition, or it may have adopted every possible variation that lies between collective and individual ownership.

But the village is a community with its own local traditional government, and the closer one gets to an Indian community the truer this is, and this village government is participated in by the entire male population. It looks after the public works, the policing and the roads; it builds a school in common, if there is a school, and cares for the church. Each individual as he grows up has in turn to share in the various tasks that the community requires. In the case of Amatanango in the State of Chiapas, Mexico, as an example, each boy begins as a messenger for the town government, takes his turn in time as one of the policemen, and after satisfying all the required offices in the civil government and in the church, ends up as an *"anciano,"* one of the elders who govern the community as a council. The Indian and the mestizo village is a community, with its own collective personality. Each member has a recognized place of his own and a defined relation to all the others. He is a participant in government and church because he has regular functions to perform in both. This village may be next to a hacienda, and there are instances where the village somehow survived surrounded by a hacienda.

Generally speaking, however, the rural world divides sharply—the hacienda in the valley and the village on the steep mountain sides. Between these two agricultural organizations there has always been friction, the hacienda encroaching upon the village, absorbing its woods, pastures, water supply; and the village every now and then rising in rebellion, protesting, going to court. The story is an old one and goes back to the early days after the conquest when the Indians crowded the offices of the Spanish officials asking for protection against the hacendado who was encroaching upon their lands.

After independence, the Indians were less able to find protection against the neighboring hacienda. The history of rural land holdings since independence is one where in the name of liberalism, equality and individual rights the Indian was increasingly dispossessed of his lands in favor of the hacienda. The struggle against the Church by the new national governments tended to increase the size of the hacienda and the power and prestige of its owner. The little villages during the same period decreased in number, size and significance. Where they expanded—in relatively small number and isolated areas, as in Southern Chile, Southern Brazil, and some places in Argentina—they had little bearing on the general trend in rural organization. The private hacienda had carried everything before it.

The hacienda is not just an agricultural property owned by an individual. It is a society, under private auspices. The hacienda governs the life of those attached to it from the cradle to the grave, and greatly influences all of the rest of the country. It is economics, politics, education, social structure and industrial development. It is a curious fact in Latin American intellectual life that the hacienda, which is so all embracing in its influence is, except for an occasional novel, never written about or seriously studied. It is, or was, so taken for granted that the intellectuals who were mostly the children of a hacienda were not conscious of its existence—like the air we breathe. When the Latin American sociologist looked for something to write about he worried about the unemployed in London or about the new sugar or banana plantation in foreign hands. The hacienda, which was the basis of the politics of the country as a whole, he was hardly aware of.

The hacienda as a society may be described by saying that it was—and is—an economic and social system that seeks to achieve self-sufficiency or autarchy on a local scale. It seeks this not as a matter of malice, but in the logic of a given institution to expand so as to have within its own borders all that it needs, salt from the sea, *panela* (black sugar) from its own fields, corn, barley and wheat, coconuts, bananas, apples and pears. All of this depends upon where the hacienda is located. If it can run from the seacoast to the mountain top, from the river bottom where sugar cane will grow to the snow line, then it can raise all of the crops that will grow in all of the climates. Not all haciendas—not any perhaps—satisfy this ideal completely, but that is the bent of hacienda organization: buy nothing, raise and make everything within the limits of your own boundaries. The big house is built from the timbers on the place—and these may be, as I have seen them, of mahogany. The furniture is made at home; the cloth is woven on the place from the sheep; the llamas that graze in the hills, the oxen, the horses, are raised and broken on the place; the saddles, bridles, harnesses, are made from the hides of the slaughtered animals. The wooden plow, the wagon, the windmill for the grinding of the corn, or the water-mill for the grinding of cane are all made on the place. The table may be loaded at a meal with every kind of meat, grain and fruit—and all of these, the table itself, the house, and the servants as well, will all have been raised, contrived, conserved, grown on the place, including the table-cloth that covers the table, the sandals of the servants, if they are not barefooted. And perhaps even the Indian musician who sits behind the screen and plays his old songs on the homemade instrument is also of the plantation. I am recalling this from personal experience on a plantation in the Province of Ayacucho in Peru.

The people on the plantation are born there. They cannot leave because they may be in debt, or because there is no place to go, for this is home and every other place is foreign. And here too their fathers and grandfathers were born and are buried. If the place changes hands, they change with it. In 1948 the leading newspaper in La Paz, Bolivia, carried an advertisement offering for sale on the main highway a half hour from the capital of the country a hacienda with five hundred acres of land, fifty sheep, much water and *twenty peons*. And similar advertisements have appeared even more recently in Ecuador and Chile. (This I have from others, one a native scholar, the other an American political scientist.) The point is that what we are dealing with is a closed economic, social, political and cultural institution.

Its administrative organization is an interesting adaptation to an aristocratic agricultural society of a non-commercial economy. For the hacienda is a way of life rather than a business. It is not an investment. It was inherited. It is operated with the expenditure of as little cash as possible. If the hacienda is large there may be a couple of hundred or more families residing within its borders. These are scattered in groups of five or ten families in different parts of the hacienda, depending on the kind of land, crops, forest. The laborer usually has a hut which he has built, and a given amount of land, which he works or shares. The hacienda provides the land, the work animals and the seed; and the peon turns over, carrying to the granary by the big house, the share of the crop belonging to the hacendado. The share is determined by the crop, and the tradition of the hacienda. In addition, the Indian also owes the landlord a given number of days' work each week throughout the year. This practice varies. It might be one day's work a week for each hectare of land, or so many days a week for living on the land. The families might also owe a certain amount of service in the big house. The point is that the hacienda has its labor supplied to it without the use of money. If there are two hundred families on the hacienda and if they each owed only one day's work a week for each of two hectares allotted to each family, it would have 400 work days each week.

The labor at its disposal without expenditure of any money for wages is used by the hacienda for working those lands which it tills on its own account. These lands might be in sugar cane, from which it can either with oxen or water power in a small homemade *trapiche,* squeeze out the juice and make *panela,* a dark unrefined sugar, and manufacture rum as well. Or its cash crop may be coffee or cacao, or other products which can be carried to the market on the backs of mules, or on the backs of men, over steep mountain and narrow gorges, to the nearest railroad station, or more recently to the nearest automobile road, or to the nearest town. The cash crop will have been raised, harvested and delivered part or all of the way to the nearest market without the expenditure of any money.

In a curious way, the hacienda is largely beyond the reach of the money economy. Internally it provides, so far as it can, for all of its needs as a going concern as well as a community without recourse to the market. The seed the hacienda supplies to the sharecroppers comes out of the store

32

houses in which it was deposited in the fall; if the laboring population living on the hacienda runs short of food or other supplies they can be purchased in the store—*tienda de raya,* in Mexican parlance, or *company store* in our own economic history. The peon will pay no cash for his purchase for he has no money. It will be written down in a little book by a storekeeper, usually some distant relative or *compadre* of the hacendado. The debt can be liquidated by labor, but it rarely is and serves to tie the laboring population to the hacienda, as they cannot leave without first paying off their debt. This has long been so. It has roots in the colonial system. It persisted all through the nineteenth century, and is still in full vigor wherever the hacienda system survives. It is as hard to kill as was the company store, token coin, or script, in the mining and lumbering camps in the United States. And token coin has its use on the hacienda, for the payment of wages, for the extra labor which may be needed beyond that owed by the peons, or for tasks which for some reason lie outside the traditional work the peons accept as theirs. These token coins, sometimes bearing the name of the hacienda, or a piece of metal stamped with *vale un día de trabajo* (it is worth one day's work) can only be exchanged in the hacienda store.

As the hacienda satisfies its own and its community's needs with as little recourse to the market as possible, it buys little, and it sells little as well. The distances, the poor roads, the primitive means of communication, make the transport of goods from one part of the country to another difficult and expensive. The relatively small income from the hacienda is, so to speak, net profit—taxes on land have always been low, the cost of production is at a minimum in monetary terms.

The hacienda is, however, not merely an economic enterprise. It is also a social, political and cultural institution. Socially it is a closed community living within its borders. Part of the hacienda population will be located near the big house, where the store, the church, the school (if there is one), the repair shops, granaries, the blacksmith, carpenter, harness shop will also be. The grist mill and the *trapiche* (sugar mill) will also, in all likelihood, be near the big house if there is water close by. The stables for the favorite horses, cows and other animals raised for household use or consumption will also be close by. The laborers about the big house tend to all these different functions. This is usually the larger part of the hacienda community. The others are scattered in small groups in different parts of the domain, tending to different duties and raising crops appropriate to the altitude, the climate, moisture and heat. Each little *rancho* hamlet is isolated and far away. It may be anything from one to ten or more miles from the next hamlet, depending upon the size of the hacienda. Their contacts with the outside world are few indeed, and the paths on the hacienda lead to the center where the big house is located, and only one rarely used path goes off to another hacienda, and to still another until the neighboring town is reached, which may be ten, twenty, thirty or more miles away.

Community activity takes place in front of the big house, on Sundays, when the peonage will have come to church, even if there is no priest in regular attendance. All burials, christenings, marriages, when they are solemnized, are social matters involving the church and as large a part of the hacienda community as is aware of the occasion. The important feast days are likely to be the saint's day of the owner, or of some other favorite member of the family. Then the entire community will turn the event into a holiday with decorations, music, dancing and drinking. A similar event is celebrating the patron saint of the church. There may be others, depending on the local Indian, mestizo or negro traditions. Beyond these festive occasions, the hacienda community has no public functions or responsibilities. It is not a political unit, an organized parish, a government, or a cooperative. If any vestige of the older Indian community survives on the hacienda, it is unrecognized by the hacendado and what functions it retains must of necessity lie outside of the hacienda as a going concern.

There may be and often is a bond between the peons and the hacendado which goes beyond the formal manager-laborer relation. The hacendado may have stood as godfather to many of the children born on the place. He may have a role not as employer primarily, but as the head of a family of which all the laborers consider themselves members. The hacienda laborers' community may have an integration resting on many years of cooperation, interdependence and mutual aid. The hacienda is an old institution. It has usually belonged to the same family over many generations, sometimes for centuries. Isolation from the larger world has tended to bring the hacendados within the same region close to each other. By intermarriage the owner of the hacienda tends to be related to most of the proprietors of the neighboring properties. Time, circumstance, and danger have brought the hacendados of the region close together, and their family connections will have knitted an extended family over a vast area where everyone knows and is related to everyone else.

One or another of these closely knitted families will have, through time, acquired an ascendancy over the others, a kind of traditional leadership in the region. And given the basis of fealty in the extended family and the godfather relation that always exists, you have the basis of political power and regional *caciquismo*. Because of the turbulence and instability that succeeded the independence, *caciquismo* served the important end of protecting its own. The interdependence of the regional hacienda owners became an essential means of self-protection and defense—either military or political. The rule that developed, logically required by the situation, was that the locality and its inhabitants followed their own leader against the national one. The leaders of the localities each had a following which

34

belonged only to them, and the great leader was dependent upon the support of the little leaders each with his own following.

In that situation the power of the great leader tended to be unstable, temporary and subject to many hazards. He really lived on borrowed strength—while the power of the local *cacique* was very great and beyond the effective control of the central government, where the great leader was located. The hacienda thus became the basis of a system of local *caciquismo,* and the local *caciquismo* the major reason for political instability. It must be clear that with the weakening of the central power, the decline in the wealth, prestige and influence of the Church, the only power that remained was that of the locality—and the locality in Latin America has meant the haciendas in the locality. They were substantial; they had a strength which was genuine. The hacienda community's fealty gave the hacendado a power which was immediate and direct. And a group of hacendados, related and interdependent, controlled a region. The *cabildo* which they controlled was for a long time the only effective government.

Before closing this discussion of the hacienda, there are certain other elements which must be brought out. The hacienda both dominated the small neighboring city and prevented it from developing economically or politically. The complaint so often heard in the Latin American smaller town, that it has no "movement" that it is "dead," is true and no great mystery. The haciendas which surround this town for many miles about buy little. Their peons have no money. The town has no important distributing function. The hacienda sells relatively little, considering its size and the number of people living on it; and what it does sell is marketed, usually, on a wholesale basis, by some agent employed by the hacienda, or by a member of the family, and is sent on, if possible to a larger city at a distance, with the result that the smaller neighboring city is bypassed. Even the mule pack carrying the hacienda goods to the city or the nearest railroad belongs to the hacienda.

The better houses in the town usually belong to the neighboring haciendas, and are occupied by some members of the extended family, probably an old mother, or a brother who does not like to live on the hacienda, or who has some professional interest. The children of the hacendado will also be in this house during the school year. The servants in the house will come from the hacienda and will be a permanent part of the household, requiring no specific money wage. In the mountains of Peru, the house will also have the service of one or more *pongos* who come to work in turn for a week, and then go back to the hacienda. This is part of their payment for the few hectares of land they till on the hacienda. In addition the house will be supplied from the hacienda with a large part of its needs—wheat, barley, rice, corn, in the grain or as flour depending on whether the hacienda has a grist mill. It will also get what fruits are raised, and depending on the distance, may be supplied with butter, cheese and what-

35

ever else the distance and the climate will allow to be transported. So the big houses in the town are not important participants in the local market.

All of this and much more has kept the town commercially inactive. If the hacienda dominates the town economically, it does so politically as well. The great family will control every local office, from the colonel of the local militia to the rural police. The tax gatherer, the mayor, the judge, the postmaster will be related to or married into or be godfathers to, members of the family. And unless the president of the country feels strong enough to be indifferent to the interest and pride of the local leadership he will not impose "foreigners" on the locality.

If we now summarize the role of the hacienda in the development of Latin America we will see that it has been and has remained, where it still exists, an isolating and conservative influence. It lived by routine share-cropping methods which prevented the use of improved machinery, methods or seeds. It tied its labor force to the property and kept mobility down to a minimum. It was a dampening influence on commercial development by buying little in the open market and selling relatively little. Its huge areas and internal system of paths leading to the big house discouraged road building. It established and maintained—and still does—a system of dependence between the hacendado and his peons which perpetuated an authoritarian tradition of master and very humble servant (I saw in Bolivia the Indians on a plantation bend their knees and kiss the hands of the hacendado) which leads directly into *caciquismo* and instability. It prevented the accumulation of capital, required no investment, called for no change, did nothing to prevent soil erosion or improve agricultural techniques. The hacienda family controlled the local political scene and set the tone socially. As a dominant influence, the hacienda paid little taxes, and neglected to, or was unable to, put all of its resources to good use.

Perhaps most serious of all is that it fostered and maintained a social ideal in which the hacendado was the representative type—ideally a superior being possessed of broad acres and numerous servants, dominant, domineering, patronizing, and paternal, with nothing between himself and the peon on the plantation. All other elements in society (craftsmen, businessmen, entrepreneurs—in the parlance of the day, the middle class) were looked upon with disdain as a necessary affliction that had at best to be suffered. The hacendado was the master of all he surveyed, and the world looked good to him. It gave him economic stability, social prestige, political power, affluence and leisure. Those of his children who did not remain on the hacienda went off to the capital of the country, attended the university and became lawyers, doctors or literary men. Many of them combined literature with a profession. They might also meddle in politics, especially if the administration was one which their family—always the extended family, always the people who come from the same region, who followed the same local traditional leadership—had helped to bring to office.

Education fitted the ideal. Primary schooling for the mass of the people was a matter of indifference; higher education in the main led to a limited number of professions—medicine, law, and to a much lesser degree civil engineering. In the earlier days, the university also taught theology. The emphasis more recently fell upon philosophy and literature instead.

The hacienda system was thus a major influence in preventing either the democratic or economic development of Latin America. If Latin America has fallen behind the United States and Western Europe in industrial expansion, politically stable and democratic government and in the growth of an educational system adequate for the present time and present need, much of the fault lies with the hacienda system.

The hacienda system has in fact reached an impasse from which it cannot escape. The pressure for economic, political and social change is building up so rapidly that the system cannot avoid the challenge to its traditional ways, and it cannot meet it. *The hacienda has no built-in device that will allow for reform of the system,* that will enable it to transform itself so as to survive and propitiate the new ways that are undermining a traditional and age-old form of social organization. It has no way of meeting the challenge and yet cannot remain indifferent to television, atomic energy—and, if you like, psychoanalysis and Karl Marx as well.

In the two countries where the hacienda has been repudiated, Mexico and Bolivia, it was by revolution. The question of whether there is another way of dealing with impending change remains to be seen. I say "impending," for it would require undue opaqueness to assume that the demands for industrialism and democracy can be met without seriously affecting the total role of the hacienda. What is happening in a small way in Peru is perhaps a suggestion that the government could if it had the energy, vision and political courage attempt a program of agrarian reform that would meet the modern challenge without a previous social convulsion. But who is there to say that the organized forces of government could move fast enough to satisfy the increasing pressure which the government would stimulate by its policies? I am not suggesting that cataclysm is inevitable. What is inevitable, if Latin America is to industrialize effectively and meet the demands for a higher standard of living and a more democratic society, is a wide agrarian reform which is not compatible with the survival of the hacienda system.

All of this discussion does not include the problem raised by the large commercial plantation in sugar, bananas and other crops raised for the international market. The fact that these large plantations may be foreign owned is only a minor complication to a difficult problem. What is involved in any attempt to apply agrarian reform policies to them is that they are efficiently operated, that they require a high degree of scientific and technical skill, that they have a foreign market which they control; or that they have to meet the world price at which the commodity is selling; that they yield a cash income per acre higher than any other crop that could be grown. These are questions of such magnitude, especially where the government gets a large part of its income from the export of a single commodity, that any policy that would price the commodity out of the market, reduce the required investment, and cut down efficiency would not necessarily improve the economic conditions either of the peasantry or of the government. The fact that the properties have to be paid for merely increases the difficulties. But it must be clear that in their modern form these enterprises are relatively new, that they are to a considerable extent foreign owned and foreign managed, and that they are so large that they tend to dwarf all other domestic enterprise.

This raises political questions that may in fact be insoluble. This is a hard thing to recognize and to accept. But politically a certain institution may prove intolerable even if economically it can be shown to be highly beneficial. The large modern plantation is probably more like a factory than a farm, and if it were possible for modern management, the workers and the government to believe that they are involved in an industrial rather than an agricultural enterprise, then issues other than land reform would control whatever controversy might arise and require attention.

The modern sugar and banana plantations are, however, not the major issue in any discussion of the hacienda. These enterprises, except in isolated areas like Cuba, are only a small part of the total agricultural plant. The hacienda is another matter; it has set the tone for a whole society— and while it differs greatly between Argentina and Peru, for instance, it has been the controlling influence in shaping the cultural development of the area and has influenced the educational system in many ways.

Education

In the kind of world we have been describing, education will take on special forms. It will have given the relatively small group of Europeans and their descendants an education fitting the aristocratic, authoritarian role that tradition and expectancy have demanded of them. It will have given them refinements and interests seemingly natural to "superior" persons in an authoritarian society, while the mass of the people will have received little instruction at public expense and that of poor quality. This whole matter is a delicate and sensitive issue, hard to deal with and hard to evaluate.

We must always begin with remembering that the universities in Lima and Mexico are a century older than Harvard; that the Franciscans carried on a most notable educational enterprise in Mexico within a few years after the conquest, where among other things Indian boys learned to read Latin, and some became good Latinists; we must also remember that the Order of Jesus had a notable career in the field of education among criollos and Indians.

All of this is in the background. But the published figures, whatever their accuracy, record that in mid-twentieth century at least one-half of the people in Latin America could neither read nor write. That would mean something like 70 to 80 million people. Countries like Argentina, Chile, Uruguay and Costa Rica can boast of a literacy rate of 80 per cent or more, while in Bolivia, El Salvador and Guatemala the people counted as literate are somewhere around 30 in a 100, and in Haiti, only about 10 per cent can read and write. These figures are probably somewhat optimistic. It has been estimated that something like four to five years of primary schooling are required before it can be assumed that the child will not fall back into illiteracy. If this is the case, then there are many more people who are functionally illiterate than is indicated by the published figures.

On the whole, the children who enter the primary school do not reach the top grade. This is especially so in rural districts, and we are dealing with a rural area. In the rural schools in Brazil, according to a United Nations study, less than one per cent of those entering reach the fifth grade, whereas urban schools have a record at least nine times as good. In 14 Latin American countries, 1.7 per cent of children of school age reach the highest primary grade.

As we have already seen, the Latin American population is growing fast, faster perhaps than in other parts of the world. This means that the number of children to the total population is relatively great. The children of school age—five to fourteen—are proportionately twice as numerous in comparison with the adults in the Latin American countries as they are in Europe. There are four adults to every child of school age in the more industrialized countries, and only two in Latin America. The relative burden, all other things being equal, of the educational costs to be borne proportionately by each individual would therefore be twice as great in Latin America as in England or Belgium. And this burden falls on people who have a much lower income and on countries where the investment per capita in industry is lower and where productivity per individual is smaller.

This however is only part of the difficulty. In many of the countries in Latin America there is the additional impediment of language other than Spanish spoken by a considerable number—in some cases the majority— of the population. This added task might well discourage even an enthusiast for popular education. How to get the teachers who know the language (Mexico lists a hundred), how to prepare the school room materials so as to make them meaningful, how to persuade the parents to send their children to school, and how to interpret to the children of an entirely different cultural universe the values derived from European antecedents might well task the ingenuity and the will even of the idealistic reformer. I always

39

recall the little Chamula child of about seven or eight, who had learned Spanish while his mother had been working in town, acting as an interpreter for his teacher to some dozen other Chamula children of about his own age. It was heroic and pathetic at the same time. Only the greatest devotion would explain the effort to pass on European culture and the ideals of Mexican nationalism through the medium of a little child. But he was the only interpreter available for the task in hand. It was pathetic, for the one or two years schooling to be had in that school would in the end avail but little to the children by the time they came to be full grown men.

At least half of the people in Bolivia, Ecuador, Guatemala and Peru lie outside the Spanish medium as a means of instruction in schools—and Indian children do not know Spanish even in families where the father speaks it. For, at home the mother tongue is Quiche, Aymara, Trique, or whatever the language of the Indian group happens to be. The language barrier is more formidable than enthusiasts for converting the Indians into good nationals like to believe.

This raises another question. How effective is a literacy campaign in a country where there are no books for the mass of the people, no magazines, no newspapers, in fact no reading matter? The literacy campaigns, and there have been a number of them, have accomplished but little. For literacy is not something by itself. It is an expression of a total cultural situation. Where reading and writing are not used because no one writes letters, because there is nothing to read, because even the first-grade primer has disappeared (mouldered away with time if one did once go to school), because newspapers are unknown—then it is difficult to learn to read and easy to forget the alphabet one acquired in the primary grade. It is hard for city dwellers here or in Latin America to visualize the poverty of the ordinary rural school and rural community in literary materials. As everything in the school usually comes from the central ministry of education the school teacher will, with the thousands of other teachers, receive a scant supply of schoolroom writing material, a blackboard and chalk, first and second grade primers. And that may be all. He may in some places receive a magazine published by the Ministry of Education filled with articles on the theory of education, which the teacher will probably not understand. For in most rural schools even the teacher may have scant book learning.

The undertaking to suddenly provide a school system adequate to the needs of a modern nation is a Herculean task. In Latin America the schools are usually maintained, supported or supervised by the national government, which appoints the teachers, builds or rents the schools, plans the program, supplies the classroom materials and orders, regulates, examines by long-range control everything, from the school desk, the blackboard, the final examination and the morals of the teacher.

A bureaucracy, well intentioned, perhaps well trained, that knows exactly what is to be done and how to do it—this bureaucracy, by giving orders in long *reglamentos* to teachers off in the jungle or in some mountain crevice fills the air with sounds of activity which make little difference in fact when one looks at the situation at a distance from the capital where the ministry is located. And in periods of political instability—and political instability is something of a norm in the last quarter of a century—the educational directors at the center change with each government. The old plans are thrown out, new plans devised because they are said to be better; and before these new plans can really take effect, a change in government will bring a new Minister of Education, who will have a newer and better plan that in its turn will fail of fulfillment.

These are pessimistic views—but how can one run away from the facts? Because of the high degree of centralization, the central government must provide for 50 or more per cent of the school population now without schools. It must find, educate, "shanghai" double the number of teachers it now has and place them on the national payroll. It must print twice as many books and notebooks, procure twice as many pencils and black-boards. It must double the school inspectors, bookkeepers, clerks, super-visors and normal schools for the training of teachers. It must do all of this and a great deal more, and it must do it in a hurry, for the population is growing so fast that at the moment the school system is losing ground. From some source the means has to be discovered to double the education budget, which in some countries is already very large. And when the President has done all of this (and no one else can do it) he will have universalized the present situation: a little over one per cent of the children of school age will complete the fifth or sixth grade, and half of the children matriculating will not go beyond the first year. The amount of literacy will have increased but slightly, and the extent of functional illiteracy will probably have doubled.

Centralization demands that the national government do it all and the central government expects to do it all, or leave it undone. But what is required within the national ideal is a school system rural and urban that will give at least a primary grade education of six to eight years for all the children everywhere, and do it soon. And this the government cannot do. Physical impediments of geography, different languages, poverty, insufficient teachers, schools and money make the demand for a universal primary education for all children an ideal that can have no present fulfillment.

To make the project a reasonable one, that is, a possible one, the country would suddenly have to be endowed with an industrial system, an economy, a social structure, a national income sufficiently large and sufficiently well distributed. It would also require the quite sudden appearance of teachers in sufficient numbers and adequately trained as well as administrators willing and able to organize and manage so large an undertaking.

41

These things are not done by sheer exercise of will. They have to grow together. And those who are concerned with education would do well to recognize that the educational system is a function of the total society and cannot be treated in isolation. One could say that a society has the school system its culture can contrive and absorb. The school system changes as the society changes, and there are no miracles to be looked for.

It is interesting to have a look at the remarkable Mexican experience in rural education. The Mexican effort came out of the revolution and had in its initial days the impulse to remake the nation and to bring the rural folk, including the Indian, into closer contact with the modern world. Beginning about 1924 under the leadership of José Vasconcelos and later of Moises Saenz and Rafael Ramirez, the attempt was made to carry the school even to the most isolated villages. Starting with inadequate funds, insufficient teachers and a not-too-clear idea of what could be done, the movement had the advantage of enthusiasm and faith in the beneficence of the revolution and its redeeming qualities, for it was to redeem the rural population from the effects of peonage and to incorporate the Indian into the nation that the school was expected to contribute to.

The important lesson for the future revealed by this undertaking was that the rural community, no matter how poor and abandoned, could become an active participant in a system of rural education. Having neither much money nor trained personnel, the ministry resorted to sending "missionaries" on horseback to the villages in the mountains to preach the gospel of education for the children. The villagers were gathered together and the problem and prospects were discussed in a kind of open assembly. It soon became apparent that the communities would provide the school— build it themselves. The missionary turned architect; and the men, women and children in their spare time, Sundays and holidays gathered and hewed stones, mixed lime, worked the adobe and built the school on land the community had given. In a short time over six thousand rural schools were built by the villages without any cost to the central government, and having built them they felt as if the schools belonged to them.

As there was no experience, no confining traditions, and as the missionaries and officials in the ministry had the ideal of using the school as an agency of social improvement, they permitted themselves to be influenced by the communities who wanted the school to be useful to the village. Out of this there developed without any initial plan a body of what came to be called "anexos" to the school. The basketball field would be one anexo. A lamp for the school that could be used by the adults in the evenings would be another anexo. A shower bath made of a tin can raised on poles was another.

It soon turned out that the anexos were the important part of the rural school. They included such things as a school garden, a house for the teacher, a plot of school land worked by the adults to provide additional income for the school or the teacher. The school also developed a kitchen where the women could learn to cook. It had a sewing machine, a barber shop where older boys cut the hair of the younger ones, a medical kit, or primitive dispensary where the teacher acted as nurse and applied iodine, bandages, and had some other simple remedies. There was no standardization in these matters. Each school adopted and contrived those anexos most convenient and useful to its particular community.

The rural school came to be judged not primarily by its reading and writing, but by its anexos. One school boasted of 33 separate activities in addition to teaching the three R's. One result was that the school was always open and members of the community participated in its goings on. Another was the formation of "committees" to look after different needs in the school sanitation, the school garden, the school plot, the furniture, the attendance, the night school and so forth. One teacher remarked that the school kept going day and night: "When I get tired I take a rest."

The most important lesson taught by this movement was that there is a latent initiative and enthusiasm in the community that once awakened can be of great help in the development of rural education.

Now, 34 years after this movement got underway, Mexico has some 20,000 rural schools, and the government prides itself on its large educational budget. But the rural schools in their vast majority do not go beyond the third grade. A large proportion of the children do not attend school beyond the first year. But more significant, half the children in the rural districts have no schools to go to. The population has more than doubled and the number of children has increased more rapidly than the adults. The government has not been able to carry a sufficiently effective campaign for rural schools. And this is the story in Mexico, which justly prides itself on its contribution to education and its efforts to meet the challenge of literacy in the modern world.

For Mexico has made important strides in converting a hacienda-dominated and peon-ridden society into one that is democratic and progressive and full of confidence in its own future. A careful analysis of what has happened in the last 30 years would show that other influences in addition to a rapidly growing population must be reckoned with in explaining the failure of the school system to keep up with the school children clamoring for schools. One of these undoubtedly has been an over-emphasis upon urbanization and a tendency to neglect the needs of the rural community. This is true even in Mexico, where the Revolution of 1910 was primarily a protest against just this kind of neglect. But rural people are on the whole voiceless and fail to bring their needs to the attention of the government immersed in the large city.

More fundamental perhaps is the simple fact that in spite of the great changes which have taken place functionally, literacy in the rural districts remains less important than in the cities. If this is the case in a country

43

like Mexico, where the hacienda system has been destroyed and where the impulse toward a fuller democracy is the outstanding feature of the present day, what can be said of the rest of Latin America? One must be on his guard against generalizations and dogmatic assertions, and no one really knows enough to be absolutely sure of his own position in matters as complex as those we are dealing with. But it seems obvious that a country divided into large haciendas on which a large proportion of the people live, lacks the motivation for organizing, and lacks the income to finance an effective system of rural education. The hacienda is chiefly responsible for the dilemma faced by Latin America in its ambition to adapt to modern ways, not only in the matter of schooling for the mass of the people but also in its efforts to industrialize or for that matter to apply scientific methods to its agriculture. The dilemma lies in the demand for modernization by the very elements who are most insistent in keeping the older social and economic institutions. They are clamoring for progress and at the same time resisting effective change. They would like to retain their hierarchical, authoritarian and centralized social structure on one side, and have the values that only come with an egalitarian, mobile, individualistic society which industrialism both needs and promotes on the other. It is, I think, clear that an effective modern school system would require so many other changes that it can only come into being as the countries develop the resources, the needs and the competencies which make universal literacy an integral part of a modern society.

Higher education in Latin America is going through a profound crisis. The older university which served a small aristocracy has been challenged to meet the seemingly impossible demands of a suddenly expanded urban population. The needs of a growing middle class and an expanding industrial system with its emphasis on science and scientific training are more than the older university with its literary traditions, its emphasis upon the humanities, its specialization in law, medicine, and civil engineering is currently prepared for. The sudden flow of students has turned the relatively small, traditional institutions of higher learning into great centers of discontent. The universities on the whole lack the means, the trained personnel, the physical room, and the scientific equipment required to train the thousands of students clamoring for instruction. In addition, because of inadequate secondary schools, the students are not always well enough prepared for the university. The professors in the majority of cases make their living by practicing a profession or occupying some post in the government. Their teaching is in a sense an honorific exercise for which they receive a modest, almost a symbolic stipend.

With a part-time teaching staff, inadequate finances, overcrowded halls and classrooms, poor or non-existent laboratories, the universities have difficulty enough to meet their obligations without the added perplexities of involvement with the government. There is a tradition of autonomy and

44

freedom from state interference in university matters. The older rule allows no policeman within the precincts of the university. But the ideal of academic inviolability has been frequently disregarded: Venezuela, Cuba and Argentina are only recent instances of the State's indifference to academic pretensions. State intervention on one side and students' demands for administrative and policy-making participation on the other make academic life exciting if not entirely peaceful and make devotion to research and the scholarly life difficult. There are many distinguished scholars and teachers who have somehow managed to find the serenity needed for creative work within this difficult environment, but there are also many teachers and students who find the going hard and the rewards inadequate. A few private, usually Catholic universities add to the educational opportunities. These are less troubled by politics, but in the broad field of education they differ but little from the nationally supported institutions.

If one is to offer a constructive comment on so sensitive a matter as the university in Latin America, it should be done humbly and with many apologies. But it does seem that it is an error to overemphasize the university in capital cities—Lima, Mexico, Caracas, and to neglect the smaller regional institutions in Cuzco, Morelia and Cuenca. This is but one suggestion. There are many others that an outsider could make, but then an outsider does not understand or have to deal with the ten thousand difficulties that stand in the path of modifying the ways of a tradition-bound university that must continue to live with a centralized, authoritarian and all powerful government.

Leadership

When Latin Americans say, as they often do in speaking of themselves, "We are a young people," they must have in the back of their mind Bolivar's remark that the inhabitants of the former Spanish colonies were neither Europeans, Africans nor Indians, but Americans. That too was the idea of the "Cosmic Race" popularized by José Vasconcelos a generation ago. These reflections by Latin Americans about their own stage of development is a way of saying that the people of Latin America are still being formed, that the "Cosmic Race" is an aspiration, an ideal to be hoped for but that in the present their character is incomplete. If this means anything—and I think that such intuitive reflections by a people about themselves mean a great deal—it is that the mestizo who is the product of this amalgam between all the races has not as yet become the universal type, the true representative of the "Cosmic Race." They recognize that the character of the Latin American has not yet been integrated. For in spite of their sensitivity about criticism from the outside, they acknowledge the validity of such painful analyses as Carlos Octavio Bunge's "Our America" and Luis Alberto Sánchez's "Does Latin America Exist?" and honor their authors for their frankness as well as their wisdom.

The meaning of the notion that "we are a young people" is that there are still Indians, negroes and Europeans and that the mestizo, the real American, is an imperfect creature because he is born and reared amid conflicting values and contradictory cultures, compared with an Englishman, a Frenchman or an Italian among whom basic attitudes have sanctions that go back beyond the memory of man, and where notions of right and wrong seem to have universal acceptance. The mestizo, on the other hand, is raised in a world where even the most intimate values are challenged and denied, among Indians and Africans and Europeans who differ in their simplest ideas of the good, and each of whom differs from the mestizo.

The import of all this is unconsciously revealed when we ask about any leader among ourselves. Who is he? Where was he born? Where did he go to school? We ask these questions not because we want to know the man's political opinions, those revealed by his party allegiance, his public statements. The queries go to the heart of the matter. They ask not what the leader thinks, but how he came to be the kind of man he is; his opinions about politics and policy are only part of the question. What kind of a character is he—regardless of his opinions. And this question of character formation in a world of conflicting values, beliefs and ideals has been answered many times and in many places. An unstable and conflicting cultural environment is not conducive to the formation of the "national" type. The contradictory cultures and differing value systems have nurtured refractory characters, especially because the mestizos are "a young people," a people just becoming. Otherwise it would be difficult to explain the turbulence and instability, the passion and the frustration, the alternatives of pride and humility, of arrogant self-assertion one day and sense of inferiority the next, frequently manifested in Latin American history.

The mestizo is a child of conquest, misfortune, denial and contempt. It is a short time between the conquest, when he had not yet appeared, and the independence when he began to emerge as an active participant, at least as a sergeant and sometimes an important leader like Morelos in Mexico. And there has not been time enough, and there will not be until in some way the fusion of the races occurs, for a national culture sufficiently broad to embrace the entire population to emerge. That is the condition of common values, and the basis of that unofficial education in right and good which precedes any schooling in a traditionally pervasive culture.

The difficulty which is widespread is clearly seen in Guatemala. Who in Guatemala speaks for all of the people? Culturally, no one. Certainly not the mestizo (Ladino, as he is called) nor the criollo (who here is also called a Ladino), nor the Indian. The Indian, of course, is voiceless. He

46

does not speak to the public at large. He is confined in a dozen mutually unintelligible tongues, is not really aware of what the Guatemalan nation claims to be. He would prefer to be left alone to go on with his own ways of worshiping God, ordering his civil affairs, dealing with the complexities of family life and tilling the land as he has always done. How far away and how indifferent to the modern world he can be is illustrated by the active use, among some Indian villages, of the ancient Maya calendar to schedule his religious activities during the year.

The mestizo who does make himself heard and has taken over the leadership of the government is indifferent if not hostile to the Indian and his ways. The mestizo talks in public and to the large world as if the Indian did not matter or did not exist, and General Jorge Ubico, so many years the dictator of Guatemala, attempted to deny the Indian's presence to the outside world. In a motion picture of Ubico's doings as president, for distribution in Central America, the Indian was cut out whenever possible. Wherever Ubico was shown, he managed to be surrounded solely by Ladinos. Only in one flash was the cat let out of the bag. An Indian face and head slipped into one very good shot—too good to be cut. Guatemala was to be shown to the world as a mestizo nation though the Indian is at least one half of the population. The criollo, in Guatemala, has largely lost his identity. There is really no one who can stand above the conflict in cultures, and speak of the body of the nation as one people. If any one did he would be driven from office by the mestizos because they represent whatever effective power there is.

It ought to be clear that this is not a matter of conservatism, liberalism, democracy, socialism, communism, or whatever other slogan may be in vogue in the next generation. It is the incompatability of two cultures with basically different value systems. The unity that the nationalist aspires to he will have only when the Indian has so completely merged in the mestizo that he is no longer aware of himself. How long it will take no one can tell, but until then there can be no national leadership, because culturally there is no nation. This example is illustrative of other cases. It applies wherever there are very large Indian groups whose presence is looked upon as a burden to the nation.

One can say something very similar about Peru, Ecuador, Mexico before the Revolution of 1910, of Bolivia until 1952 and of other countries in their degree of non-assimilated Indian groups. It is significant that in the midst of the bitterness and violence of the Mexican Revolution, the attitude of thoughtful Mexicans was that they were "making a nation" (forjando patria). That is the title Manuel Gamio gave to a book of essays dealing with the Mexican upheaval and published in 1922. It is equally noticeable that after the defeat in the Chaco War the Bolivian intellectuals were obsessed with the idea of making a nation, bringing the Indian into the public arena. That perhaps is as good an explanation of the

47

Bolivian Revolution as can be found. The question of whom the leader speaks for is a baffling matter everywhere and particularly so in Latin America.

There are few places in other regions and none in the Western world where so great a difference can be found among the "citizens" of the same nation. Culturally most of the nations of Latin America are a kaleidoscope of all types of society—from the most primitive to the most complex, from the naked Amazonian being, such as the Auca Indians on the Napo River who recently killed some missionaries because they look upon every white man as an enemy, to the sophisticated intellectual in Quito, Lima or Mexico who reads Sartre and considers himself an existentialist. And these societies occupying the same territory but standing at the extreme of human experience are more widely scattered across the continent and north of Panama to the American border than is generally assumed. The Tarahuamara in Chihuahua, the Lacandón in Chiapas, and the forest and jungle people in Brazil, Colombia and Venezuela are but the end of a line. They are more significant than their numbers would suggest. For in between the extreme of a primitive group in the jungle that sees all strangers as enemies and the highly cultured intellectuals and artists in the city there is every variety of social organization, family, structure, notions of property ownership and possession.

We have to deal with a society that has well defined groups, who have no notion of property and whose living is acquired within some roughly defined area by hunting and fishing on one hand to the intricacies of the modern corporation registered in Delaware doing business through one or more subsidiaries in Peru, Mexico or Brazil on the other. The communal villages in the highlands with their varied customs and notions, ranging from full collective ownership to the village where the agricultural lands are held by individuals but the pasture lands belong to the community are but another feature of the world we are dealing with. Within these boundaries of collective and private ownership there is every gradation of right. These many different people are as much a part of the nation as the mestizos or the criollos. Statesmanship would require the acceptance of not only the different races, beliefs and language as equally part of the nation, but it would also accept the great variety of customary law by which these peoples regulate the conduct of their members as legitimate elements of the law in the larger unit called the nation. The recognition of unity in variety, of a culture rich in its possibilities because of unique values and meanings carried by each of these groups would be the height of statesmanship. Such leadership is hard to come by. The assertion that all men are equal is an ancient doctrine deeply ingrained in Christian culture. This idea gets itself written into the constitutions of Latin America. But the idea that the various cultures within the nation are equally legitimate, and the local customs and common law by which they arrange their own affairs ought to be protected against violence and abuse has found no Rousseau even in Latin America, where the persistent variable in social structure is so important historically as well as in the present.

It may be asking too much of national leadership to be sensitive and responsive to the needs and difficulties of all the culture groups that make up the nation. But these groups are the body of the nation in a country like Guatemala. They are what leadership ought to be responsive to if it is to be national. One way of looking at the failure of national leadership is to glance at the problem historically.

The Latin American criollo had little part in government during the colonial period and lacked business experience. After the independence and all through the nineteenth century business and industrial affairs fell by default to Spaniards, Italians, Germans, Englishmen, Americans and others. The aristocratic elements who went to the universities either at home or abroad (preferably in France) became doctors and lawyers and dabbled in literature and, if they stayed home, in politics. The tradition of the hacienda opposed preoccupation with the material world, business and industry or even with agriculture. In some sense the upper classes were oriented toward Europe and indifferent to the problems facing their own country. They were after all only a fraction of the total population and because of the prevailing hierarchical society they remained "above the battle," beyond the ability, interest or necessary immersion to take effective hold of the government. They lacked the "esprit de corps" of a governing class. They were not the natural leaders of the populace. They had not risen from them or by their support. They lacked a basis in the loyalty and affections of the populace. They were not only "above the battle" but so high above the people, that the leadership of the nation could not rest in their hands.

By default, the leadership of the nation came to rest with the mestizo. And the mestizo had neither the tradition, the education, nor the experience for the task. Basically the mestizo in the nineteenth century was on the make. The leadership that he took hold of was the means of power, prestige and affluence, and he achieved these with little scruple and no conscience. But he achieved national influence and power as the leader of a faction, a political family, as the caudillo of a region, by a military coup as the "colonel" of the militia or as an ambitious and likable politically-minded officer in the national army. He was not necessarily a philosopher, a political scientist, a man of great vision. These qualities were not excluded but they were not a prerequisite. What he needed was audacity, physical courage, indifference to life, great energy, ambition, friends and a family—a political family, *compadres,* a reputation for loyalty to his friends and the qualities of a demagogue, and an ability to dazzle his followers by an unexpected trait—of some kind. He had to be generous to his immediate followers, offer and exact absolute loyalty from

49

his political family. This leadership was not dependent upon a formal political party, which did not exist.

The leader, however, did not stand alone; he had a personal party bound by ties which could not be broken except in death. For in Latin America there is always in the background a community, a tradition, a church, a family. The individual stands inside and not outside their encompassing influences as he tends to do in the United States. And in instances where these warming and protective relations have been weakened, they are replaced by an informal but compelling association that stems from having been in the same school, lived in the same neighborhood, followed the same leader. These ties have elements of fidelity and identity that will outlast misfortune, poverty, exile and even crime. It would be difficult to find such a group where either family, church or community had not entered in; but even in sophisticated clusters whose main occupation is public service and active participation in politics, there is a tradition of deference to the needs of the members of the Pleiades that takes precedence over every other consideration. To stand by your group, the members of your extended family, your classmates, those raised with you in the same village, the compadre, your companions who followed the same political leader takes precedence over efficiency, public service, budgetary restrictions or formal law.

We call it nepotism, favoritism, political irresponsibility, financial mismanagement or peculation. But that is a view of the matter peculiarly unfitting to describe the situation. That assumes that the government is everybody's government rather than that it is our government—the government of those in power for the time being. It assumes that a public official could or should disregard in the name of public service the needs and expectancies of relatives, friends, neighbors and companions, who have lived with us, protected, befriended and perchance housed and fed us. It assumes that the abstract thing called the government should displace in our affection those who have always filled the days of our lives, who came in dozens to see us off when we went on a journey, who gathered and made a festive occasion of our *día de Santo,* who filled the house with laughter and music when we graduated from school, who converted every incident in our life into a symbol of fellowship and identity and will continue to do so long after we are out of the government.

The relations with the group are permanent. Political office is temporary and precarious. And it is expected to be so. The public association, the party, the cause (outside of the Church) to which individuals can be attached does not exist. There are exceptions, of course, such as the Liberals or Conservatives in Colombia, the Colorados and Blancos in Uruguay. But these are isolated instances. The phenomenon so common in the United States of life-long service to a public cause such as the Red Cross, the Civil Liberties Union, the American Prison Association, the

50

Public Library Association, the Federation of Women's Clubs is simply non-existent. The tradition of individualism, the special complex of mestizo society, the sense of insecurity and the preoccupation with the family in its larger sense has confined and circumscribed the individual within his family clan. But inside of that particular association, loyalty and devotion are likely to be life-long and absolute, above both good and evil.

If this does not provide the best of grounds for national leadership, it gives an ideal basis for the perpetuation of local leadership, the survival of the local family, and the persistent influence of regionalism in politics. We have known something of the same sort in our own southern states. But the southern states are one influence in a highly dynamic society, which is not the case in Latin America. There the closely knit regional political family, clan, gang, party or whatever name we choose to give it—and none are adequate—exists in all parts. All of the social and political life has this basis. The region exists in the feelings and the sense of the people whereas the nation is vague and ephemeral. When we talk about leadership this is the ground upon which it stands. Even in Brazil one is a Paulista—that is, from the State of São Paulo—rather than a Brazilian, in a sense that does not exist in the United States, not even among Texans.

In some subtle way these dispersing influences have played an important role in the history of repeated dictatorship. The nation cannot be governed solely in the interest of regional political clans. The national government, however it came to power, has to make its peace with the sectional claimants, with the political gangs—factions, families—that rule the different parts of the country. If the administration, that is the president, will not surrender to the splintering influences, and if he lacks the skill to compose and compromise, then dictatorship has been the means available, if the president had the makings of a dictator in him. This is not a defense of dictatorship; it is an attempt at understanding how the dictator has played so conspicuous a role in this part of the world. This ties in with another aspect of dictatorship.

In one way the army, especially in recent years, is the only secular institution that has a national outlook and interest and can thus stand above party and region. The case of Aramburu in Argentina is illustrative of the point. The government has gone to the army for reasons too numerous to deal with here, but one of these reasons is that the army can see the whole of the nation when other institutionalized forces are only concerned with the particular. We are concerned with the source of the leadership rather than with its quality or character. It is not an accident that the leaders of the nation have so often been soldiers. One of the reasons is that the nation as a nation has a meaning to them, when there is no nationally organized power to challenge the legitimacy of the army's

51

claims to either represent or govern the nation. These are complicated matters that must not be simplified, because they may also be falsified in the process. The leadership of the nation requires a symbol, a vision, a policy and a faith which transcends the particular. But the mestizo to whom the leadership has fallen has on the whole neither the tradition nor the training for national leadership—that is being the leader of all of the people. There are, of course, many individual exceptions that could be mentioned—Lleras Camargo, Lázaro Cárdenas, José Figueres, among others, but these are not typical of the Latin American political leader.

In considering leadership in Latin America, the intellectual plays a special role. Intellectuals come to this role as influential people by the traditional prestige of university training and the high esteem placed on literary production. The recognized poet, novelist, historian, but especially poet, has a distinctive place in the affections and enjoys the regard of his compatriots. The funeral cortege of a well-known literary figure in any of the capitals of Latin America will be followed by thousands of people. Recently something like 30,000 people followed the funeral carriage of a well-known Mexican historian. The literary man is a national figure with an influence independent of government position or party affiliation. This provides him with a base for leadership in the nation which is both admirable and unique. It is admirable because he is independent, and unique because he cannot be deprived of the following that he has, or lose it except by ceasing to write and publish. He has another qualification for national leadership not shared by many of his contemporaries: he more than most is likely to have a vision of the nation as a whole. He can be above party, region, or class. He will, more than others, have had contact with the cultures beyond his own and know something of the complexities and difficulties of the world about him, and understand something of the possibilities and limits of public policy, and be aware of the temper of the age in which he lives.

For reasons that perhaps cannot be adequately explained, the intellectuals, with a few notable exceptions, both past and present, have not become the effective leaders of their nations.

To begin with, the intellectuals, and that includes the better known artists, poets, novelists, historians and literary critics, were oriented toward Europe, preferably France, rather than their own country. This was generally true until the first world war, and only gradually, and perhaps not completely even today, in some countries, have they discovered their own country. It has been remarked, truly enough, that Brazilian intellectual history can be divided into the period before Gilberto Freyre and the period after the publication of *Casa-Grande e Senzala* (translated as "Masters and Slaves"). Until the publication of this remarkable social history of Northeastern Brazil, writers were preoccupied with European subjects and paid little attention to their own country or its problems. And when

52

they did, it was to deprecate its backwardness and reflect in sadness upon the mixture of negro, Indian and white as something unhealthy if not unnatural, and as condemning their country to inferiority.

Since the publication of "Masters and Slaves" a flood of hundreds of volumes has appeared on Brazilian subjects. That is the great merit of this remarkable book. The Brazilians have discovered themselves. Instead of running away from race mixture as a scandal and a shame they find the vitality and richness of their literature, music, art and architecture in the strength and vigor which a fusion of race and culture has given. They consider Brazil a model for the world to follow and Brazilian culture as a uniquely rich contribution to world civilization.

Something similar has occurred in Mexico following the revolution, and especially after the Cárdenas regime, which greatly increased Mexican self-respect and its feeling of dignity. It was during this period that Mexico stopped living in constant fear of the United States. Whether this is the immediate cause or not, the Mexicans like the Brazilians have accepted themselves as they are and are proud of it. They are not Europeans or North Americans and do not wish to be. They have a sense of importance and pride in the vast outpouring of energy that has gone into their new art and architecture, their music and poetry, and now their fiction and drama. And all of this is Mexican. It is, I think, admittedly clear that Diego Rivera and Clemente Orozco could only be Mexicans, and no other people could have built the Mexican national University. This too is an acceptance by the Mexicans that their culture is Mexican, as is their race. They are no longer ashamed of having Indian blood in their veins and no longer drive the Indians from the main streets. But in both Brazil and Mexico this facing of the national reality is too recent to have allowed for the growth of a couple of generations to an intellectual maturity free from the sense of being culturally outcast. This self-confidence is an essential for the development of leadership in a nation whether it is drawn from among the intellectuals or not.

Beyond Brazil and Mexico, however, where does one find this kind of intellectual revolution, of a discovery of the national self, as if seeing it for the first time as it really is—and seeing that it is good? The intellectuals have lived for so long immersed in European models that they have in most places barely escaped them. There is obvious danger in overstating this proposition, and I can hear vigorous disclaimers from Argentinians, Colombians, Uruguayans and Costa Ricans, but as an outsider and a friendly one, I can only say that the willingness in gladness to accept oneself and live with oneself that has come as something of a miracle to Brazil and Mexico has not occurred in other countries. Certainly not in Peru, Bolivia, Ecuador, Venezuela or Guatemala, to mention only a few of the nations. And without this acceptance of the nation as it is, effective leadership is impossible.

53

Intellectuals interested in dealing with the important question of politics and government, of economic growth and business organization, of finance and taxation, unemployment and social security—with any one of the questions that contemporary society has to deal with—had to go to foreign books or foreign universities. And fundamentally, interest in these matters locally did not exist. The intellectual tradition was literary and theoretical. European doctrines in sociology, politics, economics and philosophy were absorbed with avidity. This has happened with positivism, syndicalism, socialism, communism, existentialism, but they were taken over as ideas rather than policies or programs. Traditionally, theory, philosophy, doctrine, intellectual attitude had little to do with political programs or social policy.

The centralized character of government, the habit of expecting the government to do whatever is to be done, the overwhelming impact of the aristocratic, authoritarian and hierarchical view of life, really meant that ideas were things to argue about, to play with, and not programs or policies. Even when ideas such as democracy or federalism get into constitutions, as the history of the last century and a half will illustrate, they remain ideas rather than norms of conduct. This has occurred more recently with the inclusion of elaborate provisions on human rights and civil liberties into the fundamental document. These too have too often remained just ideas rather than norms of behavior. A theory of democracy, communism, socialism, or what not, has to make its way against a Latin American milieu which is responsive to older and deeper attitudes, attitudes that have no formal doctrinal statement but which are nonetheless very real. For way down deep is the fact that Latin America is humanist rather than materialist. It is compassionate rather than equalitarian; it is authoritarian rather than democratic. It does not understand that authority is divisible, that the president can be defeated by a congress, or flouted by a court and yet remain president. It does not understand that other institutions than the government can exercise important public functions. The attitude is one of acquiescence in the protective power of the mighty one as long as he does not do violence to the basic moral traditions, and if he does to destroy his power by revolution, and accept a better one in his place.

Basically, Latin Americans would protect the poor, save their dignity, relieve pain and assuage sorrow rather than reform, change, improve or upset status, position, belief or ideals. It is not "progressive," and the reformers are following strange gods and using slogans that stem from other sources. In spite of their many revolutions, the Latin Americans are not either revolutionary or radical. All the revolutions would merely reestablish an older ideal society, hierarchical and authoritarian, compassionate and sensitive to the human dignity even of the least, even of the peon. And the rebellious nationalism so much in evidence is not against authoritarianism or hierarchy but against the materialism and efficiency of modern ways that have no time to be compassionate, that are so preoccupied with success as to take from men what they have most valued—their dignity.

This is perhaps a good place to say a few words about American enterprise in Latin America. The objection to American enterprise is not that it is American. Rather it is disliked because it is efficient, purposeful, direct, single-minded and materialistic. In Latin American culture, business is a part of the total scheme of things; it is part of the family, of the *compadre* relation, of the friendships, of the church. Business is done among friends in a leisurely and understanding way. Material success is at the bottom of the scale. First of all comes the protection of the family, the *compadres,* the friends. Every relation, no matter how unimportant in the business is important on the human side, for each man must be treated with courtesy and dignity, almost as a member of the family. The efficiency and singlemindedness of the American enterprise is unaware of or indifferent to the scheme of ethical and esthetic values by which life is ruled. Its very egalitarianism and familiarity are offensive. It sticks out not because it is American or foreign capital, but because it is not part of the milieu.

It cannot identify with the aristocratic agrarian tradition, or with the growing middle class. To the first it is a threat. To the second it seems a block in their own path, especially as the foreign corporation does not ordinarily (things are changing) offer the young middle class, or the young intellectuals an outlet to their ambitions, and it does not give them, or is not believed to give them, equality of opportunity within the administration. In our own experience a new industry is an opening for new careers. In Latin America a new foreign enterprise has often meant the exclusion of locally competent young people of good families. Neither the business community nor the intellectuals find it congenial. Their life is involved in the total culture, while the American businessman, or manager, stands outside their culture and is somehow beyond their reach. They have no way of bending the new enterprise to their older values and no way of losing themselves within the new venture, or of submerging it within their own system so as to cease to be aware of its irritating presence.

And Americans are not particularly helpful in this. They do not, for the most part, associate with the members of their host community, and if they have to, they often do it in a patronizing way which does not add to their good standing. Mainly Americans live by themselves and do not participate. The rector of the university of an active industrial community in which there were some hundreds of American university-trained specialists in many fields, when asked whether any of this highly select group of Americans took any interest or part in the many interesting activities of this university, replied, "These people do not associate with us."

55

If one searches into the reason for the hostility shown to Mr. Nixon, here is a key to what happened which has not been explored. And it is the burden of the complaint raised by intellectuals against "American imperialism." The economic arguments and even the political ones, though often used, are of secondary importance. They seem obvious and are part of the contemporary fashion in public debate. The other, the deeper, grievance that Americans are oblivious to and disdainful of Latin American values and sense of personal dignity, is more difficult to express and much too painful to cry in the market place. American business and American policy have often been afflicted by obtuseness and insensitivity. No amount of good will, back-slapping or offers of material aid are adequate substitutes for understanding of and sensitivity to the values that give meaning and direction to life itself. Our efficiency and purposefulness, our "go-getterness," our enthusiasm about success, qualities we greatly prize, prove most irritating and incomprehensible. If only we were less in a hurry, less bent on getting things done quickly; if only we had time for talk and friendliness and courtesy; if only we did not seem to push people around and in our haste forget, or be ignorant of, the amenities essential to friendly relations! As one Latin American expressed it, "Our greatest difficulties are over little, seemingly unimportant, things."

The Latin American intellectual, student, professor, artist, writer, and poet have found American "crudities," as they would call them, so frustrating that on occasion they have been prepared to say "Keep your good will, your material offerings and your bad manners. We will have none of them."

It is important to keep in mind that these feelings and attitudes so frequently voiced, if muted, are not confined to one country. Latin America may be divided into twenty separate nations but intellectually it is very much one community. Many of its most distinguished contemporary writers are almost household words among the literate people in the entire area, particularly in the eighteen Spanish-speaking countries. These include individuals like Alfonso Reyes from Mexico, Germán Arciniegas from Colombia, Picón Salas and Rómulo Gallegos from Venezuela, Luis Alberto Sánchez from Peru, Gilberto Freyre from Brazil, Luis Romero from Argentina, Fernando Ortiz from Cuba.

We are, as a nation, therefore dealing not with single countries even when we are only talking to the minister of Nicaragua or Argentina. Vis-a-vis the United States, there is a community of public opinion which is as wide as the land that includes all of the nations south of the American border. In many things there are sharp differences among these nations and even bitter antagonism. But as against the United States there is wide agreement on many issues and on some there is well nigh unanimity. And to no small degree this is the work of the intellectuals. It could be said

56

that the intellectuals have been the leaders in moulding a Latin American community, at least on the intellectual level, but also indirectly they have had great influence on the political attitudes of their community toward the United States. In some ways the intellectuals have been more influential as leaders of the continental community than of their own particular countries, for the intellectuals, with the exception of Colombia, rarely achieve actual political power.

They are the moderators, the critics, the gadflies, the opponents. They are not the political leaders, though they often have great influence on shaping the opinion that determines the kind of leadership that comes to office and the policies it will pursue. The intellectuals are really caught in a world where their major role is that of critic. The realities of the situation require us to recognize that they are not willing, i.e. able, to face the schizophrenic world they abide in. They greatly value all that a "patronal" and aristocratic society has given them—the ease, the unhurried life, the indifference to great wealth, the presence of many servants to make life easy and secure, the romantic notion of a heroic past, the occasion for friendships and versatility. All of this they would keep. But they also want what the modern world has to offer, or think they want it— modern cities, automobiles, airplanes, factories, the latest products of science, the gadgets of the day. They would have the best of two worlds; the patronal, senorial society and the egalitarian and industrial one, and will not recognize that they cannot have them both.

There is no way out of the dilemma by a deliberate act of will. They cannot reject either of the two worlds or remain content with one. The schizophrenic world they live in is beyond their control; and we must accept that for the next generation or longer the intellectuals will be possessed by a restless, bitter and turbulent mood. America will be the major target of this inability to square the circle; to make an agrarian feudalism fit in nicely with an industrial egalitarianism, for fortune has cast the United States as the major symbol of their dissatisfaction with both worlds.

2. Political change in Latin America

K. H. SILVERT

Merely by existing, the United States and the Western world as a whole bring to bear on Latin America a constant cultural pressure. But even though the ideas of industrialization, expanded consumption, and political egalitarianism may pour forth equally for all Latin American countries, what is absorbed varies widely from one to another. How and why and toward what immediate ends each nation moves is conditioned by its own traditions and appreciations as well as by the historical course of its particular set of involvements with the industrially advanced nations. The recurrent crises of most Latin American countries today are of a type symptomatic of a beginning maturity, of an almost accomplished understanding of what they want, what they reject, and of what methods they will use. The recently alerted awareness of the problems of Latin America in the United States is not a simply casual passage from unthinking Yankee neglect to fatherly notice; it is the direct product of a now purposively and rapidly reacting group of newly synthesizing societies.

K. H. SILVERT has combined an interest in political science and in Latin America since his undergraduate days at the University of Pennsylvania, which awarded him the Ph.D. degree in 1948. At that time he joined the faculty of Tulane University, where he is now professor of political science. Since 1955, he has also been connected with the American Universities Field Staff as associate first in Central America and then in Argentina and Chile. He has spent over five years doing research in the field itself and has published extensively on Latin America, as well as within the general discipline of political science.

59

That the internal dynamics of the Latin American countries are in part driven by the general cultural stance of the United States as well as by military aid, investments, and loans is obvious. Wittingly or not, then, the United States has had much to do with the social changes which in turn are forcing Latin America upon international attention. The uneven development of nation-states in that region is bringing Latin America closer to the problem areas and value systems of the European-type states, but what is occurring is not mere slavish imitation. Their many variations on the general themes of underdevelopment and progress toward national democracies may well eventually demonstrate to other parts of the world broad and varied possibilities in the adjustment of the individual to national social organization.

Prepared several years ago by a group of American scholars, a symposium grimly entitled, "Pathology of Democracy in Latin America," ends with these sentences:

> It is possible . . . to conclude that Latin America as a whole is groping toward a more realistic basis of political thinking in terms of its own environment, conditioning circumstances and peoples. The long-established practice of blindly following the foreign gods is slowly, but effectively, breaking down.[1]

To lump this development process of Latin America carelessly in with that of other economically retarded areas is a mistake. Commonly available statistics force one immediate exception of consequence: Argentina, Uruguay, Venezuela, and significant portions of Brazil and Mexico must be counted as intermediately developed. Even more important, Latin America has had the longest history of European colonialism in the world. While it may not bear the stamp of Western industrialism, the area has a long and varied experience with a portion of European custom and thought, not only as a superimposition but also as an internal aspect of society. Further, Latin America's underdevelopment bears not only direct lineal relation to idealized Iberian feudalism, but it also has the special characteristic of being correlated with under-population, and not with the overpopulation so evident in Asia.

And, lastly, another unusual feature is Latin America's traditionally close identification with the United States. The intimate relationship has not always been most cordial, but it is there and among the reasons for it are proximity, defense considerations, in certain measure shared ideology, and the leverage exerted by the great economic and cultural strength of the United States relative to the Latin American republics. Hemispheric readjustments from paternalism to fraternalism are becoming the order of the day as political change in Latin America mingles with the other social shifts involved in the process of going from systems of necessary authoritarianism to those of possible democracy. These devel-

---

[1] *The American Political Science Review*, March, 1950.

opments should be anticipated by diplomatic policy planners, for the period of one-man, one-family, and one-class government is just about over in a Latin America that is now doing much more than merely copying the standard recipes for democratic government.

The attempt to write about the politics of twenty different republics in one short article demands rigorous limitation, especially if the added task of relating internal political phenomena to United States foreign policy is included. This chapter will primarily consider the width of difference and, conversely, the narrowness of likeness among the Latin American countries. The basic presumption in the field of international relations is that foreign policy should not be more flexible than necessary lest it appear eclectic to the point of opportunism; and no more rigid than required by circumstances if meaningless predictions and false expectations are not to follow. The policy planner must then know to what extent the experience gained in one context is applicable in another. I have chosen social structure as the most efficient manner of classifying the Latin American republics in order to hint at the extent to which experience may be carried from one country to another. The discussions of political history, violence, parties and pressure groups are then all in terms of the measuring rod of social structure. In technical language, class structure is taken as the independent variable, and the other matters treated as the dependent variables, each brought to bear one at a time against the independent measure. The reasons for using this analytical device will be made clear as the discussion proceeds.

Political likenesses and diversities

The commonwealth notion

The justification for writing about Latin America in terms of global relationships is that such universalistic concepts are among the real symbolic tools used by political leaders within and without the area. "Latin America," "Hispano-America," "Indo-America," and "Ibero-America" are more than terms of convenience, for the opinion leaders of the area themselves recognize an emotional commonwealth. They have hardened this awareness in unique international juridical principles, in a regional organization, in their voting in international agencies, in their preferential treatment of their neighbors' nationals, and in their constitutional theories. At this formally legal level, the United States, too, has expressed its recognition of a set of special circumstances through the Monroe Doctrine in its various interpretations, particularized recognition procedures, and co-participation in regional political and economic as well as jurisprudential arrangements. Special note should also be taken of the strikingly few cases of international warfare in this cartographically Balkanized region, a phenomenon which finds one of its better explanations in the notion of commonwealth identification.

From the historical facts of politics there emerge other likenesses further serving to tie the republics together. If the common experience of colonialism stamped some similar hallmarks, whether the metropolitan power was France, Portugal, or Spain, so did the fact of independence, sweeping through all of Latin America, except for Cuba, in the same chronological period and under the same ideological banners borrowed from the United States and France. Every country underwent a "time of trouble" after independence, and every one has had at least one great integrating dictator, whether named Díaz, Portales, Rosas, or Carrera. These men are to Latin America as Louis XIV to France or Ivan the Terrible to Russia: they broke the power of the local *caciques* and established centralized control over the territories of their nascent nation-states. Where the integrating centralists could not extend their effective sway to appreciable distances, city-states emerged, as in Central America.

This forced integration almost always was loaded with ideological freight. The *caudillo,* authoritarian leader of a national arena, sought legitimacy in law, and authority in party, while he used naked power to break the *caciques.* Although *caudillismo* naturally conduces to the personalistic political parties so general in Latin America, conflicting idealisms have also been present. The Conservative-Liberal divisions of the last century, and in some countries even of this century, have echoed true policy and interest clashes as well as mere personality differences. The *caudillo,* then, has often been the personification of ideological disagreement, manipulating the power of the idea as well as the sword.

In contemporary Latin America, the emergence of impersonal political institutions is everywhere clearly visible to one or another degree. Bound into a democratic bundle, economic development, nationalism, institutionalization, and modernism are widely generalized goals. These common aspirations and a common dependence on a common world buttress the fraternal feelings of the commonwealth notion.

The historical range of political difference

A factor weakening feelings of hemispheric identification, however, is that these sentiments are restricted largely to élite leadership groups whose ideas are projected against much political divergence and politically apathetic population sectors. Variation among the countries is becoming accentuated as individual national histories become an ever stronger force pushing the Latin American nations further apart into differing political cultures and styles. They are all somewhere along the continuum to democratic nation-state status, but accident, history, and resources combine in differing ways to give varying results.

Independence sometimes came easily, for example, as in the case of Central America, heir to the greater efforts in Mexico. But in Mexico itself, the independence movement was confounded with social revolution, and the process was painful and relatively protracted. The succeeding times of trouble also varied widely in intensity and duration, from the relatively easy transition of Argentina to the fifty years of convulsion in Mexico. Where the integrating dictatorship came early, as in Chile, national life subsequently has tended to develop with comparative ease; yet other countries, such as Venezuela, show a procession of *caudillos* persisting unto yesterday's headlines. The Liberal-Conservative conflicts were usually fairly well resolved everywhere by the turn of the century, the Liberals almost invariably victorious either partially or completely. The major exception is Colombia, where the issue is still not settled. Colombia is the only country in which the two major parties still bear the names "Liberal" and "Conservative."

"National revindication," "social justice," "economic independence," "anti-imperialism," "industrialization," and "nationalism" are the words of the current Latin political lexicon everywhere. But they do not have the same tone in every country, nor even within each set of national boundaries does this vocabulary generally permeate all the population strata. Even though the generalized aspirations of the leadership elements may have ingredients in common, the development of an adequate American policy vis-a-vis the entire area must take into account not only the vast differences of the present, but also the fascinatingly diverse manners in which further development is certain to manifest itself.

Political values and types of polities

Social class

A hobby of Latin Americanists, their hands forced by the variety of their area of study, is to develop social character types within which to squeeze all twenty republics. One of the efficient ways in which to set up a distribution is in accordance with social class, a most obvious feature of Latin societies which is visible in clothing, speech, occupation, habitation, education, and of course, political power. The allied subjects of social class and social mobility tell us whether a society is open or closed, and thus are essential to predictions concerning stability and the probabilities for democratic processes. Social structural analysis is also indispensable for an understanding of nationalism and potentialities for economic growth.

The simplest societies in Latin America are those ordinarily called semi-feudal, ruled by a small élite, the holders of major economic power, recipients of the highest social status and prestige, monopolists of the political organism. Under them can be found a shrivelled administrative and professional group charged with the operation of the cities, the public service, and the discharge of the necessary professional functions, especially law and medicine. At the bottom are the peasants, migratory or tenant farmers, sometimes the owners of their own small plots; and in the cities, those persons necessary to the more menial functions. In some countries the lowest agricultural group is divided ethnically into Indians and other persons considered Europeanized, no matter what their physical race, by virtue of their speaking a European language, their wearing of non-Indian dress, and their feeling of being a part of the national life, even though most tenuously.

Guatemala is an excellent case of a structure only slightly more complicated than that described above. Of a total population of about three million, perhaps only 125,000 can be counted as effective actors in the reaching of political decisions at the national level. This figure is arrived at by subtracting the Indian population, those rural *mestizos* who are not truly national in their concepts, the illiterates, persons under eighteen, and a part of the female population.

At the other end of the scale is Argentina. Almost a third of the twenty million Argentines live in Greater Buenos Aires, and in the country as a whole, two-thirds live in towns and cities of over 2,000 population. About a third of the Argentines are in the middle and upper occupational levels. Except for scattered and isolated Indian and mixed rural groups, the population is European. Agricultural labor is not rooted to the soil as in Peruvian and Chilean haciendas, for example; farm workers and ranch hands may and in fact do make use of the channels of social mobility, forming one of the important mass groups supporting ex-dictator Perón and contributing to the huge increase in the city populations of the past fifteen years.

Caste-like racial distinctions and a sharp cultural cut between the city and the country make popular sovereignty and the dispersion of political power at best a very limited possibility in such countries as Guatemala. The homogeneity of Argentina speeds communications, distributes aspirational goals almost universally, and promotes mass participation in politics for good or ill.

The velocity of Latin American social change, and it is in some fundamental respects the fastest moving part of the world, can create very complicated class systems. Mexico and Brazil, to take two examples among various, have what may be called double systems. There is an old and a new upper group, the former generally agrarian and clerical in orientation, the latter urban industrial and secularist. The old service middle group coexists with the new white collar and professional elements, while the industrial blue collar groups find little in common with depressed agrarian persons. Add the racial complication of the Indian populations

64

of Mexico at the village cultural level, and this somewhat oversimplified picture is complete.

The most important class phenomenon from a political viewpoint is the rapid growth of middle groups. Fomented by the exploding cities, the complex skills demanded by the new industries, the expanding welfare functions of government, and the extension of the professions, the middle sectors are already the decisive voice in at least half of the Latin American countries. Their presence spells the doom of traditional *caudillismo,* but not necessarily the immediate and automatic stability and democracy which popular myth attributes to them.

Nationalism

An ordinary view of nationalism is that it is a negative sentiment, backward looking, exclusivist, anti-foreign, and at times even insane, as in Nazi Germany. A cooler reaction would be to think of nationalism as a social value elevating loyalty to a state and to the citizenry included therein to a supreme position. In the event of a clash involving, say religious institutions or even the right of a parent to beat his child, a national society would assume ultimate adherence to the dictates of the state within a broadly prescribed realm rather than of any intervening, buffer institutions. Some of the usual historical manifestations of nationalism are citizens' armies, such symbols as flags and anthems, a public education system, reverence for the past as well as glorification of the future, and so on. Supernationalism, the product of totalitarian systems, is the extension of this loyalty to make it fit a disintegrating situation; historical nationalism, on the other hand, is an integrative and generalizing mechanism.

The creation of new middle (as well as upper and lower) economic positions, which occurs in developing countries, forces apart the traditional social structure, introducing the middle classes which are such a dynamic part of the new Latin America. These complications are at the same time rationalized by nationalism, a loyalty pattern to cover not only the geographical areas involved, but now also the new identifications across class lines which build consistency and stability into the higher degree of interdependence that industrial urbanism always implies. Where there are middle groups, there is nationalism, the basic political value of Westernism.

Despite a lack of hard data, some informed guessing may be done as to the degree to which various Latin American countries have become truly national societies. In point for this subjective evaluation are such criteria as ethnic integration of the population, political history as it may indicate cohesiveness or disorganization, complexity of the city and the occupational range of the economic apparatus, degree of autonomy or dependency of the countryside and the political power of the peasantry, if any, mobility factors, and so on. Closest to nation-state standing in Latin America are Uruguay, Argentina, Costa Rica, and Chile, and perhaps in that descending order, although to be so exact as to give rankings within the categories is to open the door to much wrangling. The next category might well include those countries moving rapidly toward nationhood with a solid social consensus approving the trend. Again in questionable descending order, these countries are: Mexico, Colombia, Brazil, Venezuela, and Cuba. The third category includes those in which the upper groups are moving violently toward nationalist aspirations, but with sluggish response in the body social. They are Peru, Bolivia, Guatemala, Ecuador, El Salvador, and Panama, once again in dubious order. And lastly, slow rates of movement, with almost all social sectors stagnant, are to be found in Honduras, Paraguay, Nicaragua, the Dominican Republic, and Haiti.

Class, nationalism, and democracy

The social value of nationalism is a necessary condition for democracy, but not a sufficient one. Without it, the almost universal acceptance of the rules within which democracy works and the necessary belief in the reciprocating continuity of acquiesence and opposition cannot function.

Democracy presupposes a toughminded and tenacious acceptance of the nation as deserving a continuing loyalty which transcends loyalty to class. Democracy assumes that the proper adjustments and accommodations among classes, probably accompanied by vigorous debate and pulling and hauling, will be made peacefully within the framework provided. If loyalty to a class, whether a proletariat in the professional sense or an élite group, supersedes the common loyalty then democracy suffers accordingly.[2]

National loyalty identifications, however, are not sufficient to guarantee democracy, since the sentiment may also be employed for the implementation of totalitarian, as contrasted with authoritarian rule. Latin American dictatorships, even including the Perón one, so far have been more closely related to the works of a Cromwell or a Frederick the Great than to a Hitler or a Mussolini. Totalitarianisms are so called precisely because they seek to destroy completely the institutional buffers between the individual and the state, to erase all non-state loyalties, and to void all doctrines propounding governmental self-restraint. When scientific techniques are not well developed, then the full weight of the dictator can fall directly only on the visible élite; others escape for negative reasons, saved by the sheer impossibility of the police task. With IBM machines, radio patrol cars, and modern propaganda techniques, the state gains the power to "finger" anyone, to minimize if not erase the cushioning effects of religious, kin, and class shock absorbers. If technological complication implies

---

[2] Russell H. Fitzgibbon in "Pathology of Democracy in Latin America," as cited.

middle classes and middle classes imply nationalism, then nationalism in turn also implies possibilities for sterner autocracies as well as fuller democracies. In short, nationalism is a neutral factor, its color a reflection of other choices.

What we may call "political culture," notions of civic goodness and badness, the attitudes of innovating groups, and the pressures from the international world all contribute to throwing the choice toward more or less freedom. In Latin America, even the harshest dictators customarily attempt to clothe themselves in legal legitimacy and to talk in the name of democracy, tutelary or otherwise. This pose is not mere farce; it conditions future action most importantly.

Latin American constitutions are an excellent case in point of the orienting power of expressed traditional goals. Over two hundred constitutions have been adopted in the more or less 150 years during which the Latins have been at work on organic law. Most of the changes have been in the hortatory and the distributing clauses as one or another philosophy or this or that administrative gimmick has been experimented with. But the aspirations outlined in these documents have often served to condition the actions of future governments. As a Latin American jurist has said in commenting on the advanced theories contained in constitutional law, "After all, before you embrace a woman, you tell her you love her." Through the schools, law, the writings of impassioned leaders, Latin Americans have been told for almost two centuries that democracy is desirable. The writings of Locke, Bentham, the two Mills, *The Federalist Papers,* the Constitution of the United States, and the Declaration of the Rights of Man, among many other such expressions of man's dignity, have all been imported to help in solidifying this predisposition. While the economic and social conditions in most of Latin America have not been of a type to support full-blown democracies, these political values have constantly served as a prod for the changing of the opposed root conditions. Small wonder, then, that the 20th Century is so often called The Age of Politics in Latin America.

It is thus no accident that included in the list of these countries which are most nearly nation-states are also to be found those usually considered most democratic. A noted American historian, Arthur P. Whitaker, suggests that "the countries which have approximated most closely to the democratic ideal have been—Argentina, Brazil, Chile, Colombia, Costa Rica, and Uruguay." A typology developed by a political sociologist (Seymour Martin Lipset, in a recent issue of *The American Political Science Review*) posits only two categories, "Democracies and Unstable Dictatorships" and "Stable Dictatorships." He puts in the former Argentina, Brazil, Chile, Colombia, Costa Rica, Mexico, and Uruguay; and in the latter, all the rest of Latin America. While two categories are insufficient to explain all of Latin America, the reappearance of the first seven in high position on all three listings, "The National," "The Democratic," and "Democracies and Unstable Dictatorships," clearly indicates certain factors common to all. Nationalism plus the long belief in the value of democracy may well be in combination as the common denominator.

It should not be expected that such a fundamental change as the flowering of national democracies can occur without great disturbance.

The uses of force

A Chilean political figure has written that some Latin Americans want "order even if in despotism," and that others want "liberty even if in anarchy." Before an ordering of liberty is attained, there will probably be much more trouble in Latin America. But the real amount of violence as such should not be overestimated. The number of revolutions in Latin America is accentuated by the North American, who tends to forget that there are twenty different republics all having their own troubles, and who does not understand the patterning of Latin violence, the often reduced numbers of persons involved, and the built-in limitations of the impact of civil disorder on daily life.

"Unpredictable" and "unstable" are the two adjectives most often applied to Latin American politics. The implications of both pejoratives are partially erroneous. First, to be "unstable" is not necessarily to be "unpredictable." As a matter of fact, one of the easiest things to predict is instability itself. And second, some types of revolutionary disturbance do not indicate instability. If the normal way of rotating the executive in a given country is by revolution, and if there have been a hundred such changes in a century, then it is not being facetious to remark that revolutions are a sign of stability—that events are marching along as they always have. A country can afford such adventures only if they are contained and if there are built-in safeguards against excessive violence. The right of asylum, recognized legally by all Latin American governments, is one of the insurance policies provided to cut down deaths by revolution. Top-level corruption—a kind of saving against a rainy day—is another of these insurance devices. In addition, very strong kinship ties, a sense of class identification, and colleagueship all offer protection against the vicissitudes of politics. Many revolts, then, cost few lives, immediately affect persons only in the élite groups, and do not perturb the normal functioning of society.

In addition we should not forget that some countries have enjoyed very long periods without violence. Mexico has experienced peaceful political transitions for the last thirty years. Of the 105 years between 1839 and 1944, only three presidents in Guatemala occupied 61 years of the time. And yet, not to be too sanguine about the matter, some revolutions have

68

been extraordinarily bloody and deeply disturbing. Let us see whether some order can be breathed into this matter.

Types of revolutions and their incidence

There are many different families of violence, and their incidence depends absolutely on the type of society concerned. Here are the more common varieties, past and present:

The Simple Barracks Revolt—More outbreaks have been of this kind than of any other. Highly characteristic of the rudimentary bi-class societies, the army plays out the disposition of force, sometimes in its own name, or in that of a given leader, sometimes with ideological justification, and yet again in various combinations of these three rationalizations. The barracks revolt rarely causes much public commotion, even though at times substantive shifts in policy may emerge from one.

The Peasant Revolt—Only in bi-ethnic countries, or where the rural group is maintained in deep subservience, do peasant revolts take place. They are rarely reported internationally, since by definition they occur in a restricted area and are not of direct significance at the national level. Very few are now seen, although they were quite common in the colonial and early independence periods.

The Regional Revolt—Another type now almost never seen, regional uprisings were characteristic of the conflict period attending the rise of the centralizing *caudillos* and the liquidation of their provincial rivals. The history of Argentina, for example, is often written in terms of the "port," Buenos Aires, as opposed to the "interior," or the provinces. Brazil offers many examples, as does Colombia. Regional rivalries are now often played out in party politics through the activities of local bosses, who in many places have inherited the name *"cacique."*

The Complicated Barracks Revolt—The commonest of all at present, this kind of insurrection involves civilian as well as military groups. The immediate events are largely in terms of military action, but the issues are clearly ideological and involve political parties and interest groups. The fall of Perón is a case in point, as well as the defeats of Pérez Jiménez in Venezuela in 1958 and Rojas Pinilla in Colombia in 1957. This type tends to be somewhat costly in lives, although there are some examples (such as Guatemala in 1944) in which almost no one is killed. The issues may be entirely political, or the civilian participation may be so heated and widespread as to verge on the attitudes and aspirations of social revolution, as was the case in Cuba with the recent overthrow of Batista. The Cuban example is on the borderline, for although Havana fell and Batista fled as the direct result of an army defection, civilian opposition had previously so eroded the Batista Government's ability to impose itself as to leave the military with no choice.

69

The Civilian Political Revolt—Because of the active role of the military in politics, there is no abundance of this kind of action. Chile, in its 1932 year of revolutions, saw the military discredited and many examples of entirely civilian action in forcing governmental changes. This kind of undertaking becomes more difficult when the military are equipped with jet planes and tanks. The establishment of irregular armies and the practice of civilian terrorism were easier in the days when the rifle was the common arbiter. The general strike is the contemporary civilian phenomenon most closely allied to this category of revolt.

The Social Revolution—The Mexican Revolution, at its most heated between 1910 and 1917, is the only relatively complete example of social revolution in Latin America. This revolution combined all the other types, involving as it did simple and complex barracks revolts, a large measure of peasant protest and action, civilian participation at all levels, and regional disturbances. The result was to change the nature of the social hierarchy and partially to reorder it, thus fitting the classical definition of social revolution.

Unstructured Violence—(1) The Street Riot: *"Manifestaciones,"* as they are often called in Spanish, usually take place to protest particular governmental actions, such as a rise in bus fares or the arrest of political or labor leaders. University students are very prone to this kind of disturbance; for example, the student riots in Mexico in 1958 and those in Chile in 1957 were both sparked by an increase in bus fares. Deaths are not uncommon in these incidents. (2) The *Bogotazo:* This phenomenon takes its name from the mob violence in Bogotá in 1948, when the assassination of the leader of the Liberal Party touched off mass rioting resulting in wholesale looting, burning, and killing. These occurrences are undirected, a kind of explosive social vomiting. They indicate that the normal channels of access to the decision making areas have been closed off for too long to bleed off protest pressures. The *bogotazo* is rare, but there are sufficient cases in history—and, dangerously, enough street riots which have had all the preliminary elements of the *bogotazo*—to make this category worth including.

Complicated barracks revolts, civilian political revolts, social revolutions, and unstructured violence are all characteristic of periods in which the middle class is growing and seeking an adjustment. Those countries denominated as quite national (Chile, Uruguay, Argentina, and Costa Rica) as well as those on the verge (Mexico, Colombia, Brazil, Venezuela, and Cuba) are susceptible to these types of disturbance, or already have partially outgrown them. Since these nations either have large, complicated industrial cities or the self-conscious and cohesive landed peasantry of Costa Rica, civil strife is inevitably vastly punishing to major parts of the population, or at best a very grave threat. Bloodless strife is impossible to these countries; the best they can hope for, should they have recourse to revolution, is the stylized combination street fighting and barracks revolts of Argentina, an arrangement which may not hold even for that country should their troubles become more galling.

The more underdeveloped republics will tend to stick to the spread ranging from simple barracks revolts to complicated ones, probably with some peasant and regional difficulties thrown in, particularly in the cases of Peru and Bolivia. But no guarantees against a build-up to social revolution can be given even for the least developed countries, although the probabilities are against it. The uncontrollable factor here is the nature of international ideological and economic stimuli and the intensity of local reactions to them.

The prognosis must be for continued revolutionary activity in many of the countries as they shake their way further into this century. If Europe drew itself from mercantilism to capitalism by way of the French Revolution, Latin America is doing it by way of the Mexican Revolution and its forebears, as well as all those smaller conflicts in which so much valor, idealism, and youth are spent.

The role of the military

The obvious part played by the military in Latin American politics is a normal concomitant of oligarchical governments. Where democracy is impossible, as in the non-national states, then government is by definition the creature of only a part of the body social. Thus, knowledge of the law, not to speak of respect for it, must be limited and the degree of anticipated obedience to be expected is low. In carrying out its internal political policing functions, the military interacts with its peer groups or with those whom it desires to emulate. There is no divorce, then, between the armed forces and the social elements making up the effective political groups in the less developed nations; on the contrary, the identification is all too close.

The patterns of the military-civilian relationship change with the nature of the society and the development of the political value system. The simplest relationship is, first, in the traditional caudillistic form, in which the leader is almost always an officer in the armed forces and uses this power position to cement himself into office. Second, there is the modern variant of this practice, in which the military rule in trustee fashion, but are dependent upon institutional forms and maintain a degree of impersonalism, so that a *caudillo* does not emerge. The government which succeeded Perón in 1955 was of this type, a tutelary military rule which prepared the way for the holding of elections and the reinstitution of constitutional government. The Venezuelan provisional administration of Admiral Wolfgang Larrazábal, which recently ceded to the legally elected Rómulo Betancourt, also falls into this category.

71

A third variant is the military acting as the general orienters of policy. The Mexican situation is thus viewed by some specialists; that is, that the military defines the outside limits within which the constituted authorities may work, thus taking into its own hands only the ultimate tutelary role in partial control of the civil functionaries. The Argentine armed forces are certainly playing this role at the moment in limiting the actions of President Arturo Frondizi with respect to the unions, communism, *peronismo,* and the Church. Closely allied to this category is the fourth variant, the situation in which no government can exist without at least the tacit consent of the military. Peru falls into this classification, as do Brazil and Guatemala, at least for the moment. Any one of these first four situations is unstable, for slipping from one to another relationship is always a possibility unless social inhibitions against military interventionism have grown strong, as in Mexico.

Fifth, we find the military acting as a veto group only insofar as their own interests are concerned, but otherwise quite powerless politically. It may be that Chile fits this classification, or it may even fall into the sixth, in which the armed forces are professional and apolitical. Uruguay is in this last fortunate position. The ultimate possibility is that the military should be nonexistent. Costa Rica is the lone example, the only country in Latin America which has simply abolished its armed services on the dual grounds that the good citizen himself is enough to defend the country against any neighboring enemies, and that no one is able to defend it against the mighty nuclear weapons of the world powers.

Military intervention in political affairs is a long-standing impediment to the development of responsible government, a constant invitation to the dissatisfied to seek adjudication by bullet. Even though the military, armed with their World War II weapons, have not always been on the side of the devil, by and large they are a hindrance to the development of experience in the peaceful transfer of power. They can be hemmed in effectively only by the development of a complex of parties and pressure groups to orient the collective power of the citizenry. Certainly the growing complication of Latin American governments makes it ever riskier to entrust public administration to untrained and *ad hoc* military governors.

Parties and pressure groups

Party systems

Among other functions, political parties organize the electorate for their periodic interventions in decision making. They serve to carry ideas back and forth between the government and the populace when campaigns and elections are not in process. That they also act as employment agencies is well known. Not every Latin American group bearing the title *"partido"*

72

is really a political party by these criteria. When what is called a party merely performs policing functions for a dictatorial government and serves as a housekeeping agency for the imposition of views from the top, then we are not dealing with a functional party. Of this one-way control type are the single party "systems" of such a country as the Dominican Republic. The party is so closely identified with the administration that to be of an opposition group is to be subversive or even treasonous. Venezuela has also operated so in the recent past, as have other Latin countries in their periods of harsher caudillistic authoritarianism.

Mexico, however, offers the case of a single dominant party playing out its role without crudely repressive practices. There are opposition parties, the most important of which are the clerical PAN (National Action Party) on the right, and the Communist Party on the left. Membership in these opposition groups is no crime, and they legitimately serve to organize dissident opinions. But they have no ability to win an election, even though they may campaign, publish, meet, and speak without interference. The PRI (Institutional Revolutionary Party), the official entity, embraces everyone from the industrialist to the government employee to the trade unionist. Sometimes it is argued that the PRI is analogous to the Democratic Party of the American South, in truth representative of many factions, with the real decisions among opposing views made in the primary elections. In Mexico, the arguments take place among the leaders representing their rank and file supporters, and then the party makes known its official position. PRI is not monolithic; it is part of the trust arrangement in which Mexico's development is held by the military, the intellectuals, the new economic élites, the trade unions, and the middle class groups. Labor difficulties offer some hint that the PRI may eventually break into its component interest parts, but it would be a rash man indeed who would presume to predict when this split will occur.

Aside from the false and the real one-party systems named above, there are also a few two-party structures to be counted. Traditionally political development, as has been said, revolved about Conservatives and Liberals. In Colombia, where this division still exists, we have the most consistent case of bi-party politics. Uruguay, with its *Colorados* and *Blancos* ("Reds" and "Whites") has been considered by many political scientists as not a true example of a two-party structure, for the *Colorados* had won office uninterruptedly for almost a century. But in 1958 the Whites finally won a national election, and so we may presume Uruguay to be in the two-party class.

There are also mixed cases, in which two major parties contend at the national level, but a multiplicity argue over the municipal and provincial posts. Argentina is the most complicated case of this kind, for since 1945 only two major parties have presented themselves for the presidential elections; unhappily for simplicity, they have not always been the same two parties. In 1945, there was the Peronista Party, with virtually all the opposition in a single coalition. The traditional Radical Party led the opposition in the hopeless elections of 1951, but later, in 1958, the Radicals split into their two historic blocs, the Intransigent Radicals and the Radicals of the People, they being the only two serious contenders. The Conservatives, Socialists, Christian Democrats, Peronists, and Communists continue to be forces of some consequence, however, so that Argentina is on the borderline between a two-party and a multi-party system.

The electoral laws of Argentina, modeled as they are after those of the United States, including an electoral college, favor a two-party system even though social practice and the diversity of new interest groups favor a multi-party structure. Chile's laws, however, have until this year provided for an extreme form of proportional representation within the neoparliamentary governmental organization established in the Constitution of 1925. The result has been one of the most stable multi-party systems in Latin America running, from right to left, from Conservatives through Liberals to Radicals in the center, and on left to Christian Democrats, various branches of the Socialists, and the Communists. The close similarity both in Chile and Argentina to the political party spread of France and Italy is clear, and is no accident, for both countries are deeply influenced by those two European idea sources.

The multi-party system of Brazil, however, is more indigenous in origin and orientation, and also includes phenomena peculiar to the size and population of that huge country. The ideological distribution is strongly influenced by entirely internal considerations and is only peripherally liable to influence from abroad, while the extent and diversity of the country has been propitious for the development of sectional parties. Although these regional groups, or what are sometimes called "particularistic" parties, have died out almost everywhere in Latin America, including Brazil, the regional origins of a political party have much to do with setting present day attitudes. The Province of São Paulo has been particularly noteworthy in its influence on national politics through party mechanisms.

What the parties carry along in terms of substantive programs is also considerably varied. There are the well known "somebodyisms," the personalistic parties which identify with a charismatic individual. Thus arise the labels, *peronismo, batllismo, porfirismo,* and so on, referring to the conglomeration of attitudes, ideas, and loyalties surrounding Perón in Argentina, Batlle in Uruguay, and Porfirio Díaz in Mexico, to take only three of numerous examples. An ideational tone accompanies these personalistic designations: a kind of Black Populism in the case of Perón; secularist, middle class reform politics identified with Batlle; and the classical marriage of Liberal Positivism and *caudillismo* associated with Díaz.

74

When the party is totally personalistic, a condition almost invariably associated with the fraudulent one-party systems, then the suffix *"ismo"* is not used, and only *"ista"* is employed. It would sound foolish to say *trujillismo* or *perezjimenismo* to denote the "philosophies" of Trujillo of the Dominican Republic and of ex-President Pérez Jiménez of Venezuela. For them, only *trujillista* or *perezjimenista* makes sense. Only the more ideological leaders can have their names enlarged with either suffix.

There is little meaningful relationship between party system and the social order, except in the most backward authoritarianisms. In those cases, it is only by classificatory generosity that one can speak of parties at all. A better clue to political development is derived from party programs and approaches, rather than from counting the number of parties and relating them systematically. A reasonable hypothesis is that the more national a country, the less personalistic will be the parties, the more they will adjust conflicting interests within their own mechanisms, the greater will be their concern with institutional self-preservation and the winning of elections as a good in itself. As is to be expected, then, Argentina, Chile, Uruguay, and Costa Rica all have long histories of impersonal party politics.

Professional parties coexisting with single-interest and personalistic parties are readily observable in Brazil, Venezuela, and Cuba; these nations are among those in the second level of adjustment to nation-state status. Mexico and Colombia, heading the list of countries in the second level of adjustment, have unique structures for Latin America, but their parties may with confidence be called impersonal, and broadly based in the interests they represent, regardless of their ideologies. In Peru, Bolivia, Guatemala, Ecuador, El Salvador and Panama, the parties tend to be narrowly based, many are shortlived, and in numerous cases little difference can be observed between a party and the single interest it represents.

A preliminary non-public mediation of interest disputes is necessary so that the electorate may choose among alternatives not at the level of detail, but of policy. Without an impersonal political party structure aiding in the day-to-day mediation of disagreement, substantively good voting is difficult if not impossible in anything more than a town situation. The weeding out of issues to simplify national politics is a major party function. This function has international effects. The introduction of this level of debate may slow down the process of diplomatic negotiation but is necessary when a national consensus, rather than a mere executive opinion, is required for lasting agreement on substantive issues. In brief, it is intrinsically more difficult to negotiate truly important matters with democratic nation-states than with dictatorships. It is only good sense to make the effort, however, especially when we recognize that the age of *caudillismo* is drawing to a troubled close, as surely it is in Latin America.

75

Marxism and communism as special cases

Marxist thought and Communist ideology, as Western phenomena, have no market in non-national cultures. Naturally, then, the general social and economic development of Latin America opens up possibilities for the growth of communism as it does for the evolution of middle classes. Communist parties seem especially important in situations either of rapidly developing nationalism, or in cases in which normal processes are being bottled up by intransigent opposition. Robert Alexander, in his *Communism in Latin America,* argues that wherever a democratic trade union movement is allowed to flourish, the Communists lose their major source of mass support and become ineffectual. He cites Mexico as the most pertinent example, adding that in a period of national construction Communists may play a very important role, but thereafter they can be "withered away," to turn their phrase against them, by the open play of normal democratic politics.

A Senate investigating subcommittee released in 1959 the following figures on Communist Party membership in the various Latin American countries during 1958:

Argentina	70,000 to 80,000
Bolivia	4,000
Brazil	50,000
Chile	20,000 to 25,000
Colombia	5,000
Costa Rica	300
Cuba	12,000
Dominican Republic	Negligible
Ecuador	1,000
El Salvador	500
Guatemala	1,000
Haiti	Negligible
Honduras	500
Mexico	5,000
Nicaragua	200
Panama	500
Paraguay	500
Peru	6,000
Uruguay	3,000
Venezuela	30,000 to 35,000

There might be some disagreement as to the numbers given, but nowhere do Communists comprise a truly mass party, one which could conceivably win at the polls. The confusion arises when parties of the center and the democratic left combine with Communists, either officially or informally,

76

to attain given national objectives. This kind of alliance takes place either in times of such acute political crisis that polarization is an obvious necessity, as is the present situation in Chile; or else it occurs when the objectives are massive and all-embracing, such as the secularization and nationalization of politics, as in Guatemala during the ten-year period of Juan José Arévalo and Jacobo Arbenz from 1944 to 1954. A similar coalition occurred in Mexico during the decade of the Thirties, but the period of subsequent consolidation drastically reduced the advantage of alliance with the far left, and the center-left and center have now succeeded in weaning away from the Communists much of their popular and emotional support.

There is almost no chance that a Communist regime will implant itself directly anywhere in Latin America. In combination with other parties lies their only chance of formal penetration into affairs of state. During the post-World War II East-West honeymoon, Communists held many and important offices in several countries, including Brazil and Chile. But in those two republics, as well as many others, the outbreak of the Cold War saw the parties outlawed and diplomatic relations broken with the Soviet Union. There has been a gradual relaxation of these legal restrictions, but communism has not regained the status it had a decade ago.

Outside the realm of party politics, an unsophisticated blend of economic determinism is a common way of thought among educated Latin Americans. In areas where economic necessities loom large, where the example of the external world continuously pushes toward expanded consumption, to put primary attention on economic factors as the key to social change is natural. The United States has also contributed to this kind of easy analysis by an accent on economic development and the ingenuous insistence that people with full bellies don't become Communists. It is not only Communists, Trotskyists, and left Socialists who have Marxist ideas; in an amorphous way, anyone who subscribes to the absolute premise that "Money Talks" contributes to a dime-store variety of economic determinism.

Pressure groups

Interest or pressure groups are few in Latin America. Where caudillistic one-party rule holds sway, there is insufficient complication to give much room to variegated pressure groups. And where multi-party systems operate, except in the most developed countries, the parties represent small middle and upper groups and speak in the name of the economic interests themselves.

But still, there remain some extremely important associations which can be called pressure groups. Foremost in rank is the Church, although some analysts go so far as to presume the religious institution almost an integral part of government. The intellectual ground here is very treacherous. Probably nowhere is the Church less than a veto group; i.e., it may not be able to innovate policy, but it can make action against it very costly if not impossible. In Ecuador, where the Church is at its strongest, it probably transcends veto status and can institute action, as it probably also can in Colombia. In other lands where the Church has great strength, such as El Salvador and Peru, it probably cannot act in the nature of a party as it does in Ecuador and Colombia.

Legal separation of Church and State exists in Brazil, Chile, Cuba, Ecuador, El Salvador, Guatemala, Honduras, Mexico, Nicaragua, Panama, and Uruguay. The Church is established in Argentina, Bolivia, Colombia, Costa Rica, the Dominican Republic, Haiti, Paraguay, Peru, and Venezuela. But this legal categorization tells us little, for while almost all the established churches have this legal status as a holdover from the rights of the Spanish monarchy and while the purpose of establishment is to make the religious institution subservient to the state, the degree of control varies widely. There has, for instance, been active persecution of the Church in Venezuela, in contrast to an impressively strong Church in Colombia. And where legal separation exists, the same range of attitude is also to be found, from the past bitter attacks on the Church in Mexico, to the comfortable adjustment in Chile, to Church ascendency in Ecuador.

Another variable is the Church itself, which is by no means the same in its politics everywhere. The Gallican-influenced Churches of Brazil and Chile have very different political traits from the Spanish and Italian Church of Argentina. Most of the Chilean clergy now favor Christian Democracy; in the main, the Argentine clergy backed Perón for all but the last years of his regime, and still support many of the ideas of *justicialismo*. The long-range trend everywhere is for the Church to throw in with the rising middle groups, to oppose *caudillismo,* gently to support labor, and to drift slowly toward the official support of Christian Democratic parties. There is much opposition within the Church itself to certain of these temporal decisions, of course, and it would be highly incorrect to indicate that there is a general Latin political consensus in the Church.

The students, notorious political actors that they are, also constitute a pressure group. Latin American universities, organized on the European system, introduce their students immediately to subprofessional life; the social class gulf between student and professor is also minimal, for almost all students in Latin American universities are of middle and upper occupational group parents; their chances to participate at reasonably high levels in the national life after graduation are thus high to begin with. University elections are often good indicators of public elections, a kind of academic Maine and Vermont. Political division among the students parallels that of the major political parties, and student political activities train youngsters for active life outside. There are few Church universities of high prestige in those Latin American countries where they are allowed to exist. Although students in religious universities are also political activists, the

78

incidents about which one reads in the newspapers almost invariably are initiated in the state universities, citadels of the new, rising, nationalistic middle youth.

Other pressure groups are what one might expect: associations of land-owners, mine operators, industrialists, chambers of commerce, and prestige social clubs nudging into the political sphere. Then there are union groups, invariably politically militant if they are not subservient arms of the state. At times, they are both. Where labor is fairly free of governmental supervision, it tends to group in Socialist, Communist, and Radical camps; and in three countries—Argentina, Chile, and Uruguay—unionism also accepts Anarchists. The union movement of Mexico has been closely allied to the growth of the single party, whatever its name may have been at any particular period. In the most retarded countries, unions are either *de facto* or even sometimes *de jure* illegal. Honduras, for example, legalized labor organization only as recently as 1954.

Another kind of occupational pressure group is the professional association, often intimately tied in with the universities from which they depend in many countries.

Groups-in-interest are another crucial index of impersonalism and maturity in the political process. To the extent to which they exist, a polity of countervailing powers becomes a possibility, assuring the operation of lateral controls in the political system and making possible government by decisions as the result of compromise through bargaining instead of by fiat through uncontrolled self-interest.

Some international echoes of internal politics

The wide variation in the political development of the Latin American republics precludes the application of overly narrow rules to the processes of interpretative analysis and policy making. But even this simple homily is difficult to apply in practice, for not only are Latin American countries broadly dispersed on almost any scale of social measurement, but also, in many short-run, operational respects, they are almost exactly what the United States is not, a fact which makes for difficulties in cross-cultural recommendations. Latin America in general wants revolutionary changes, whether with violence or without; the United States is moderate in its views and skepical of wrenching change. Latin American countries are in the early, romantic stages of nationalism; the United States is emerging into a cautious internationalism. The Latin intellectual enjoys high social prestige and excellent chances for political power; the "egghead" in the United States is trusted only in his specialty. Latin American labor leaders are devoted to political unionism; his American counterpart is convinced of the advantages of economic unionism.

Most Latin Americans see the state as a legitimate agency for directing capital accumulation and investment; avowed American ideology is *laissez-*

faire, despite the mixed economy of the United States. Latin Americans are more worried about their internal Communist Parties than about the Soviet Union, and have no direct emotional involvement in the Cold War; the United States views the international clash with Soviet Russia as a struggle for survival in the deepest sense. Latin America wants steel mills and the other monuments of industrialization against a background of the technical full employment of underdevelopment; the United States is dealing with problems of automation and employment. Latin American governments are frankly tutelary; the American government is charged with the opposite task of reconciling numerous conflicting issues among laterally competing interests. Their culture includes many Catholic as well as generically Mediterranean notions of collectivism and syndicalism; the United States is generally Protestant and individualistic in its approach to matters metaphysical. This list of divergences could be extended almost indefinitely. The major point is that North American groups cannot talk directly to their Latin American peers, for the immediate aspirations and methods of each are not the same.

It is only in terms of broader and more long-range objectives that the community of interests becomes apparent. The ultimate dedication of the United States to democratic process is clearly reflected in Latin America. Unhappily, discord invariably appears over means to that common end, and the daily decisions of diplomacy suffer accordingly. The United States has often demonstrated itself insensitive to the currents of internal Latin American politics as well as to the variety of solutions possible to those countries. Too often have we defined private ownership as equal to capitalism without taking into account notions of competition and countervailing powers; we have viewed expropriation as equal to socialism, and nationalism as the same as supernationalism; the governmental authority of dictators has been treated as an honorable equivalent of legitimacy, and rote anti-Communism as full partnership in the community of free nations.

Many Latin American countries, for their part, have dedicated themselves to a maintenance of the privileges of the old semi-feudalism at the same time as they seek the revolutionary advantages of modernism. Between the transcendental ideal and the grubbiness of daily administrative practice there is often a yawning gulf filled with ineptitude and sometimes corruption. Latin Americans have a long way to go to translate their notions of dignity and the good life into the reality after which they yearn. But, of course, that point is what this chapter concerns. The exciting variety of response being developed in Latin America is a most encouraging sign, and at the same time a challenge to the scholar, the businessman, and the policy-maker. This variety cannot be understood by narrow ideologues thinking in bromides.

Many roads lead to democratic Salvation.

3. The role of the press and communications

EDWARD W. BARRETT AND PENN T. KIMBALL

It is a truism to say that the United States has entered finally and irrevocably into the global community. American national policy must respond to issues that circle the planet and even extend into the cosmos. Moreover, in the years ahead the nation will have to make vital policy decisions on short notice—without the former luxury of waiting for the public to become informed, for public opinion to jell, and finally for that opinion to make itself felt in the Congress.

Never before has there been so much to report from so many places. Even the modern miracles of communication can scarcely cope with the

EDWARD W. BARRETT, Dean of the Graduate School of Journalism, Columbia University, worked on Birmingham, Alabama, newspapers, edited the college daily at Princeton, and worked with the Columbia Broadcasting System after graduation. Later, with *Newsweek* magazine he served as Washington correspondent, national affairs editor, and, from 1946 to 1950, as editorial director. During World War II he set up the world-wide news and photo service of the Office of War Information and succeeded Robert E. Sherwood as director of OWI's overseas operations. From 1950 to 1952 he was Assistant Secretary of State for Public Affairs. Dean Barrett is author of *Truth Is Our Weapon*.

PENN T. KIMBALL is Professor of Journalism at Columbia University. He has been a senior editor of *Collier's*, feature editor of the television program *Omnibus*, and a member of the Sunday staff of *The New York Times*. Professor Kimball participated in a 1957 study of American government and business personnel in Latin America under the auspices of the Carnegie Corporation of New York and the Maxwell School of Citizenship and Public Affairs at Syracuse University.

potential torrents of news, background information and interpretation which flow from world-wide complexities. The individual citizen is engulfed in print, pictures and sound. And yet he runs farther and farther behind the racing developments of current history.

Latin America, for all its importance, is not vastly more important in the lives and future of thoughtful North Americans than Quemoy, or Berlin, or the Congo, or the Middle East. Everything, everywhere is important today. No one knows enough about anything, not excepting the sweep of events in our own country. We live in varying states of relative ignorance, each of which poses its peculiar dangers.

If our media of communication in general cannot or will not adequately cover a running domestic story as vital as inflation, it should not be surprising that there are gaps in our information concerning economic developments in Brazil. If American readers do not keep adequately abreast of news from their state capitals, it is not surprising that they will be stunned by a burst of news from the capital of Cuba.

Today the average educated and articulate Latin American is far better informed about the United States than is the comparable North American about Latin America. The score or more excellent newspapers in the other Americas feature large quantities of news about the United States—most of it news supplied by the two great North American news services. The additional scores of fair-grade newspapers—and the radio and television stations—generally give greater proportions of their output to news of world affairs than do comparable media in the United States.

Whether this be cause or effect can never be ascertained. The intelligent Latin American may get more world news because he is more interested and less self-satisfied than the average North American; or he may be more interested because he is supplied regularly with more news of the world. In any event, there is no doubt that the sizable flow of North American news sustains and maintains the educated Latin American's interest and knowledge.

In the United States, the case is far different. With a few notable exceptions, newspapers give relatively little space to news of the world and minute space to news of the other Americas. Whether this be cause or effect, the level of interest in and knowledge of Latin Americans among even educated United States citizens appears shockingly low.

Yet every North American who returns from a trip through Latin America comes back with wonder over what he sees in Mexico City, Caracas, São Paulo or Buenos Aires. Part of this wonder is amazement over the bustle and growth of the great Latin cities. Part is confusion over monumental contrasts between wealth and poverty or economic crises laid at the doorstep of Yankee policies. Part is apprehension over explosive political situations where nationalism and communism and anti-imperialism swirl in the streets. And a part is exhilaration over contrasting societies, exotic cultures, staggering scenery and the warmth of Latin personalities.

The brashness of youth and the mellowness of age mix in a startling way in Latin America. The traveler from middle-class North America sees only extremes among his southern neighbors. The experience is fascinating, baffling, but never dull.

Why, then, should there be a problem about United States press coverage of Latin America? And, in view of the historic common interests of the New World, why is the problem suddenly so acute?

Why proper coverage means so much

The special importance of adequate public information about Latin America could hardly be appraised more clearly than in the first of Dr. Milton S. Eisenhower's reports to the President (November 18, 1953).

Security in the Western Hemisphere

We believe deeply that we must constantly be alert to maintain and to build better political, economic, military and cultural relations with our neighbors to the South. Good relations in this Hemisphere are crucially important to our own future and to theirs, and indeed to the future progress of the entire world.

*   *   *

To comprehend the interdependence of the nations of this Hemisphere in the event of war, one need only to recall the determined attempt of enemy submarines in World War II to sink all shipping between the Americas and how near to success they came.

*   *   *

The Doctrine enunciated in 1823 by President Monroe was designed to protect the newly won independence of all the nations of this Hemisphere and to permit the community to grow to maturity free from domination by any transoceanic power. The Monroe Doctrine was obviously based upon considerations of our own security; if the arguments to justify it were strong in 1823, they are truly mighty in the shrunken world of today.

The possible conquest of a Latin American nation today would not be, so far as anyone can foresee, by direct assault. It would come, rather, through the insidious process of infiltration, conspiracy, spreading of lies, and the undermining of free institutions, one by one. Highly disciplined groups of Communists are busy, night and day, illegally or openly, in the American Republics, as they are in every nation of the world. While many persons may now think of Latin America as not being in the line of attack

83

in the modern world struggle, success by the Communists in these nations could quickly change all the maps which strategists use in calculating the probabilities of the future.

* * *

The building of permanent peace involves the establishment of abiding cooperation among nations of great cultural diversity . . . The cultural diversity of the Western Hemisphere, while notable, is primarily within the philosophic framework of Western civilization, a civilization which seeks to establish and maintain institutions and processes conducive to the attainment of the supreme human purposes and rules of conduct proclaimed by its religious concepts . . . In this Hemisphere, despite great cultural diversity, there is no real impediment to the development of that understanding on which effective cooperation among our peoples can surely be built.

* * *

The efforts of those who are concerned with developing good relations among nations must be directed first of all to the multitude of methods by which there may be developed among peoples and governments that understanding on which economic, political, military and cultural cooperation may successfully proceed.

The key to better understanding

We found misunderstanding of the United States in South America . . . misunderstanding and disagreements in the economic field especially.

* * *

We must in all candor say that many in the United States do not understand adequately the economic difficulties and potentialities in South America— in Latin America as a whole.

In short, overcoming the present lack of information and understanding on both sides with respect to economic problems constitutes in our judgment the greatest single opportunity to strengthen relationships between the United States and the republics of Latin America.

* * *

We should look to the free mass communication media of the United States, and especially to the press associations and newspapers and magazines with Latin American correspondents and circulations, as a major means of promoting essential understanding. Certainly the information media of the United States have a profound effect on attitudes in both the United States and Latin America, and thus on official and unofficial relationships. It would be helpful if these media regularly found it possible to do more than report the spectacular occurrences in the Latin American coun-

84

tries. A revolution will merit widespread attention by the press, radio and television, but the long-term underlying causes may not. Yet the basic causes may have more to do with the future welfare of our country—and with international relationships—than did the revolution which brought new leaders to power.

I believe deeply that adequately informed peoples in the Americas can find cooperative and mutually advantageous solutions to hosts of problems, but partially informed citizens are likely to foster tensions, disputes and serious ill-will.

It is recognized that the primary function of the press is to convey news, not to promote understanding and good will among nations as such; but in the modern world struggle, in which we need all the friends we can get, citizens must depend greatly on mass communication media for the evidence relevant to valid judgments. The media which have correspondents in Latin America should consider that part of the world so important to the United States that they will assign their best men and women there, as indeed some of them now do.

Similarly, United States dispatches to Latin America can faithfully interpret or grossly misrepresent our intentions and actions . . . The press and radio of South America daily bulge with news gathered and dispatched by our great free information system . . . Unfortunately, the functioning of our free press and its value as an independent medium of news and opinion are not too well understood. A good many leaders with whom we talked, while indicating their comprehension of our free, competitive press and news agencies, nonetheless expressed the belief that the United States Government could, if it wished, influence the attitude of the press insofar as their news stories and editorials impinge upon foreign relations. They seem to believe that press criticism of their domestic policies, sometimes based on inadequate understanding of their local conditions, reflects a governmental attitude and that thus, while maintaining an official policy of non-intervention, we do in fact intervene by indirect means.

Misunderstandings grow

Five years later, in another Report to the President on United States-Latin American relations (December 27, 1958), Dr. Eisenhower declared:

I reaffirm essentially all I said in my report of 1953, but now I must add a note of urgency to my general recommendation that the nations of Latin America and the United States re-examine their attitudes and policies toward one another and constantly seek to strengthen their economic, political and cultural relations, to their mutual benefit . . . I now must report that misunderstandings seem to me to be even more serious than they were in 1953.

85

In the United States, the problem stems primarily from a lack of knowledge. We wish to be a good neighbor. We want the Latin American republics to regard us as a faithful friend. But our people generally do not truly comprehend the problems and aspirations of our neighbors, and thus we sometimes take actions which are detrimental to the good relationships we wish to foster. Thus it is possible that the people of the United States would have favored actions different from those that were taken in the area of trade relations if they had been in possession of all relevant facts.

*   *   *

Responsibility for informing the people of the United States about Latin American policies, attitudes and developments—to the extent that this is a government duty—rests with the State Department. Responsibility for informing the peoples of Latin America about similar matters in the United States rests with the United States Information Agency.

I recommend that the information facilities of the State Department be increased . . . and that special efforts be made to induce the mass media of the United States to maintain competent correspondents in Latin America and to carry a steady flow of news and interpretive material from all twenty republics.

A report on United States relations with Latin America was submitted by the subcommittee on Inter-American Affairs of the House Committee on Foreign Affairs on May 12, 1959. The subcommittee, headed by the Hon. Armistead I. Selden, Jr., Congressman from Alabama, recommended "Sustained news coverage of Latin American development by the news media" and declared:

> United States citizens should be kept informed regularly of Latin American developments and trends, which has not always been the case. It is true that world crises compete for space and time, but we feel, since public opinion is a major force in the formation of U.S. foreign policy it is incumbent on the news media to make every effort to present a rounded coverage of trends and events in Latin America.

Most of the subcommittee report dealt with Latin American grievances against the United States, rather than with the problem of United States opinion about Latin American affairs.

> The demonstrations against the Vice President last spring and the more recent hostile outbreaks in Bolivia are indicative of continuing misunderstanding as between the United States and some of its Latin neighbors. Underlying these misunderstandings are several real conflicts of interest, such as the effect of our trade policies on key Latin American commodities.

Although the report did not say so directly, the implication of its recommendation on press coverage is that the state of information about Latin America in this country is partly responsible for many irritations and misunderstandings, and that a better informed American public must precede policy changes which might alleviate some of these problems.

A frequently heard complaint among Cubans is that we supported the Batista government, although, technically, the United States discontinued military aid to the Cuban government some nine months prior to its fall, the subcommittee reported.

Nevertheless, the use by the Batista government of limited residual military aid equipment during the Cuban revolution, in violation of the mutual aid agreements, has created deep resentment against the United States among many Latin Americans.

These fires were obviously fed when the American press reacted violently to the public trials and executions by the new Castro regime, as the riots in Bolivia were touched off by an article in *Time* magazine quoting alleged disparaging remarks made by a member of the United States diplomatic mission there. Where misunderstandings exist already in a climate of incomplete information on both sides, the occasional spot news story often does more harm than good in these circumstances. Irregular coverage can sometimes be worse than no coverage at all.

American knowledge of Latin America

The vicious circle

The flow of news northward over the Tropic of Cancer and into the sphere of attention of the American public is conditioned by attitudes which are not easily explored. How much do North Americans really know or care about Latin America? The question is a practical one for the newspaper and magazine editor and the television producer or radio news chief who has a budget to meet and a boss to please. Their performance is often measured by the response of the audience. Missionary zeal carried on in a vacuum of non-readers and non-listeners does not enhance many careers in private-enterprise communications. In those areas of news where the risks seem highest, there is a tendency to blame failure on the exasperating public and fall back upon sure-fire material like crime and the marital troubles of movie stars.

This brings us to what Herbert Matthews has outlined as the vicious circle of Latin American coverage: the reader will not read or listen to Latin American news because he is neither informed nor interested in it. The newspapers, magazines and broadcasters will not give Latin American news because they believe their clients do not want it. The failure to provide the news perpetuates the ignorance of the reader, and this ignorance leads to the lack of interest.

Implicit in this circle of assumptions is the further assumption that when Latin American news falls on deaf ears, if indeed it does, the fault rests not with the story-teller but with the uncaptive audience.

The truth is difficult to gauge, because we really know so little about what interests the general public. Some of our most brilliant editors navigate this murky question, they admit, with the seat of their pants. A good hunch has probably led to more Pulitzer Prizes than have readership surveys. Great publishing successes have been scored by winning audiences no one else had the vision to anticipate. Skill of presentation has been part of the process as well as the "discovery" of latent enthusiasms.

The pessimistic view of what North Americans will read about Latin Americans prevails, however, even in circles fervently hopeful of an opposite result. There is an air of resignation about many of those who make their living covering and editing the news. Publishers who come home inspired from Pan-American junkets are dashed with cold water when they pass on their ideas to the realistic, shirt-sleeved pros on their news desks. Latin American news, like British soccer scores, is a luxury which "only a New York *Times* can afford."

Such apprehension has its roots in what tangible evidence is normally available to those trying to communicate to the public. The mail is light. The cover doesn't sell. The survey shows reader traffic is low. The coverage is dropped and few complain. The Trendex sags. The sponsor's merchandise doesn't move. Imperfect as the evidence may be, the burden of proof on the other side rests heavily on declarations of faith and conscience.

If the United States public is truly not overly informed or interested in what it gets about Latin America, is there a case to be made that this might not last forever?

The level of information

A nationwide public opinion survey conducted on behalf of a United States business concern contained a question in which respondents were shown a blank outline map of South America, divided into three parts. Those interviewed were asked in which part they thought Venezuela was located—the top, middle, or bottom third of the continent. Thirty-nine per cent correctly placed the country at the top. Twenty-eight per cent incorrectly located it in the region actually occupied by such countries as Bolivia and Brazil. Fifteen per cent pointed to the wrong end of the continent, actually containing Argentina, Chile and Uruguay. Eighteen per cent had no idea at all.[1]

Thus, the wrong answers outnumbered the right ones on this test of simple geography. When Vice President Nixon was stoned in Caracas three years later, this poll would indicate, six out of ten Americans had only vague ideas about where this outbreak of anti-American feeling had occurred.

---

[1] Data from 1955 survey by International Research Associates furnished by The Roper Public Opinion Research Center, Williams College.

It has often been said that while it is risky to overestimate the information possessed by the American mass public, it is equally foolish to underestimate public intelligence. The lack of basic information illustrated above should be considered in the context of the fact that in a similar nationwide poll conducted by the National Opinion Research Center of the University of Chicago on behalf of the United States Department of State, only 52 per cent of those interviewed could correctly identify John Foster Dulles in his cabinet post as Secretary of State nearly three years after he had taken the oath of office.

Is it possible for a nation in which only a bare majority knows who is Secretary of State and in which only a minority can locate Venezuela in its approximate position on the South American continent to reach the kind of judgments required by the subtle and complex issues of our relations with Latin America? Before leaping to a gloomy conclusion to that question, it is worth recalling the number of occasions in our history when the American people have risen magnificently to meet sterner challenges.

Our educational system in recent years has been moving away from the concept that mastery of a subject can be transferred by cramming young heads full of facts. We need to know how to think for ourselves. And while information is essential to intelligent thought, the ability to recite what bounds Liechtenstein on the four points of the compass is not necessarily the key to following affairs in Central Europe.

It is entirely conceivable, for example, that Americans can grasp the essence of collective security in the American hemisphere without being able to name the heads of state in Nicaragua and Costa Rica or to place those countries on the correct side of the Panama Canal. Opinion polls are valuable instruments, but the most skillful practitioners would not claim ability to measure the human mind with the nicety of calipers applied to a rod of metal.

A check among the major United States polling agencies indicated they have compiled relatively little data concerning the level of interest and/or information among Americans concerning Latin American affairs. This in itself would seem to reflect a lack of demand. The vicious circle is in operation again: no demand leads to lack of information; lack of information reduces the demand for new information.

The most extensive information was apparently compiled in a series of surveys on American opinion carried on for the State Department between 1946 and 1956 by the National Opinion Research Center. These continuing polls were financed out of special, unearmarked funds in the office of the Secretary of State, and when Congress objected to this method of financing in 1956, the polls were suspended.

The major attention of these samplings was upon areas of major concern to United States policymakers in the years immediately following the

89

second world war: Western Europe, Russia and the Far East. But some of the questions asked included references to our policies in the Western Hemisphere as well as the rest of the world, and in a few instances dealt directly with Latin American problems.

The level of interest

Whatever Americans may know about their neighbors to the South, these polls indicate a degree of consensus on the necessity for standing together with them to resist outside attack that is greater than that for any other area of the globe:

NORC POLL—June 24, 1947

Suppose some country attacked one of the countries in South America. Would you approve or disapprove of the United States sending armed forces along with other American countries to stop the attack?

Approve	Disapprove	Don't Know	Qualified Answer
72%	12%	9%	7%

NORC POLL—April 19, 1949

Suppose some big country attacks (a Western European nation; a South American nation). Would you approve or disapprove of the United States using its armed forces to help stop the attack?

	Approve	Disapprove	Don't Know	Qualified Answer
Western Europe	55%	25%	7%	13%
South America	62%	19%	11%	8%

NORC POLL—September 16, 1949

Would you approve or disapprove of the United States using its armed forces to stop any attack on a country in (Western Europe; South America; India)?

	Approve	Disapprove	Don't Know	Qualified Answer
Western Europe	43%	39%	7%	11%
South America	50%	30%	12%	8%
India	25%	53%	17%	5%

NORC POLL—April 20, 1956

Under our defense alliance in South America and Central America, the United States and those countries have promised to defend each other against any attack. Do you approve or disapprove of this?

Approve	Disapprove	Don't Know
85%	7%	8%

The spread in the percentages answering these differently phrased questions at different points in time illustrates how risky it is to make firm generalizations about popular attitudes toward other parts of the world. A graphic example of this is contained in this same series of polls.

In February, 1948, the NORC asked a national cross-section whether they took a "keen," "mild" or no interest at all in our policy toward Korea. The answers broke down as follows:

	Keen	Mild	None	Don't Know
Interest in Korea	12%	29%	46%	13%

In April, 1953, the situation had spectacularly changed:

	Great Deal	Some	None	Don't Know
Interest in Korea	71%	25%	4%	0%

The fact remains that the United States public, over a span of nearly ten years, registered opinions consistently on the side of collective security in the Western Hemisphere. This concept is embodied in the 1947 Treaty of Rio de Janeiro, which broadened our historical policy under the Monroe Doctrine to encompass the proposition that an attack on one American republic is now considered an attack on all, whether such aggression takes place from within or without the hemisphere.

Such attitudes do not spring from thin air. They indicate that North Americans are not indifferent to our strategic interdependence with the American Republics. Since, as Dr. Milton S. Eisenhower reported to the President after his 1953 tour, "cooperation must be based on genuine understanding," one might conclude that if Americans recognize the need for cooperation, it should not be impossible to interest them in information bearing upon this goal.

A NORC poll taken in November, 1954, shows that a substantial proportion of Americans interviewed then wished that the United States government would pay more, not less attention to the problems of South and Central America.

91

Do you think our government is paying too much attention, or not enough attention to the problems of South and Central America?

Too Much	Not Enough	About Right	Don't Know
5%	41%	22%	32%

The same cross-section also voted overwhelmingly on the side of United States economic and technical assistance to Latin American countries.

Do you think the United States should help these countries in South and Central America to build up their industries, or shouldn't we concern ourselves with this? Do you think the United States should help these countries improve education and health?

	Should Help	Should Not	Don't Know
Build up industries	66%	24%	10%
Improve health and education	82%	13%	5%

Interestingly enough, this is the identical poll in which only 52 per cent could correctly identify the job held by John Foster Dulles. It also contained a question on whether those interviewed thought of Senator Joseph R. McCarthy favorably or unfavorably. That turned out 44 per cent favorable toward Senator McCarthy, 35 per cent unfavorable and 21 per cent in the "don't know" category.

The typology of respondent who thought favorably of Senator McCarthy, but was unable to identify John Foster Dulles, and who at the same time thought our government should pay more attention to Latin America and help build up its industry, education and health—a phenomenon familiar to pollsters—raises awesome problems in communication. Who is brave enough to predict what this person will or will not read about Latin America? Yet it is foolish to deprecate the American mass audience, on the one hand, just because it does not conform to a logical ideal, and, on the other hand, to equate confusion or ignorance with lack of interest.

The following table, compiled from NORC polls which asked how much interest Americans took in a whole host of domestic and foreign issues during the ten-year postwar period, would indicate that Latin America does not fare badly in comparison with other matters in the forefront of attention during those years. (Dates indicate when question was asked).

How much interest do you take in (items described): a great deal of interest, some interest or practically none?

Date	Area of Interest	Great Deal	Some	None	Don't Know
		%	%	%	%
10/13/48	The cost of living	82	15	3	0
4/ 1/53	The war in Korea	71	25	4	0
9/16/49	A possible depression	62	28	9	1
3/ 1/50	Strikes in this country	60	29	10	1
10/13/48	The coming election for President	60	33	7	0
9/16/49	Our relations with Russia	49	35	15	1
3/11/55	The hydrogen bomb tests	47	41	11	1
2/25/48	Our relations with China	40	39	18	3
3/11/55	The Formosa situation	37	41	20	2
10/13/48	The Berlin question	36	47	16	1
8/ 4/55	What happened at the Big Four Conference in Geneva	32	47	19	2
4/ 1/53	The Congressional investigation of the State Department	36	39	22	3
2/25/48	The Marshall plan for European recovery	31	45	20	4
6/23/55	The question of unifying Germany	28	48	21	3
2/25/48	*Our relations with Argentina*	25	43	29	3
3/11/55	*Our relations with Central and South America*	23	42	32	3
2/25/48	*Our relations with Brazil*	22	40	35	3
3/11/55	The United Nations	21	59	19	1
5/14/53	War in Indo-China	21	50	28	1
8/ 4/55	Visit of Russian farmers	20	52	26	2
9/16/49	The spread of Communism in Asia	20	36	39	5
9/16/49	What is going on in Germany	20	42	35	3
2/25/48	The way the State Department handles its job	19	45	30	6
9/16/49	England's present financial crisis	17	46	35	2
5/14/53	Our government's tariff policy	16	42	38	4
10/13/48	Our policy toward Palestine	16	50	31	3
4/29/55	Publication of Yalta papers	18	29	46	7
10/13/48	Our policy toward Spain	12	39	43	6
4/29/55	The work of our Foreign Service	11	48	38	3
3/ 1/50	Our relations with Yugoslavia	9	32	52	7
8/ 4/55	What UNESCO is doing	9	34	49	8

Obstacles to better coverage

The most stinging indictment of United States press coverage of Latin America comes from the editor and publisher of *Editor & Publisher,* the leading trade magazine of the newspaper business. Robert U. Brown, in the issue for January 31, 1959, devoted his whole column—"Shop Talk at Thirty"—to the problem.

"It now seems to be unanimous that U. S. news coverage of the Cuban revolution left something to be desired. Criticism by various U. S. editors centers around erroneous reports of a Batista victory over the rebels during the last few days of December. Herbert L. Matthews, Latin American specialist for the New York *Times,* summed it up last week by saying: 'In all my 36 years in journalism, I've never seen a worse job than the reporting during the last three weeks in Cuba. It was pretty bad before that.'

"In fairness to the reporters who were present it should be noted that Cuban censorship under Batista was pretty tight. It probably accounted for some of the difficulty in getting at the truth. But some of the blame should come right back to the newspaper editors who are now doing the complaining, with a few exceptions.

"In general, they are the ones who have had a continuing lack of interest in legitimate news from Latin American countries. They have failed to instruct their own deskmen and wire editors in the importance of news from that area to the U. S. and to our citizens. They have ignored most of the solid news about Latin America that has been delivered to them over the wires because they have felt their readers were not interested.

*   *   *

"There haven't been enough Latin American news specialists to cover the whole area so that good reporters, but inadequately trained in language and customs, have sometimes been assigned only when seemingly 'hot' stories develop.

"It will be argued that a good 'savvy' reporter ought to be able to cover any story, any place, any time. True, perhaps, if the story develops in the U. S. But it overlooks completely the differences in language, social customs and political philosophies of Latin countries."

To the practical problems enumerated by Mr. Brown—censorship, newspaper editors' lack of interest, a shortage of adequately trained reporters—most publishers would certainly add at least one more: the high cost of covering an area as large and as complicated as the twenty American republics.

The high cost of foreign coverage

John Wilhelm, head of the McGraw-Hill Publishing Company's foreign news service, estimates that it costs his organization $25,000 a year to field one foreign correspondent, without the extra expenses which spot coverage for a daily publication would entail. A conservative estimate for transmission tolls on copy comes to another $12,000 a year, based on the correspondent's filing about four stories per week. Thus, to maintain a single full-time American correspondent in only five Latin American capitals would cost about $185,000 a year. Few newspapers feel they can afford even one man abroad working exclusively for their readers at these prices.

The New York *Times,* which spends $4,000,000 a year on its foreign news service, supports no more than four North Americans on permanent assignment in Latin America. Although Time, Inc. maintains somebody in every Latin American country except the Dominican Republic, only four are American staffers sent out from New York. The newspaper or magazine editor who aims at adding the depth of photojournalism to a Latin American story must provide in the budget for the added expense of sending along a photographer as well as a reporter. Often the complications caused by deadlines or local conditions require the dispatch of personnel all the way from the States to cover a single story.

In television, the costs of foreign coverage are compounded fantastically when camera crews and technicians are added to the upkeep of the staff correspondent assigned to the story.

This is reflected in a quick review of the television news logs of the Columbia Broadcasting System and National Broadcasting Company networks between July 1 and December 31, 1958. CBS put on one special half-hour report dealing with Latin American news, and NBC two during that period. All three dealt with Argentina. (The NBC shows won George Polk Memorial Awards for commentator Chet Huntley and producer Reuven Frank.) The day-to-day flow of Latin American news in the regular television and radio news reports is more difficult to estimate, but it does not bulk large.

After the Castro upheaval in Cuba, which occasioned a temporary pickup in spot coverage, the CBS network also produced a half-hour report on the Cuban rebel which was shown on prime evening time in January, 1959. In May, 1959, CBS aired a two-part report titled "Is Cuba Going Red?" which was telecast on Sundays from 6 to 6:30 P.M. The sound track was broadcast on radio later in the evening. The production costs of these two programs were approximately $25,000 for a total of one hour of programming. On a once-a-week basis this type of coverage would thus cost more than a million dollars a year, exclusive of time charges.

During the first six months of 1959, NBC put on a total of three half-hour, special TV reports from Latin America, two of them on Cuba and one from Colombia.

The grand total for these two major TV networks over a one-year period works out to eight special programs on Latin America lasting four hours. Three-fourths of this was occasioned by the unusual crisis in Cuba.

NBC has estimated that the cost of producing regularly a fifteen-minute weekly film roundup of Latin American news, using three full-time bureaus and a corps of stringers to cover the area, would exceed $2,000,000 a year.

The twenty Latin American republics encompass an area two and one-half times the size of the United States. Although the phrase "Latin America" is convenient, it is a gross oversimplification of a diversity which persists in spite of the common bond of language in eighteen of the twenty

95

countries. The area cannot be adequately covered as if all twenty countries were a single unit. Moreover, when one leaves the capital cities, the problems of transportation and communication often become difficult. Furthermore, local journalistic traditions in some of these republics are altogether different from those prevailing in the United States. The supply of local nationals who can write within the specifications of the North American media and interpret local events from the perspectives of the North American audience is highly limited. Caught between the economics of fielding specially trained Americans to cover this vast area and the editorial risks of relying upon local stringers, even the best intentioned editor or broadcaster often feels frustrated.

The role and problems of the wire services

There are 1,761 daily and 546 Sunday newspapers in the United States, plus 3,663 radio and 512 television stations. Coverage of Latin America—except in a handful of cases—is provided for these outlets principally by the two great news-gathering wire services—Associated Press and United Press International, both of which also service several hundred Latin American clients.

Each receives 5,000 to 10,000 words a day on the Latin American desk in New York City. Only a fraction of this flow, however, goes out on the wires to North American clients.

"After more than 20 years of pushing Latin American news on the wires," says a UPI general news manager, Earl J. Johnson, "I've concluded that very few editors are really interested. Much is said at inter-American press meetings about the importance of printing more news from Latin American countries. But not much is done about it when the North American delegates return to their desks."

Paul Sanders, in charge of the AP Latin American news desk, confirms the fact that "there is not much push from members for Latin American news. We put out 1,000 words a day, but only a small percentage is actually used."

Sanders thinks part of the problem is a matter of timing. The biggest and most important papers throughout Latin America tend to be morning papers. Local news sources, he says, are in the habit of releasing material late in the day with local distribution in mind. Hence, a flood of copy reaches New York between 8 and 10 o'clock in the evening—a poor time for anything short of a front-page story to develop for use in most North American morning papers. By the time next day's afternoon papers are being made up the news item has grown stale and is discarded on the desk in favor of late-breaking developments elsewhere.

Although Associated Press employs 200 to 300 persons in Latin America, only 11 of these are North Americans working out of six full-time bureaus (Mexico City, Havana, Caracas, Rio de Janeiro, Santiago de Chile, and Buenos Aires). Other points are covered by local nationals exclusively, most of them on a part-time basis. UPI has eight North Americans on full-time assignment as correspondents in Latin America.

The wire services concede that it costs them twice as much in some cases to use a North American correspondent as it does to fill the post with a local national. They claim a local national can do a better job sometimes, because it is easier for him to develop local contacts and escape the suspicion toward foreigners. Local nationals are backstopped by periodic swings made by North American staffers throughout the region. After the debacle when the Associated Press reported a Batista victory over Castro only a few hours before the former fled Havana, however, an extra North American was permanently assigned to the one-man Havana bureau. When things begin popping in one of the smaller countries, as they did when rebels "invaded" Nicaragua in the spring of 1959, the wire services have to rush a man to the scene from a permanent bureau such as Mexico City.

The more subtle difficulties

The fall of Batista punctuated a period of Latin American history that had also witnessed the fall of dictators in Argentina, Colombia, and Venezuela and a general improvement in the free flow of information throughout Latin America. A report by the International Press Institute, released in 1959, praises the Inter-American Press Association for acting "tirelessly on behalf of press freedom." It cites the Dominican Republic, Paraguay, Bolivia, Batista's Cuba and the Somoza regime in Nicaragua as the principal remaining areas of censorship. The I. P. I. notes that press freedom has been restored in Colombia, Venezuela and Argentina.

The problems of newsgathering in Latin America are thus more largely the subtle difficulties of dealing with government bureaucracies that are not organized to service the representatives of the local press in a manner comparable to United States agencies, much less the needs of foreign correspondents. The same is true of potential news sources in business, labor, agriculture and the like. Anti-United States feelings, the explosive character of political and economic developments, sheer physical difficulties and the normal obstacles of cross-cultural reporting, all compound the task of getting at the background and interpretation so necessary to United States understanding of the volatile Latin American situation.

The Latin American beat calls for the highest professional skills. Yet, realistically it should be pointed out that Latin American posts are not considered "prestige" posts in most organizations maintaining a world news organization. Reputations are easier to make in Europe or the Far East. The Latin American specialist often finds himself in a dead end within his editorial hierarchy. Latin American posts which offer such drawbacks to family life as high altitude or sub-tropical climate, uncertain health and school facilities, plus vast distances from relatives at home, are sometimes spurned. World War II helped create a correspondent corps with backgrounds and attachments in many parts of the world, but few of these veterans have ever been South of Havana or Mexico City.

There is no logic, not even good sense, to these factors, perhaps, but they nevertheless exist. The recruiting of able correspondents in this age of suburban man suffers everywhere from the fact that when the children start to grow up, the family wants to come home. The British tradition of picking up stakes for a lifetime abroad, albeit a lifetime surrounded by exports from home, is not typical of our North American culture. (Many Latin American stringers for United States publications are British.)

The training of news specialists in Latin America is inevitably governed by the laws of supply and demand. Limited opportunity to land a job constricts the number willing to acquire training sufficient unto the requirements of sensitive and thoughtful reporting. There are conspicuous examples of journalists motivated by a sense of mission about Latin America who, regardless of frustrations, have literally forced their way into the field. Some have sold their publishers and their news desks on the idea that Latin America is not only important, but also that readers will respond to excellence by devouring stories which are readable and meaningful. But these have been—and still are—pioneers. By and large, North American journalism has not followed their trail.

A spot check of Latin American news

A spot check of the number of column inches of space devoted to news and interpretation of Latin American affairs in newspapers published in three American cities gives some indication of how small this coverage is.

The check was made in the morning and evening papers which appeared in Louisville, Kentucky, Kansas City, Missouri, and Portland, Oregon, on two dates six months apart. These three cities were chosen on the basis of an extensive study made previously on behalf of the Carnegie Endowment for International Peace. In a detailed analysis over several months the Research Division of the School of Journalism at the University of Minnesota found that the quantity of foreign news appearing in the six papers involved was closely comparable to that which was found in a probability sample of 100 newspapers representing a cross-section of the whole United States.

The dates selected were October 8, 1958, and April 8, 1959—the second Wednesday in each of these two months. These dates fell roughly three months before and three months after the unusual flow of stories out of Cuba caused by the overthrow of Batista. Although, there is no claim of precise scientific accuracy for this procedure, it seemed a fair, yet economical, way to sample the flow of Latin American news into the American press.

The papers thus involved were The Louisville *Times* and *Courier-Journal,* The Kansas City *Times* and *Star,* and the Portland *Oregonian* and *Oregon Journal.* The twelve issues under study were scanned to determine (1) the total quantity of editorial matter in each and (2) the percentage of foreign and Latin coverage of each. A distinction was made between items that could be called "substantive"—politics, economics, diplomacy, etc.—and the general run of foreign news, which also includes accidents and disasters, entertainment, light features, etc. Editorial comment and stories out of Washington dealing with international and Latin affairs were included in both categories.

The accompanying table shows the results of this check.

Space devoted to Latin America

The figures indicate that an average issue of these six American dailies contains more than 2,000 column inches of editorial matter. The space devoted to foreign items of every description varied from a low of 92.3 column inches to a high of 393.6 column inches, but the overall average came to 274.8 column inches per issue. This amounted to an average of 12.5 per cent of total editorial space. The percentage of "substantive" foreign news and comment averaged considerably lower, 7.7 per cent.

Latin American items of all kinds ranged from nothing at all to 51.4 column inches per issue. The top proportions of editorial space devoted to Latin America were 2.4 per cent in the Louisville *Times* for April 8 and the 2.1 per cent in the Kansas City *Star* of the same date. "Substantive" Latin coverage in these two issues total 1.9 per cent and 1.7 per cent respectively of total editorial content. It came to less than one-half of one per cent in four of the twelve issues studied and to less than one per cent in nine of the twelve.

On the whole, the evening papers ran slightly more Latin news than morning papers. The highest total of column inches was in the Kansas City *Star,* but the Louisville *Times* was a close second. The latter ran a long editorial on April 8 dealing with Castro's forthcoming appearance before the American newspaper editors.

The only Latin news to make the front page in any of these issues was a short squib in the October 8 copy of the Louisville *Courier-Journal* headlined "30 Killed in Bus Plunge" in western Colombia and another one-paragraph item in the April 8 Kansas City *Times* on the Senate Foreign Relations Committee approving a new ambassador to Bolivia.

Latin American Coverage in Three Cities—October 8, 1958 & April 8, 1959

	Total Col. In. Editorial matter	Col. In. Foreign	% Foreign	Col. In. Latin	% Latin	Col. In. "Substantive" Foreign	% "Substantive" Foreign	Col. In. "Substantive" Latin	% "Substantive" Latin
Louisville, Kentucky									
(m) *The Courier-Journal*									
Oct. 8	2126.6	256.5	12.0	15.0	0.7	239.8	11.3	10.3	0.5
April 8	2265.0	92.3	4.1	0	0	76.8	3.4	0	0
(e) *The Louisville Times*									
Oct. 8	2058.1	237.3	11.7	31.5	1.5	93.4	4.5	27.1	1.3
April 8	2131.8	221.9	10.4	51.4	2.4	144.7	6.8	40.6	1.9
Kansas City, Missouri									
(m) *The Kansas City Times*									
Oct. 8	1748.5	256.6	14.7	11.0	0.6	189.2	10.2	7.9	0.5
April 8	2225.0	393.6	17.8	23.3	1.1	285.4	12.8	21.8	1.0
(e) *The Kansas City Star*									
Oct. 8	2404.7	374.8	15.6	40.8	1.7	165.4	8.5	30.8	1.3
April 8	2099.8	334.9	15.9	45.1	2.1	166.9	7.9	36.4	1.7
Portland, Oregon									
(m) *The Oregonian*									
Oct. 8	2149.5	316.6	14.6	5.5	0.3	213.9	9.9	0	0
April 8	2308.4	260.9	11.3	21.4	0.9	173.2	7.5	13.4	0.6
(e) *The Oregon Journal*									
Oct. 8	2496.6	284.0	11.4	8.3	0.3	123.8	4.9	1.0	0.04
April 8	2301.3	268.1	11.6	11.2	0.5	169.5	7.3	11.2	0.5
Average:	2192.9	274.8	12.5	23.7	1.1	167.7	7.7	16.7	.76

Col. In. = Column Inches.
"Substantive" refers to topics dealing with politics, economics, social affairs, diplo-

Proportion of background and interpretation

The inside pages of the *Courier-Journal* which carried the bus-plunge story on page one carried on page nine an AP roundup of world "hotspots," which included short items on the Castro rebel forces and the Hollywood activities of Rafael Trujillo, Jr. On page sixteen appeared a story out of Mexico City headlined "Circus Denied Permit For Making Too Much." The lead page of the second section announced the award of a $2,500 Inter-American Press Association scholarship to a newspaperwoman in Colombia. The Latin content for that day was completed by a one-paragraph AP story out of Havana covering an announcement by Batista army headquarters that seven Castro rebels had been killed in the provinces and a sports-page story of a tennis victory by Pancho Segura of Ecuador.

The Kansas City *Times* for the same morning contained three Latin items: a one-paragraph AP story out of Quito, Ecuador, "Find Pre-Inca Citadel" (page 3); an 8-inch Reuters story from Buenos Aires (page 9) on a student protest march against a new government education law; and a sports-page story on a match made by Argentina's Pascual Pérez, world flyweight boxing champion.

The *Oregonian* for October 8 carried the Segura tennis story, the "Pre-Inca" find in Ecuador, and a boxing story about Mexico's Gaspar Ortega.

In the afternoon papers that day, the Louisville *Times* carried 31.5 inches of Latin copy. Two-thirds of this was taken up by a story and picture on page 4 about a group of Chilean industrialists making an inspection tour of local wood-working plants under the auspices of the I.C.A. The remaining three items were the Ecuador find, a Mexican golf tournament and a UPI short on a priest attacked by a Venezuelan mob.

The Kansas City *Star's* quota was 40.8 inches of Latin American news. This included a 16-inch AP background story on statehood for Puerto Rico, which technically might not qualify. The *Star* of that day also contained a long background article on Costa Rican politics and economics written by George Beebe of the *Chicago Daily News* service headed "Charts Course for Costa Rica." Also seven column inches on the teaching of English over Mexican TV (AP) and a short on Caribbean fishing.

The *Oregon Journal* ran only 8.1 column inches of Latin copy: the Batista army report on slaying seven Castro rebels; an AP story on the damage caused by a tropical storm in Mexico; and the match made by the Argentine flyweight.

The number of stories on this list which might be classified as contributing to better U.S.-Latin understanding is relatively sparse. In fairness, one would have to know everything that was made available that day. But the pattern of what was found newsworthy is interesting. The Louisville *Times* gave heavy play to a Latin story with a good local angle.

101

Storm, disaster, riots, sports made all the papers along with the archeological find in Ecuador. Special services—Reuters and the Chicago *Daily News*—subscribed to by the Kansas City papers—gave their Latin American coverage a depth not found in other services.

The lead stories for the day in all papers was a serious relapse suffered by Pope Pius XII and the naming of Judge Potter Stewart to the U. S. Supreme Court. Otherwise, the run of news was average.

A straw in the wind

The figures indicate a small rise in Latin-American content and in the proportion of "substantive" Latin-American news in April, 1959, over October, 1958.

The exception is the Louisville *Courier-Journal* which ran nothing that day. Its companion afternoon paper, The *Times,* however, ran the heaviest Latin-American schedule of all on that date. These included the Castro editorial signed by Editor Emeritus Tom Wallace, the front-page short on the ambassador to Bolivia, plus three "substantive" news stories: the expulsion of Russian diplomats after riots in Argentina; a request by Somoza foes in Nicaragua for the United States ambassador to leave; a story headed "21 Countries Plan Inter-American Bank" out of Washington; and a report on the first American ship to carry cargo from the Great Lakes to Latin American ports.

In Kansas City, the morning *Times* played the Argentine report on page 11, plus a Chicago *Daily News* feature on women's rights in Colombia. The afternoon *Star* contained seven Latin American items, including two local items concerning a lecture on the Caribbean by Cornelius Vanderbilt, Jr., and a Pan American fiesta. An AP story on Cuban currency regulations and the rebellion in Panama also appeared along with a short on Mexican newspapers and another story on deep-sea fishing off Peru. The editorial-page feature column, "Starbeams," carried two Batista jokes.

The Argentine riots made both Portland papers, and the Senate confirmation of the ambassador to Bolivia appeared in the morning *Oregonian.*

Although the sample is thin, this turned out to be a more sober collection of items than those that turned up before the upheaval in Cuba. It is hard to tell how much the psychology of awakened telegraph desks may have been responsible. The lead stories that day were Adenauer's announcement that he would give up his West German chancellorship (on which he later changed his mind), the Connie Nicholas murder trial in Indianapolis, and Oklahoma's repeal of state prohibition.

The salient finding is that these six newspapers, which have been found reasonable reflections on national press trends, gave an average of 1.1% of their total editorial space to Latin American news of all types and 0.76% to "substantive" Latin American news.

102

Noteworthy efforts to improve coverage

The work of the IAPA

The Inter-American Press Association, which has been cited for its job in improving the climate for press freedom internally in Latin America, has also held conferences and trips to Latin America to create more interest among United States publishers in covering Latin America for North American readers. Individuals who have been active in IAPA activities—such as John O'Rourke of the Scripps-Howard Washington *Daily News,* William H. Cowles, of the Spokane, Washington, *Spokesman-Review,* William Pepper of the Gainesville, Florida, *Daily Sun,* John R. Herbert of the Quincy, Massachusetts, *Patriot Ledger,* among others—have made a point of trying to present Latin America news intelligently in their own papers.

Queried concerning the impact of such efforts in their local communities, most of these publishers admitted that it was difficult to produce concrete evidence. However, Mr. Cowles writes from Spokane:

"There seems to be no doubt that more interest in Latin American news is being shown in this community than formerly. Of course, we have recently had some stirring events there, of which the rise of Castro is the most noteworthy.

"The wire services find usage of general Latin American news to be low. It seems to be difficult to interest either readers or telegraph editors in material with which they merely 'ought' to be concerned. When stories are delivered that have strong emotional interest, as in the case of the Cuban revolution, the Nixon episode, the overthrow of Perón, and the assassination of Castillo Armas, news staffs will publish them without urging, and the public will read them eagerly.

"The problem, obviously, lies with the significant but undramatic news that necessarily makes up the bulk of the report. In that connection, I think the horizons of North American readers are gradually but steadily enlarging. This process probably is enhancing readership of the kind of news about which we are concerned. The big, violent stories, unfortunate as they often are, perhaps whet interest in Latin America, so that gradually the public's normal receptivity to ordinary news from there increases. I presume that is what is happening in Spokane.

"One of the good suggestions that has come out of the Inter-American Press Association is to send news editors and telegraph editors to the meetings of IAPA. By this means, they should develop a better appreciation of Latin America as a source of news. This suggestion is against the background of the fact that the news services are sending a voluminous report from Latin America, only to have much of it fail to go out on the

United States domestic wires and again to have much of what is delivered to the newspapers go unused."

An experiment by UPI

In November, 1958, United Press International experimented by mailing out an entire page of UPI Newsfeatures devoted exclusively to Latin America. The venture was tied in with a National Latin American Week and Latin American Day. "The special page . . . got a big editorial page play in the Quincy *Patriot Ledger*," general manager Earl J. Johnson reported. "Otherwise, this layout . . . evoked only minor attention."

Editor John R. Herbert says "the situation in Quincy may be due to the fact that I have a personal interest in the subject. When I attended a meeting of the IAPA board in New York, many of the publishers present were not conscious of the fact that UPI had sent out such material. This suggested a need for greater liaison between publishers and editors in this matter and brought about the suggestion that something should be done to get publishers to bring their editors to the IAPA annual meeting so that the enthusiasm of publishers for IAPA could be transmitted to the men who actually handle the news."

Joseph Jones, UPI vice president, says UPI does not intend to repeat the trial balloon in that form. "Instead, we will look more determinedly for Latin American copy which can be incorporated into the regular feature service."

Jones adds that the UPI services a special one-hour Latin American news report on its wires to a few newspapers like the *Christian Science Monitor,* Washington *Daily News,* Los Angeles *Times,* San Diego *Union,* Miami *News* as well as *Time* magazine. The UPI business wire also "carries a good chunk of economic news from Latin America. But we find that even good spot news from Latin America is vulnerable to ditching on the desk in favor of other world, national and local news. We get the feeling sometimes that the service we provide from Latin America is not welcome. In the Middle West last December, just before the blow-up in Cuba, newspaper editors complained that we were giving too much play to Castro. It's hard to improve something which doesn't spark much enthusiasm anyway.

"Of course, the telegraph editor is always jammed for space. He never has enough room for everything he would like to handle. He tries to get things into the paper he *knows* people are interested in. The space situation makes it tough for him to pioneer.

"If you have what you believe to be an important story, you have to find a way to get the client to use it. We sometimes put a spot lead out of Washington on top of a Latin American story, and find that the Washington date-line increases its chances of getting into the paper."

David Hellyer, Latin American editor of The San Diego *Union,* writes in *The Quill,* published by the professional journalism fraternity Sigma Delta Chi:

"Many conscientious United States editors, aware their readers' news diet is deficient in Latin American items, would like to keep the readers better informed on important hemispheric developments in the political and economic fields. They find the task extremely difficult. They find it hard to make such news meaningful to the average American, mainly because few American readers possess a sufficient background in continental affairs to comprehend the significance of an isolated news story.

* * *

"The average American news editor, faced with critical space problems and a shrinking newsprint allotment, gives play only to those stories which he, in his judgment, believes his readers must comprehend to keep abreast of the times.

"The smaller the paper, the greater the difficulty. Let us assume, for example, a small daily in our own Midwest publishes a five-inch story reporting the fall of another cabinet in Chile. The story, cut to the bare essentials of its lead, can do no more than state that the cabinet has fallen due to disagreement between the president and one of his ministers.

"The casual reader of this hypothetical small-town daily—lacking the perspective against which to view this item—may glance at the story (or perhaps just its headline), shrug his shoulders and say: 'Just another revolution in South America.'

"Now it's not just 'another revolution' at all. Indeed, there has been no revolution. Nonetheless, the item is charged with significance, a significance which conceivably could extend to the Midwestern town in which our hypothetical reader lives. Behind the story is the tragedy of spiralling inflation, the story of a nation of seven million people fighting for its life. This the reader does not know, of course, unless he is much more intellectually curious than the average."

The Copley News Service

The Copley chain of newspapers in California and Illinois, of which The San Diego *Union* is a part, inaugurated a special Latin American news service in 1955 to supply background and trend stories for this deeper insight into hemispheric affairs. Hellyer contributes to its "Pan American Report" which is prepared five times weekly and tailored to the space problem by being limited to a maximum of 450 words. The service also includes a weekly feature called "Know Your Hemisphere." The Copley News Service now serves 15 newspapers in addition to the 15 members of the Copley group, including the Richmond *Times Dispatch* and the New Orleans *Times Picayune*. It maintains a full-time correspondent in Buenos Aires and stringers in fourteen other Latin American cities. Hellyer, editor William Giandoni and John Abney, a former correspondent in Mexico City, make periodic swings to the field on special assignment.

"The Copley papers in Illinois," Hellyer reports, "use just about as much Latin copy as the California dailies do. They use it on both editorial and news pages, averaging from four to six columns weekly. A year ago they used between one and two columns weekly.

"There has been no spontaneous writing-of-letters that I know of by readers. We are not too concerned about the absence of specific reader reaction yet. This is pioneering work, the slow drip-drip of water on the rock. Readership habits have been a long time building in the U.S., and we don't expect to force acceptance of a Latin American readership habit overnight.

"Either the Union or Copley News Service has staffed a number of big events in recent Latin American history, including the Castro trials, the Nixon trip, the IAPA meeting, the Rio finance ministers' conferences and the Panama conference of American presidents. This represents a considerable outlay of money, and is one measure of the conviction we all have here in the need for better Latin coverage."

The Kansas City Star

A special effort on a local community basis was sparked by another young reporter, Hal Hendrix, when he was a member of the staff of the Kansas City *Star*. Hendrix now covers Latin American news for the Miami *News*. Working in Kansas City in 1953 as a City Hall reporter, he persuaded publisher Roy Roberts to assign him to Dr. Milton Eisenhower's Latin American tour. When he returned, Hendrix dug out the fact that several Kansas City firms did a considerable business with Latin American customers and that one local bank handles as much as $100,000 per week in Latin American transactions. The *Star* helped to promote a trip of thirty Kansas City business and civic leaders through South America, and a special Latin American weekend in Kansas City attended by eighteen of the twenty Latin American ambassadors in Washington. Meanwhile Hendrix was writing a thrice-weekly Latin American column in the *Star* and circulating through the hemisphere.

"As the coverage grew so did the mail from readers in outstate Missouri and Kansas as well as Kansas City. With the mail came requests to talk to luncheon groups, schools and churches. At every appearance, the audience fired questions, questions, questions. We discovered the schools were using the columns to supplement history and geography work, and the churches were using them in adult discussion groups."

The column was dropped when Hendrix left the *Star* in 1957. But, reports *Star* editorial writer Roger S. Swanson, "our coverage of Latin America has not declined. Often we will run several editorials a week on Latin America (which I write). Our news coverage of Latin America, I believe, is more extensive than that of most papers. On numerous occasions we have queried the Associated Press for situation stories about political developments. Or for greater, clearer details. Earlier this year two of our staff members visited in Mexico, Panama and Cuba. I spent a week in Washington this spring, visiting the Pan-American Union, the State Department, embassies and legislators.

"The *Star* believes Latin America to be of growing importance in world affairs. We feel it often is neglected. Latin America is important to Kansas City. Our local firms annually conduct a large volume of business with Central and South American countries.

"I think the *Star's* readers, too, have a big interest in Latin America. Kansas City, though in the heart of the nation, is internationally minded. Pan-American day is observed annually. We have a sizable Mexican colony.

"Summing up, then, I would say the *Star* believes Latin American news and opinion to be highly important; and believes that it will grow more important in the years ahead. The *Star* feels obliged to give its readers the best possible coverage in this area."

The New York Times

The Latin American staff of the New York *Times* was originally organized back in 1928 when Arthur Hays Sulzberger, now the publisher, made a personal swing through South America and established part-time correspondents in four Latin cities. The *Times* now maintains full-time bureaus, each headed by a staff correspondent, in Mexico City, Havana, Rio de Janeiro and Buenos Aires, plus a network of part-time correspondents in nineteen other Latin American locations. Seven of these stringers are North American, seven are British (mostly in Britain's Caribbean settlements), one is Dutch and three are local nationals in Guatemala, Bolivia and Ecuador. Periodic tours of Latin America are made by members of the news and editorial staff.

The *Times* editorial crusade to restore *La Prensa to* Dr. Alberto Gainza Paz and Herbert Matthews' exclusive stories from the mountain headquarters of Fidel Castro are dramatic examples of the *Times'* enterprise and interest in covering Latin America. In the past decade *Times* staffers have won three Maria Moors Cabot medals for the advancement of "sympathetic understanding" in the Western Hemisphere. On the occasion of one of these awards, Mr. Sulzberger defined the role of the United States press in covering Latin America in these terms:

"What we need is a wholesome climate of public opinion in which prejudice and indifference bred of ignorance are dispelled. We need to know each other better—and that is a job for the press. Not that the press can accomplish the purpose single-handed. The schools, government agencies, cultural and trade associations—all have vital roles, but the principal responsibility for conveying information and interpretation to a broad public falls on the press.

"Up to now this responsibility has been perceived by but few newspapers in the United States. Latin America, by and large, is a neglected area of news . . . It is fair to say that the countries south of the Rio Grande generally have been under-reported and that the trickle of stories that have appeared have tended to give a distorted, unbalanced picture of Latin American affairs.

*　　*　　*

"The press has the obligation to fulfill its true purpose by bringing the people all the information they need for effective citizenship . . . This responsibility has two aspects. First, the facts must be reported fully, accurately and in proper balance. Then, because the bare facts are usually complex and many-sided, readers must be given expert interpretation to guide them through the maze."

Emanuel Freedman, the *Times* foreign news editor, believes that in covering Latin America, as anywhere else in the world, the success of the *Times* is based on supplying "a continuity of coverage on the main stream of developments" over and above the day-to-day spot news. This involves a good deal of editorial planning and thinking as well as a network of available manpower. Freedman adds that the *Times* often prints mail copy from its Latin American stringers with datelines a week or ten days old if it considers the story significant. "We have long since gotten away from the concept that it isn't news if it doesn't carry yesterday's dateline," Freedman reports.

This attitude has practical aspects in view of the fact that Latin America is a high-cost area for the transmission of news. (Charges range from five cents to ten cents a word.) More favorable press rates, Freedman suggests, might make a difference in the case of those newspapers which are reluctant to follow the *Times'* policy on Latin American mailers.

One cannot leave the subject of the New York *Times* and Latin America without further mention of Herbert L. Matthews. The point is not perhaps Mr. Matthews' individual accomplishments as a reporter and editorial writer on the Latin American scene, although these are considerable. But

108

more important the wisdom of the *Times* in cultivating and encouraging specialists who are permitted to function at the top editorial level has been demonstrated in coverage, like that in Cuba, which provides insight and understanding to its readers in advance as well as after climactic events make front-page news.

The weekly news magazines

Both *Newsweek* and *Time* pursue a policy of earmarking space in every issue for coverage of Canada together with Latin America. In practice, *Newsweek* allocates three columns of space to one or both areas as the run of the news dictates. *Time,* which publishes special editions for distribution in Canada and Latin America, runs special four-page sections in each of these "exports." In its domestic edition, United States readers receive two pages of news boiled down from these eight in *Time's* "Hemisphere" department. This was increased from one page a few years ago.

Harry B. Murkland, *Newsweek's* Hemisphere Affairs editor, has written in "Americas": "On the basis of my own experience, I believe there is a good deal more reader interest than most editors realize. But clearly there is no irresistible public demand for more news of Latin America.

*   *   *

It seems to me that the basic reason for the paucity of serious Latin American news in our papers and for the lack of reader interest that is both the cause and the result of that paucity, is simply the presentation.

*   *   *

Given U.S. ignorance of Latin American backgrounds, and given the way the North American press presents Latin American news, the result is bound to be confusion in the mind of the reader. And because he is confused, he is almost sure to be uninterested. He will become interested only when he begins to understand.

"The way to do this would be to treat the Latin American news that comes into the newspaper office not as a finished product but as raw material . . . handed over to an editor qualified by experience and knowledge to handle it. He would add the necessary background, identification, and interpretation, and only then would the story be printed."

This, of course, is in essence the way all news is processed by the news magazines. Without becoming involved in evaluating the dangers of mixing "slant" with "interpretation" under this system, this technique, when skillfully and responsibly employed, has frequently enabled the news magazines to make Latin American news more meaningful.

Time reports that, of its mail received from U.S. readers last year, its Hemisphere section reportedly ranked fifth out of all 23 departments of the magazine in reader reaction.

109

The example of the news magazines has undoubtedly been an influence on the general increase of "explanatory" writing and news-summary sections in American newspapers. The increased use of maps, charts, biographical and geographical background has particular application to coverage of Latin America. Where information gaps exist among readers, editorial imagination can help to bring stories within their grasp.

The Pulliam papers

Eugene C. Pulliam, publisher of The Indianapolis *Star and News* and the Phoenix, Arizona, *Republic,* believes that "any newspaper which conscientiously tries to serve the best interests of this nation should give special attention to the coverage of Latin American countries. There is nothing soft or theoretical about this comment. It is in our own self-interest to help develop the great frontiers which lie all through South America and where we could have as close friends as the Canadians if we had only pursued the correct policy.

"Too much of the news we get on South America comes through various government agencies and is little short of being pure propaganda. What we need is straight reporting by reporters who are giving the facts, telling the truth and presenting the story in an interesting way—without any effort to praise or condemn some government agency.

"I think we have increased the readership interest in foreign affairs on the part of our readers principally by giving them interesting stories, day after day after day. Frankly, I think the fact that we have the best foreign editor in America [Michael Padev], plus the fact that we send people abroad almost continuously, either to Europe, Asia or South America, writing with a personal touch, adds greatly to the interest of readers in a news story and gets them to read stories that otherwise they would probably pass over.

"We make periodic surveys of readership of all classes of news in all of our papers. It is absolutely amazing what we have been able to do in increasing the interest of our readers in international news.

"In Phoenix the interest in South American news has increased more rapidly than it has in Indianapolis, but even here the interest is high. When I bought the *Star* in 1944 there was a general average readership of international news of about 18 per cent. Today it exceeds 65 per cent both here and in Phoenix."

This astounding increase in these two heartland American cities casts doubt on the popular premise that Americans are not good customers for foreign news. The way this news is written and presented is a key factor to the audience it can reach.

Conclusions

Summary

The flow of news and information between Latin America and the United States, important as it is, is but one stream in a worldwide torrent of vital communications. The staggering quantity of such intelligence strains our modern technical resources and engulfs individual understanding. The problem of promoting adequate press coverage of Latin America must be viewed in the context of a much larger problem—the challenge of keeping abreast of extraordinary developments all over the globe.

The nations of the Western Hemisphere, nevertheless, have a special relationship which makes mutual understanding of critical importance. Such understanding rests on more and better information than now exists. The mass communications media—press associations, newspapers, magazines, radio and television—exert a powerful influence on Latin American and North American attitudes. And there is authoritative evidence that irritations and misunderstandings have been increasing. The climate of opinion in these countries has a profound effect on the policies of their governments—strategic, economic and social.

Popular attitudes are not only influenced by what is transmitted by the mass media but they also help to shape the character of this output. In the United States there is widespread feeling that North Americans do not know or care very much about Latin American news. Some editors say that is why they do not supply more coverage for their audience. This produces a vicious circle: first, the claim is made that Americans are not interested; next, the failure to provide the news perpetuates ignorance; finally, ignorance leads to the lack of interest described by the editors.

When one looks into the assumptions behind the dilemma, it is by no means clear that Americans are as uninterested in Latin America as we have been led to believe. We have sparse data. Public opinion polls indicate serious gaps in basic factual knowledge about our Latin American neighbors. At the same time, these polls also suggest that many Americans do *care* about what is going on in these countries. Their ignorance may be a reflection of the quality of information they have been offered rather than an index of an inherent lack of interest.

To achieve better United States coverage of Latin America involves practical problems, however, which it is foolish to underestimate. High quality foreign correspondence is expensive. Publishing and network profits are narrow. Furthermore, Latin America must compete for available resources against the demands of other crucial and underreported areas. These are only some of the factors that have made the press associations the fundamental source of worldwide news flowing to the vast

111

bulk of the North American audience. And the press associations are responsive to the demand of their clients.

The managers of these newsgathering organizations report that only a small percentage of the Latin American news they presently distribute to their clients actually finds its way into print or onto the air waves. Latin American news is receiving only a tiny proportion of the total space in our newspapers. Even these fragments run heavily to accidents, violence or sports rather than to the solid substance of politics, economics and social affairs. There are straws in the wind, however, that the shock of recent events in Latin America has sharpened the eyes of desk editors for more meaningful background and interpretation of the Latin American scene.

Requirements for understanding

If the nation is to have the kind of public understanding that will prompt and support intelligent policies toward Latin America, two requirements seem inescapable:

1. The thoughtful, articulate segment of the population must be at least broadly informed about the other Americas. This need not involve a detailed knowledge of geography or of the names of the heads of all governments. It does involve comprehension of the importance of the other Americas, some feeling for their backgrounds, cultures, and sensibilities, and some knowledge of political, economic and social trends.

2. The small minority of true opinion leaders across the nation should be able to keep themselves informed about current developments and trends in the Americas.

Neither of these goals is likely to be achievable in a nation whose newspapers and other news media generally neglect Latin America.

Possible remedies

From all the available data, no clear, pat solution emerges. We do find, however, certain clues that suggest possible and partial remedies.

1. The compilations of public opinion survey findings suggest that, while there is profound public ignorance of Latin America, there is latent interest in the area and a through-the-pores sense that the other Americas are of great importance to this nation. The right kind of reporting and presentation of news might well awaken the subsurface interest.

2. Any individual working on a study of this type finds himself gravitating toward the feeling that, in this area in particular, "there is no dull news, just dull writing." Fragmented reporting of isolated political events in a given country, for example, evokes little reader response. There are

112

signs, however, of a real readership potential for the skillfully written article setting such events in perspective and showing their relation to broader trends.

Whatever their other faults, the news magazines have demonstrated much about how to present Latin American news interestingly and meaningfully.

3. The experience of the Kansas City *Star* and Hal Hendrix point to interesting possibilities. Here a newspaper man set out to develop and nurture interest in Latin America among leading citizens; this whetted an appetite for more news and editorials on the subject; the newspaper endeavored to meet the demand, and so on.

4. One of the obstacles to adequate Latin American news, not only in the press but also in the magazines and electronic media, has been the sense of news editors that they were "playing to an empty house." The appreciable audience that has a genuine interest in the area has not written to applaud good reporting or to condemn bad or nonexistent coverage. Those who know something and want to know more of Latin America could do much to break the vicious circle by expressing their approval or disapproval to the news media.

5. The Inter-American Press Association has undoubtedly proved constructive in drawing a dozen or two United States publishers to meetings in Latin America every year or so. While some doubtless were lured initially by the prospect of a tax-deductible business trip, the net effect has been to heighten understanding of the area, not only among the informed publishers but particularly among some who could not previously distinguish Brazil from Costa Rica.

This suggests the possibility that some of these publishers might see fit to build on this foundation by sending on future trips to the other Americas their news editors who customarily make the decisions as to what foreign news is published in their newspapers.

6. If maintenance of full-time correspondents abroad is extremely expensive, the occasional survey-reporting trip is less so. The responsible news editor, sent on a trip as mentioned above, can not only improve his perspective and freshen his outlook but can also report back to his readers in terms that they understand and appreciate. A number of newspapers have effectively employed the technique in Europe; few have done so in Latin America.

7. An interview survey of New Yorkers during a recent newspaper strike pointed up the phenomenon that Americans often do the "right" thing for the "wrong" reason: Many of those interviewed indicated that they read the news daily not purely for the sake of informing themselves but rather to avoid seeming uninformed among friends, neighbors and business associates.

113

This suggests that the monopoly newspaper, now the rule in 90-odd per cent of American cities, has an opportunity that was less evident in the days when it felt compelled to outshout its competition in sensationalized reports on murder, rape and miscellaneous skullduggery. By giving the vital or broad-gauged report from Latin America the prominence he feels it deserves, the editor can possibly induce readership among those who are looking for social cues as to what is important. Here, in brief, is a case where the dubious characteristics of monopoly and of keeping-up-with-the-Joneses might well be harnessed for constructive purposes.

8. The press has a responsibility to lead as well as follow the aspirations of its audience. And this can be practical as well as right. If Americans are capable of becoming better informed about Latin America, someone must provide the opportunity. The history of our press is rich with examples of audiences that awaited only the chance to be cultivated.

Isolated experiments in improving the flow of news and background from the twenty American republics tend to support the points suggested above. Some of these experiments have already stimulated a heartening reaction, both from the public and the individuals responsible for editorial planning. If it can be demonstrated not only that better United States news coverage of Latin America is an issue of press responsibility, but that there is a real market for such efforts, we will have gone a long way toward piercing the curtain of frustration that envelops this subject.

4. The economic picture

REYNOLD E. CARLSON

Introduction

The central feature of the Latin American economy in the postwar period has been a broad drive toward economic development. Almost without exception, every government has taken the position that its policies in the economic area will be to direct the available resources and to create the conditions necessary to achieve a substantial increase in the national production of goods and services.

There are several reasons for placing economic development as the top priority. In the first place, the population growth in Latin America is one of the highest in the world, increasing at an average rate of 2.5 per cent annually since the war, which means the total population will double in 25 to 30 years, from its present level of 180,000,000 to 360,000,000.

A second source of pressure for economic development may be found in the revolution of aspirations that has been evident since the war. The Latin American countries have been subjected for some time to what economists call the "demonstration effect," in which people's wants and

REYNOLD E. CARLSON is Professor of Economics at Vanderbilt University. He has also directed the Institute of Brazilian Studies and taught at Johns Hopkins University. He has served as an economist and consultant on Latin America for the United States government and the United Nations; he has been senior economist in Latin America for the World Bank.

tastes have been sharply stimulated through easy access to such media as the Hollywood movies and American magazines, as well as direct exposure through travel to the higher standards of living in the United States and Western Europe. To be sure, this demonstration has been under way for many years, but somehow it seems to have caught hold in the postwar period, so that even the rank and file of the population feel they should have a larger share of the economic goods which other countries, and, indeed, some groups in their own countries seem to possess. Prior to World War II, these aspirations took the form of widespread legislation in social security and welfare, in some cases virtually copying the legislation of the more advanced countries. As will be seen subsequently, these aspirations for social betterment have been largely disappointed because, almost without exception, no country possessed the resources necessary to implement the elaborate legislation. The cost of social welfare benefits has been a heavy addition to the wage bill which, in most cases, was not compensated by increases in productivity. In other cases the competition for the limited resources between social welfare on the one hand and the need for capital formation on the other, has been a potent factor in the inflationary pressures plaguing many of the countries.

A third factor behind the drive for economic development is the structural problem existing in most of the countries, especially in the area of foreign trade. It is well known that the exports of Latin America consist largely of primary products such as foodstuffs and raw materials, the prices of which are subject to wide fluctuations in the world market. These fluctuations have served alternately as accelerator and brake to the rate of growth. Out of this situation has grown a whole school of thought that the only solution is industrialization in order to reduce the vulnerability of the economies to changes in their terms of trade.

Another factor of a structural character is the state of agriculture, which still provides the means of employment for 50 and 60 per cent of the population in most countries. Yet agriculture has generally lagged behind other sectors with respect to the adoption of known techniques, and has been less successful in attracting capital than industry and commerce. As a result, agricultural productivity has either declined or stagnated. Total output in physical terms has, of course, increased and has generally kept pace with population growth, but this increase has been achieved almost entirely by continual additions to the labor force working with the same primitive techniques that characterized agricultural production fifty years ago. The fact that the agricultural sector is overloaded with population is, for the most part, the real reason for the low statistical per capita income. As with foreign trade, so with agriculture: there is a strong feeling that economic development cannot be achieved without massive industrialization in order to take people from the farms and to increase the productivity per man of those who remain.

Some notice must also be taken of the growing disposition toward nationalism and the increasing role of the national government, in seeking to accelerate the rate of economic development. Two aggressive elements are abroad in the economy of Latin America. One is found in the private sector where powerful industrial and commercial groups are emphasizing the advantages of a nationalistic policy designed to reserve the exploitation of domestic resources for nationals and generally to discourage the foreign investor or businessman. The other aggressive element makes itself felt through the government sector. It actively seeks to expand the role of the government in the economic field as a supplier of capital, as an entrepreneur of new industrial undertakings, and as the architect who designs and influences the economic structure by means of various measures, channeling the forces of economic development in one direction or another according to some judgment as to what is "best" for the economy. In this connection, the position of the military in many of these governments ranges from the relatively quiet role of domestic police force to the other extreme where decisions on the allocation of scarce resources can be made and implemented only with the sufferance of the military group. To be sure, this is an old story in Latin American history, but it is singularly out of place in a region which has "officially" committed itself to promoting economic development while at the same time trying to support a military establishment that absorbs 30 to 40 per cent of the national budget.

Each of the elements set forth above may now be examined in some detail, but the framework of the discussion which follows will be that of economic development and its inevitable consequences for the economy of the United States.

Diversities and growth rates

It must be made clear at the outset that the region known as "Latin America" is not a single entity with uniform characteristics about which easy generalizations can be made. It will be useful, therefore, to spell out some of the broad differences found among the 20 Latin American countries. In the first place, the obvious differences are in the size and population of the countries. The Latin American countries range from Brazil, at one extreme, with a population of 60,000,000 and a geographic size greater than continental United States, to Panama and Costa Rica with populations of barely 1,000,000 and of equal size with West Virginia or South Carolina. The rates of growth of these populations also vary from a high annual increase of 3.1 per cent in Venezuela to a low of 1.2 per cent in Guatemala and Bolivia.

117

Next, with respect to the structure of the economy, the range is again very great. At one extreme is Venezuela, with a per capita income of $500 and, at the other extreme, Haiti with a per capita income of only $85, which places it on a par with some of the poorest countries of Southeast Asia. Illiteracy varies from 13 per cent in Argentina to 89 per cent in Honduras (ten years of age and over). The productive sectors are marked by the fraction of the population gaining a livelihood from agriculture (i.e., rural population) which is 38 per cent in Argentina and 75 per cent in the Dominican Republic. Dependence upon foreign trade (measured by exports as a percentage of national income) ranges from a low of 13 per cent in Argentina to a high of 49 per cent in Venezuela and 41 per cent in Costa Rica. Four countries have a single export commodity accounting for 80 per cent or more of total exports. An important distinction arises between those which export minerals (Chile and Bolivia), those which rely upon exports of foodstuffs (Argentina and Ecuador), and those with exports of fiber (Uruguay and Paraguay).

In terms of financial stability, the range is again very great. Some countries are on the brink of runaway inflation, such as Chile and until recently Bolivia, in contrast with other countries enjoying a price level even more stable than that of the United States, such as Cuba, Haiti, Panama, and the Dominican Republic.

There is no point is laboring the obvious fact that diversity does exist in Latin America, but this fact needs to be remembered in the discussion to follow. The problems of Latin America are no different from those of the other underdeveloped countries of the world, and a more meaningful analysis might be based upon some classification other than mere geographical location. Thus, the mineral exporting countries of Latin America have some problems probably closer to those of Africa and Asia than to the semi-industrialized countries of Argentina, Brazil and Mexico, which are operating at a level far removed from the poorer agricultural countries like Paraguay and Haiti. In short, the Latin American countries are a heterogeneous group. They are lumped together because of their long historical association through such institutions as the Pan-American Union and the special interest which the region has for the United States on grounds of mutual security, foreign trade and investment.

In real terms, production in the Latin American region increased at an annual rate of about 4.5 per cent over the seven years 1950-1957. With a population growth of approximately 2.5 per cent annually, this means an annual net advance per capita of about two per cent. If Venezuela were excluded from the calculations, the growth of production would still be about four per cent, or a per capita increase of 1.5 per cent annually.

This rate of growth may be contrasted with that of other regions. Gross national production of the United States in the postwar period increased 4.2 per cent annually, or 2.5 per cent per capita. In Europe, taking the

118

countries of the Organization for European Economic Cooperation, the postwar growth was 5.2 per cent, which is a per capita rate of 4.4 per cent. In Asia postwar growth ranged from 8.5 per cent (7 per cent per capita) in Japan to 2.5 per cent (1 per cent per capita) in Pakistan. The sharp difference between the growth in total production and the per capita growth figure in Latin America, draws attention to its high rate of population increase in comparison with other regions of the world.

The principal factor in the growth rate is the volume of investment. Thus, in the period 1950-1957, 16 to 17 per cent of total national income was invested in plant and equipment, construction and inventories. In absolute terms, the increase has been substantial because production has risen by one-third. It remains to be seen whether this rate can be maintained in the next decade. It must be remembered that sharp increases in commodity prices have taken place during the last seven years, in part because of the Korean War, which drove mineral prices to new highs, and in part because of the sharp reversal in the world coffee situation which caused prices to double in 1949-1950 and to increase again in 1953. In view of the role of minerals and coffee in the balance of payments of the Latin American countries, these gains greatly increased the capacity of the countries to invest and thus contributed to the high growth rate achieved. The prospect for these commodities in, say, the next five years is much more pessimistic. Coffee prices have already declined drastically because of the huge increase in world production now coming on the market from the new plantings stimulated by the high prices of 1953-1955.

The rate of investment may also be analyzed in terms of the amounts needed to maintain the capital stock and to provide for new population growth. Although gross investment was 16 to 17 per cent of the total output, roughly one-third of this comes from meeting the depreciation of existing plant and equipment and goes to maintain—but not to increase— the existing stock of capital goods. Another one-third is required just to maintain the per capita stock of capital, that is, to provide the housing and tools needed to equip the annual increase in population and simply to maintain them at the existing low level. Finally, the last one-third of the investment serves to increase the production level of the country. When viewed in this fashion, it appears that even a high investment rate of 16 to 17 per cent results in a net increment of growth which is fairly small. If, as noted above, per capita income increased by two per cent, it would be necessary to maintain this level of investment for a period of 35 years in order to double the present standard of living. This is a sobering thought which is likely to be overlooked by the more zealous advocates of economic development.

The second element to be stressed is the origin of the investment in these countries. In general, it may be said that well over 90 per cent of the

119

capital growth comes from domestic resources, such as depreciation reserves, undistributed profits, collective savings from social security institutions and personal savings, while only ten per cent represents foreign capital entering the country. Evidently, the region's rate of growth has been achieved with its own resources, which raises additional problems. The increasing pressure to expand consumption is in direct competition with the need for capital formation. In view of the low levels prevailing in some countries, the pressure to consume is formidable, and many popularly elected governments have come to power on a platform promising to expand consumption or to improve welfare. Nevertheless, if sustained economic growth is to be achieved, it will be necessary to syphon off substantial fractions of the new increments in production in the direction of capital formation. On the basis of the past seven years, for example, gross production increased one-third, but the rate of investment remained roughly unchanged.

The experience of 1958 seems to confirm the hypothesis that the growth rate for the past seven years for the region as a whole has been tapering off. In 1958 gross production increased about three per cent in contrast with five per cent the year before, which in per capita terms meant an increase of less than one per cent in 1958. When account is taken of the deterioration in the terms of trade, the increase in per capita income was zero for 1958. In fact, over the last three years per capita income rose only two per cent—that is, less than one per cent a year. It would be excessively optimistic, therefore, to project the average achievement of the last seven years into the immediate future.

One of the characteristics of economic development is the changing structure of the economy and the emergence of particular sectors to positions of importance. As noted earlier, gross national production expanded 35 per cent in real terms between 1950 and 1957. It remains to note the growth rates in particular sectors over this same period.

In agriculture, production increased 26 per cent, or somewhat less than the rate of total production. Per capita, the increase was only eight per cent, which over the seven-year period means an improvement of barely one per cent per year in living standards. With particular reference to row crops and cereals, the increase was 31 per cent in the period 1950-1957, or a gross increase of ten per cent over the seven-year period; livestock and meat production increased 18 per cent in this period, but with zero increase on a per capita basis.

Output in mining increased 70 per cent in these years, reflecting the substantial developments in Chilean copper, Brazilian iron ore and manganese, and Venezuelan iron ore.

In the manufacturing sector, the increase over the same period was 37 per cent. This rate is not much greater than that in agriculture, con-

120

sidering the pressures for industrialization in many countries and the forced draft measures taken to promote industrial projects for purposes of import substitution, often with little or no reference to factors of comparative advantage. The process of industrialization in countries like Argentina, Brazil and Chile has been accelerated by a variety of measures and incentives. Since all three countries maintain exchange controls and have supported overvalued exchange rates for varying periods of time, the incentives to import capital equipment for industrial purposes have been very strong. The same incentives have been applied to imports of raw materials, fuels, and spare parts needed to operate these industrial plants. Protective devices are not lacking and often prove more effective than the tariff, the classical device for protecting national production from the foreign imports. Exchange controls have been administered for the purpose of protecting established industry from the competition, not only of foreign imports, but also of foreign factories which would otherwise be attracted to a country because of growing markets and earnings prospects.

Nationalism has reached one of its more virulent forms in the industrial sector. It is possible for industrialists, already entrenched in an economy, effectively to close the door to new enterprises from abroad which would probably compete for the growing market. Many of the so-called industrialization laws purporting to invite expansion are so designed as to exclude entrants to an industry on various grounds. In some cases existing firms can demonstrate that their capacity or their plans for expansion of capacity are adequate to meet the domestic market at existing prices. In other cases it is considered "unfair competition" for a foreign firm to enter a country with modern equipment and make use of the latest technologies in order to produce at substantially lower costs and therefore lower consumer prices.

In short, the rate of industrial expansion is inhibited by the defensive tactics of existing producers who hope to reserve the expanding market for themselves without being under pressure to rationalize their techniques of production or to meet price competition.

Another element tending to retard the expansion of industries is the absence of the necessary investment in economic overhead capital, particularly in electric power and transportation. These continue to be bottlenecks in the rate of industrial growth. Surveys that have been made in cities like Rio de Janeiro or São Paulo indicate a substantial waiting list of industrial firms unable to get into production or to expand existing facilities until new generating capacity will permit an increase in the connected load. Similarly in transportation, existing firms find that their rate of expansion depends upon widening the domestic market, which can be achieved only by substantial investment in railways, highways and auxiliary services. In fact, the growing realization of industrialists that power and transportation are essential to their own growth is probably a major reason for the pres-

121

sures now being placed upon governments to invest heavily in such overhead capital. Not many years ago these same industrialists were indifferent to such developments and begrudged the allocation of resources to those sectors. Private power companies in Brazil, for example, have been able to capitalize on this new awareness and to absorb a substantial amount of new capital in the form of domestic equity participation from the very industrialists who have now come to recognize the critical importance of electric power in their own plans for expanding operations.

Other sectors in the economy continue to grow at comparable rates. Thus, construction increased 28 per cent, transportation 50 per cent, and government 23 per cent in the period 1950-1957. Services are also a sector showing considerable expansion (31 per cent in the period under review), and in terms of employment their role is actually increasing relative to agriculture and manufacturing. In 1948, for example, agriculture accounted for 54 per cent of the labor force; seven years later in 1955, the employment created by agriculture was down to 50 per cent. Manufacturing and construction remained relatively unchanged, accounting for 18 per cent of the employment over the entire period. Services, on the other hand, have shown a steady increase from 26 per cent of the labor force in 1948 to 30 per cent in 1955.

This suggests the interesting hypothesis that the manpower being released from agriculture is not going into industry as is frequently alleged, but into services. It is possible, therefore, that the familiar phenomenon of disguised unemployment known to exist in agriculture is simply being shifted to the service sector. Anyone visiting Latin America must be impressed by the large number of domestic servants, restaurant waiters, parking lot attendants and the like, who almost certainly represent some degree of disguised unemployment. Their productivity, for an urban area, is probably not much higher than if they had stayed on the farms. Industry, meanwhile, does not appear to be absorbing increasing fractions of the population but is barely holding its own as a source of employment.

One must hasten to add that these inferences are based upon overall statistics for the entire region. It is undoubtedly true that in certain countries, like Mexico or Brazil where industrialization is moving rapidly ahead, industry is increasing its relative position as an employer of labor. Even in such countries, however, it is likely that the services are also absorbing substantial amounts of the labor being released from agriculture. The problems of urbanization, therefore, should not be viewed as a by-product of industrialization alone. They are generated in part by the substantial increase in the number employed in services. These people earn incomes substantially less than industrial labor. They make up the bulk of those miserable souls who occupy the hills around Caracas, the *callampas* outside Santiago, and the hillside *favelas* in Rio de Janeiro.

Latin American trade and the United States

The countries of Latin America find their closest ties with the United States economy in the two broad areas of foreign trade and foreign investment. The United States received one-third of all its imports from Latin America and shipped 20 to 25 per cent of its exports to this region during the last few years. Early in the postwar period the fractions were even larger, for the obvious reason that other sources of supply in the world were not in a position to resume trade with Latin America until they had gradually recovered from the effects of the war. With respect to particular countries, the United States role as trade partner shows considerable variation. In countries like Colombia, Guatemala, and Mexico, the United States accounts for 70 to 75 per cent of their total exports. The only countries where foreign trade is oriented toward Europe are Argentina and Uruguay. Here the United States accounts for only 10 to 12 per cent of their exports.

The fact that 15 countries ship 40 per cent or more of their exports to the United States makes them peculiarly vulnerable to conditions in the American economy. These countries often feel that their economic dependence upon the United States is excessive. Whenever difficulties arise with respect to prices received for their exports the tendency is to put the entire onus upon the United States rather than upon the world market. The notion that the price of coffee is "set" in New York is widespread.

The composition of Latin American exports to the United States in 1958 is roughly as follows:

	Billions
Petroleum	$ .8
Foodstuffs	$1.9
Minerals and other raw materials	$ .8
Total	$3.5

Although all these major commodities are produced in various parts of the world outside Latin America, and world market prices obviously reflect total world production, the question of stability in most raw material prices, including foodstuffs, is one of the topics most frequently spotlighted by the Latin American countries. No international conference of an economic character can take place without putting the issue of price stability for raw materials high on the agenda. The belief that the United States should assume responsibility for organizing and implementing some scheme to achieve greater price stability is widespread through the region.

United States policy has, until recently, been adamant against any institutional arrangements to support international prices of raw materials, but this traditional view is now being reexamined. Numerous illustrations can be found in the period since the Korean War wherein prices of certain principal commodities have fallen drastically in the world market, crippling the exchange position of the exporting country, compelling it to cut back sharply on imports, and casting doubt upon its ability to maintain payments on its foreign obligations. In these circumstances the United States has taken steps to ameliorate the situation partly to maintain the flow of its own exports in competition with Western Europe, and partly to prevent a default on contractual obligations abroad. Thus, when the price of copper or coffee plummets to low levels, the United States feels constrained to compensate at least in part for the loss in foreign exchange. Large Export-Import Bank loans, sometimes called "bailing out loans," are made to the countries having difficulties. When, for example, the price of copper dropped from 36 cents a pound to about 20 cents in a period of a little over one year, Chile received loans from the Exim Bank plus standby credits with the International Monetary Fund which, in the aggregate, were practically equal to the amount of foreign exchange lost through the decline in copper prices! While these operations made it unnecessary for Chile to cut back on imports of American goods, it left the economy with a heavy debt burden of relatively short-term maturity. If the price decline persists beyond a year, these short-term obligations tend to be renegotiated, rolled over, or stretched out; and in the final analysis one discovers that a substantial amount of United States or international resources has been committed. It may well be that some institutional arrangements to dampen the fluctuations in international prices of raw materials and foodstuffs would be "cheaper" than the present measures to shore up sagging economies.

Intra-regional trade continues to be fairly small, with approximately ten percent of Latin American exports absorbed within the area. Historically, trade among the Latin American countries has been complicated by geographic conditions, lack of transportation, and perhaps most importantly, by the fact that principal export products are competitive rather than complementary. Moreover, as long as currencies continue to be inconvertible, triangular trade of the classical variety cannot be achieved. The area's import needs are largely for capital goods and semi-finished as well as finished manufactures, and these are not available at competitive prices except from industrialized countries.

In the postwar period numerous attempts have been made to use bilateral trade agreements between countries within the region to expand trade, but generally speaking this device has proved ineffective. A country will usually put its marginal export items on the bilateral list in an attempt to push them into trade channels while commodities with a normal world market are usually kept off. Thus on the bilateral list Chile tries to push the sale of nitrate, but not copper. Brazil will push lumber and fruit, but will omit coffee, and so on.

Bilateral agreements are inevitably inefficient and costly, to both exporter and importer. They are usually associated with systems of exchange control, import and export licensing, and multiple exchange rates. In general, the consumer of the commodity traded through bilateral agreements tends to pay more than if the same commodity were available through regular trade channels. This is the real economic cost of such arrangements.

The pattern of foreign trade is important to the extent that its volume and composition reflect the varying rates of growth in the Latin American countries. Gross national product—as already noted—increased in the years 1950-1957 by 35 per cent from $40 billion to $54 billion in terms of 1950 prices. Gross capital formation (fixed capital, excluding inventories) increased 56 per cent from $6.6 billion to $10.3 billion.

The value of total foreign trade in real terms increased 55 per cent in imports, and 25 per cent in exports. Evidently, exports increased somewhat less than the rate of increase in real production, whereas the growth of imports was substantially higher than that in production. For the region as a whole, therefore, imports in 1957 represented 15.5 per cent of gross output, in contrast with 13.5 per cent in 1950, while exports were relatively unchanged from 15.5 per cent in 1950 to 15.2 per cent in 1957. The fact that imports are increasing more rapidly than gross production in real terms runs counter to expectations and suggests that the Latin American economies are becoming increasingly vulnerable to balance of payments difficulties in spite of considerable progress that has been made in import substitution.

Notice may be taken of the composition of the imports over the period 1950-57. The data below reflect the volume of imports in terms of 1950 prices.

Imports in 1950 Prices
(Millions of Dollars)

	1950		1957		Percentage Increase 1950-57
	Amount	Per Cent	Amount	Per Cent	
Consumer Goods	$1,383	26	$1,841	22	33
Fuels	429	8	739	9	72
Raw Materials	1,807	33	2,727	33	51
Capital Goods	1,781	33	3,039	36	71
Total	$5,400	100	$8,346	100	55

It is surprising to note that consumer goods imports have actually increased 33 per cent, which is the same rate as for gross production. It is true, of course, that a substantial part of this increase represents foodstuffs, the importation of which has been steadily going up in the period under

125

review. Import substitution in agricultural commodities is evidently going very slowly. Even in durable consumer goods, the one area in which the pressure to industrialize is supposed to be most effective, imports appeared to have risen 40 per cent, or again roughly the same rate of increase as for gross production. Fuels and raw materials together have maintained their same relative position, about 41 per cent, but there has been a marked increase in the quantity over this seven-year period. As the above table shows, fuel imports increased 72 per cent, or twice the rate in gross production. This can be explained by referring to such countries as Brazil and Argentina, where imports of petroleum products have jumped and efforts at developing domestic resources have lagged far behind.

With respect to raw materials, the rate of increase is again considerably greater than gross production, which suggests that much of the current industrialization must be based upon imported raw materials. This could have serious consequences for future balance of payments difficulties; in fact, the large increase in fuels and raw materials taken together (55 per cent in the period under review) suggests that an element of rigidity is being built into the balance of payments, and that in the future it will not be possible to cut back on these imports without seriously dislocating domestic production.

Finally, capital goods imports have not only increased twice as rapidly as the rate of gross production—which is to be expected—but have also constituted a larger fraction of total imports.

The analysis serves to emphasize once more the important connection between a country's balance of payments position and its rate of economic growth. If export earnings decline for any reason, the country must, barring financial help from abroad, cut back. Since fuels and raw materials cannot be cut back, and much of the consumer goods category consists of foodstuffs, the full impact of balance of payments adjustments must fall upon the capital goods sector. In these circumstances, the economic growth in the next decade may be considerably more irregular than in the past when, in balance of payments crises, it was possible to cut back at various points. Now, however, the axe must fall on capital goods whenever trouble emerges unless, of course, foreign sources of capital—private or official—can be induced to close the gap.

Inflation

For a number of Latin American countries, inflation has become a major economic problem, although the causes have varied between countries over the last ten years, and the rate has varied from virtual stability to galloping inflation.

During World War II and shortly thereafter, export surpluses were a cause of inflationary pressures. Then the cause of the pressure shifted to the private sector, especially in those countries with an active entrepreneurial group which, by repeated demands upon the domestic banking system, brought about increases in the money supply for investment purposes. Inflation generated by these private pressures to invest becomes particularly acute when a government embarks upon a development program while at the same time placing no restraints upon expansion in the private sector. Inflation from private investment pressure is apt to be found in those countries with overvalued exchange rates and which use extensive direct controls to maintain some semblance of equilibrium in their balance of payments. In these circumstances, importation of capital goods and equipment at an overvalued exchange rate is an enormous incentive to construct industrial plants with relatively cheap equipment. This seems to have been the pattern in the countries with the most virulent inflation—Argentina, Brazil, Paraguay, Chile, and Bolivia.

Fluctuations in the balance of payments has, under some circumstances, also been a cause of inflationary pressure. When terms of trade turn favorable for a particular country, there is a disposition to expand on all fronts rather than to accumulate exchange reserves. A new level of investment is somehow built into the expectations of the entrepreneurs, both government and private. Then when a downturn comes and exchange earnings drop back to previous levels, or lower, a country may turn to inflation in an effort to maintain its rate of investment and overall growth at a level higher than can be sustained by the reduced availability of resources. When the terms of trade turn against the country, it frequently happens that unemployment appears in sectors that had previously been booming. Thus, pressure for public works projects is generated to alleviate the unemployment. A sharp decline in the price of copper, for example, will close down marginal mines in Chile; and the government seeks, by all measures including inflation, to soften the blow by make-work projects.

In recent years, the principal causes of inflation are found in fiscal deficits at the national level which are monetized through recourse to Central Bank borrowing. One source of such deficits is the dependence of the national government upon certain taxes, the yields of which may rise or fall with changes in the terms of trade. The pattern tends to be repeated when a sudden windfall of revenue is used, not to retire debt, but to finance new projects. In fact, each upsurge in export prices seems to raise government expenditures to a new high. When the downturn comes, these expenditures, for political or other reasons, cannot be cut back, and a government finds itself resorting to inflation.

Still another source of inflation in the fiscal sector is found in the social security legislation of a country seeking to maintain pensions and other welfare payments at levels beyond its capacity. Welfare payments of this type soon bulk large in a government's budget. In Chile, for example, government employees may retire on the basis of years of service regardless of age at full pay, and their pension benefits are automatically raised every time active government employes receive a wage increase.

In some countries, the government may operate public services such as railroads below cost, whereby enormous operating deficits are incurred. At times, in countries like Brazil and Chile, deficits on government railroads alone have accounted for one-third to one-half of the total fiscal deficit of the national government.

Finally, a new source of inflation has recently emerged with the stockpiling of products such as coffee in an effort to arrest the decline in the world prices. Unless a government is strong enough to shift the financial burden of stockpiling backward to the producers, the cumulative effect of monetizing an annual increase in coffee stockpiles creates enormous pressure for inflation.

It will be instructive to examine the record of inflation of the various countries for the period 1950-1957. The table below gives the increase in prices as measured by the cost of living index for each of the countries.

The effect of inflation upon the rate of economic growth is a topic that attracts wide attention, and there are different schools of thought. One point of view suggests that a moderate rate of inflation, say 3 to 5 per cent annually, facilitates the structural changes that are a necessary feature of economic growth. Others feel that inflation tends to force savings upon the wage earning group which normally has a high propensity to consume and which is difficult to reach by taxation. According to this argument, inflation tends to reduce real wages and thus increase the entrepreneur's incentives to expand. This point may be illustrated by comparing minimum wages in the Federal District of Brazil at two points of time, 1956 and 1959. The minimum wage applicable in 1956 was 3,800 cruzeiros per month, and was sharply raised in early 1959 to 6,000 cruzeiros per month, an increase of 45 per cent. However, the expansion in price levels over a period of two and one-half years probably yielded a net decrease in real wages. Using the free market exchange rate for a rough approximation, the monthly minimum wage in 1956 was equivalent to $57.50, whereas the 1959 rate was equivalent to $44.50. It can probably be demonstrated that real wages in an industrial center like São Paulo—excluding a few new and highly capitalized industries—have remained relatively constant over the last decade. This means that increases in productivity have been substantially syphoned off to the owners of the equity interest.

Rate of Inflation: 1950–57

	Cost-of-Living Index 1957 (1950 = 100)	Annual Growth Rate, Real Terms (%) 1950 - 1957
Panama	104	
Venezuela	104	8.0
Cuba	105	
Guatemala	109	3.5
Ecuador	111	5.5
Haiti	112	
Dominican Republic	113	
Costa Rica	113	
UNITED STATES	117	3.5
Honduras	119	4.7
El Salvador	125	
Colombia	152	5.0
Nicaragua	154	
Peru	161	6.0
Mexico	170	6.0
Uruguay	207	
Argentina	326	2.0
Brazil	329	5.2
Paraguay	1,113	
Chile	1,173	1.5
Bolivia	6,937	

Another school of thought suggests that inflation is, at best, ineffective and may actually be detrimental to the rate of economic development, especially if the rate increases fast enough to discourage capital formation. Chile offers an illuminating example of what can happen to capital formation under accelerating inflation. Gross investment as a fraction of gross national production declined in the following pattern:

Gross Investment Under Chilean Inflation

Year	Investment as a percentage of GNP
1946	16.6
1948	12.5
1950	11.1
1952	8.3
1954	6.7
1956	1.0

Since the above ratios refer to gross investment, it appears that net capital formation was zero or negative in recent years. There were, of course, other elements in this situation, such as government attitudes unfavorable to foreign investment and discriminatory taxes through the exchange rate. Nevertheless, the above series is a striking example of the corrosive effect of rapid inflation upon capital formation and economic growth.

The earlier table on rates of inflation included, for a number of countries, the annual growth rate in real terms for the period 1950-1957; but the evidence is mixed, and there is no constant relationship discernible between the rate of inflation and the rate of growth. Argentina and Chile, to be sure, show very low growth rates and virtual stagnation, but Brazil appears exceptional, and one notes the phenomenon of rapid growth in the face of steady inflation. Nevertheless, Brazil's growth seems to have been achieved in spite of inflation and not because of it. Such factors as the expansion of the enormous and growing domestic market, the emergence of an active entrepreneurial group, the substantial inflow of foreign capital, both private and official, and the favorable terms of trade, especially in coffee prices, are probably the major reasons for Brazil's good showing over this period.

In summary, the effects of inflation upon an underdeveloped country will vary according to the institutional arrangements, but in general inflation probably tends to serve as a brake upon economic growth. There are five effects which can be imputed to inflation:

1. It destroys incentives to save, without which there can be no capital.
2. It creates pressures on the balance of payments, generating a chronic shortage of foreign exchange; meanwhile artificial exchange rates discourage exports while encouraging imports, thereby aggravating the problem.
3. It distorts the pattern of investment in favor of urban construction, diverting capital away from the basic sectors of power and transportation.
4. It makes difficulties for entrepeneurial planning and weakens the incentives to reduce costs or develop new techniques.
5. It creates serious social tensions as different groups in the economy are competing to preserve their respective standards of living.

All five effects can easily be documented in the experience of the Latin American countries over the last decade.

The role of foreign capital

As noted above, approximately ten per cent of total investment in Latin America came from foreign sources, including retained earnings by foreign companies. Gross investment in the whole region totaled $65 billion over the last seven years, of which $4.6 billion (seven per cent) came from private United States investors. Of the latter amount, two-thirds was net outflow of "new" capital and one-third was reinvested earnings. Another $1.5 billion (2.5 per cent) was the net increment in official capital from the United States and international agencies; and finally, approximately $345 million (.5 per cent) came from countries outside the United States, practically all from Western Europe.

Latin America ranks in first place in private direct investment of United States capital; and in terms of total long-term private investment, including portfolio, it is exceeded only by Canada. In the decade 1946-1957 the United States stake in Latin America in direct investment rose from $3 billion to $8.8 billion. In 1957 this represented 35 per cent of total direct investment abroad; Canada was second with 33 per cent. In addition to this volume of direct investment, private capital also holds approximately $1 billion in portfolio investments in Latin America. The composition of the direct private investment is as follows:

Petroleum	$3.2 billion	36%
Manufacturing	$1.7 "	19%
Public Utilities	$1.3 "	15%
Mining and Smelting	$1.2 "	14%
Trade, financial institutions and others	$1.4 "	16%

An interesting analysis of United States direct investment in Latin America was prepared by the Department of Commerce based on a survey of operations in the year 1955. The survey covered some 300 United States companies representing 85 per cent of the total United States direct investment in Latin America. The purpose of the survey was to develop some evidence of the total impact of United States private investment on the Latin American economy. An earlier publication (*Foreign Capital in Latin America,* New York, 1955) by the United Nations had produced a somewhat distorted view by looking only at the balance of payments effect, namely the inflow and outflow of capital. Since the balance of payments is only one aspect of the problem, the Department of Commerce survey explored the total impact on Latin America including purchases of domestic raw materials, payrolls, local taxes, and reinvestment of earnings. One of the erroneous inferences derived from the United Nations publication was an attempt to compare the volume of annual remittances of profits and dividends with the annual inflow of new funds. There is, of course, no connection between the two factors. Nevertheless, the inference that United States private investment was "decapitalizing" Latin America received widespread publicity in the newspapers and economic journals of the region. The amount of annual remittances must be compared to the total investment in the country and not to the movement, purely coincidental, of new capital funds into the country. It would seem obvious—although many Latin Americans failed to see it—that the annual remittance on a capital investment (book value of $6.6 billion) would have no relation to new increments of capital coming in annually from abroad. One is an income factor and the other is a capital factor. The "decapitalization" argument alleged that in the period 1946-1951 United States income received from direct investments was $3.1 billion, whereas net outflow of capital was $1.6 billion, suggesting that United States direct investment was taking out approximately twice as much as it was putting into Latin America.

The Department of Commerce survey showed total sales in 1955 of $4.9 billion, of which 55 per cent was for domestic consumption and the remainder for export. The operations may be analyzed as follows:

Local Payments and Accruals	*Millions*	
Wages	$ 878	
Materials	1,498	
Interest and Dividends	62	
Other	300	
	$2,738	55%
Taxes	1,017	21%
Total Local	$3,755	76%
External Payments and Accruals		
Imports	554	11%
Remittances: Branch Profits and Dividends	555	11%
Other	82	2%
Total External	$1,191	24%
Total Payments and Accruals	$4,946	100%

Remittance of branch profits and dividends as shown in the 1955 survey amounted to approximately 11 per cent on the book value of the reporting companies; if petroleum were excluded, the returns on book value would be only four per cent. However, book values in countries subject to chronic inflation usually understate the real value of the direct investment. Hence profit remittances on industries other than petroleum would be considerably less than four per cent if assets were given a more realistic valuation. The same survey showed the reporting companies invested $569 million in exploration and development, plant and equipment, and inventory, which is an amount roughly equal to the remittances in 1955.

132

It is also worth noting that local taxes including income taxes, customs duties, and other indirect taxes amounted to $1 billion, or an amount roughly equal to profits remitted and new investment in that year. Even excluding petroleum, the same order of magnitude appears; total local taxes were $458 million in comparison with remittances of $154 million and new investment of $262 million.

The prospect for attracting foreign private capital to the Latin American countries has received much attention in recent years; and two general points of view may be identified. On the side of the United States investor, emphasis is usually given to the investment climate, which is a composite of various elements including freedom of entry and exit, equal treatment before the law, prospects for earnings, absence of discrimination, and so on. The other point of view, which might be called the Latin American, is inclined to underplay the investment climate and to substitute a series of so-called incentives designed to attract private capital. Many of the countries have enacted special legislation in the postwar period designed to give special treatment to foreign capital in matters of foreign exchange or taxation. Nine countries offer some form of foreign exchange incentives designed to create certain exemptions under exchange control regulations, while seventeen countries have enacted special tax privileges to attract foreign capital. Most of the latter relate to exemption from customs duties on capital goods entering the country, which in some cases is extended to include raw materials, fuels, and spare parts. Three countries (Venezuela, Uruguay, and Peru) have refrained from enacting specific legislation of an incentive character.

In general, the effect of such incentive legislation has been minimal and many of the so-called "incentives" are nothing more than a relaxation of impediments to investment which were created in earlier periods. The Latin American countries are also inclined to argue that United States taxation of earnings from foreign investments is an inhibiting factor and that special concessions should be made in United States income tax laws beyond the provisions which already exist for enterprises qualifying as "Western Hemisphere corporations." These receive a reduction of 14 points on corporate income tax, reducing the effective rate from 52 per cent to 38 per cent. The United States Treasury takes a negative view of additional concessions of this type. The case of Canada may be cited as a good example of what private capital will do when the investment climate is attractive irrespective of corporation tax rates.

It is instructive in connection with this question of taxation incentives to note some of the effective tax rates on locally incorporated subsidiaries of United States corporations. The Canadian rate of 43 per cent compares with 42 per cent in Brazil, 44 per cent in Chile and Mexico, 45 per cent in Peru and Colombia, and 48 per cent in Argentina. These are total effective rates based on generally applicable rules and do not account for

133

special incentives such as initial tax exemptions or accelerated depreciation allowances.

The United States government did, however, move in the direction of incentives by offering a plan for the guarantee of private direct investments against risks of exchange convertibility and expropriation. Investment guarantee agreements have been negotiated with ten countries in Latin America, but as of December 31, 1958, only $30 million had been underwritten in four countries—$26.5 million on exchange convertibility risk and $3.5 million on expropriation. It is interesting to note, however, that those countries suffering from chronic balance of payments difficulties and instability of exchange rates (Argentina, Brazil, and Chile) are among those which have refrained from negotiating such agreements. Considering that Mexico, Venezuela and Peru also abstain from these guarantee agreements, it appears that six of the most important countries, which account for 73 per cent of total United States direct investment in Latin America, have not seen fit to participate. Evidently the flow of private direct investment into these countries has been unimpaired by the risks of convertibility and expropriation, or else the private investor calculates that the cost of such insurance may be excessive, considering the risks that it covers.

As noted earlier, private investors in the United States hold approximately $1 billion in portfolio investments in Latin American countries. These represent for the most part the old bonded debt which went into default at the time of the great depression. Over the last decade, however, one country after another has negotiated agreements with its bond holders and has resumed service on the portfolio debt. Bolivia in 1958 was the last of the Latin American countries to resume service on the old bonded debt. Notwithstanding this attempt to re-establish their credit, none of the Latin American countries have yet been able to borrow new funds through the issue of securities in the capital markets of the United States or Western Europe. The record of financial management in many of the Latin American countries over the past decade has not inspired confidence in world capital markets. Resumption of service on the old debt thus proves to have been a necessary, but not sufficient, condition to gain access to foreign capital markets where nations may borrow with no other security than the full faith and credit of their governments. Since this condition is likely to continue for some years, the emphasis has shifted to the use of official or international capital for purposes of economic development.

Official capital

The principal sources of official capital for lending to Latin America are the Export-Import Bank, the International Bank for Reconstruction and

Development (World Bank), the International Monetary Fund, and more recently the Development Loan Fund and the International Finance Corporation. A new agency, the Inter-American Development Bank, was organized in April 1959 and its articles of agreement are pending ratification.

The Export-Import Bank

The Export-Import Bank, an agency of the United States government, has been active since 1934 in providing capital for public and private projects in Latin America. Over the life of the Exim Bank, Latin America has received 35 per cent of the total resources made available. For the purpose of this report, attention will be directed principally to the lending activities in the last five years, 1954-1958, in order to gauge the net investment which these lending institutions have made possible in Latin America. Moreover, the significant data refer to disbursements rather than authorized credits; years may sometimes elapse between the authorization of a credit and its disbursement, and it is the latter which measures the actual inflow of capital.

Attention may first be directed to the Exim Bank, whose activities in Latin America are summarized in the table below:

Export-Import Bank
(Millions of Dollars)

	1953	1954	1955	1956	1957	1958
Outstanding Balance Year's End	857	897	897	849	963	1,314
Loans Disbursed		109	118	70	234	485
Repayments		70	119	117	120	134
Net Investment		40	0	−48	114	351

Over the five-year period disbursements were $1,016 million, while repayments, that is, amortizations of previous loans, amounted to $560 million, leaving a net increment of $457 million. Examination of the above table also reveals the interesting fact that for a period of three years from December 1953 to December 1956 the Exim Bank not only failed to provide any net capital investment for Latin America but actually slightly reduced its stake in the region. This stagnation was the result of a policy decision by the new United States administration that declared the World Bank to be the lender of first recourse for development capital; the Exim Bank was left to operate in the limited area outside the range of World Bank operations. This policy was evidently reversed in 1957 with the reorganization of the Exim Bank and a rapid acceleration in the

135

net capital provided for Latin America; in fact, the net investment of $457 million noted above took place in the last year or so.

The principal borrowers from the Exim Bank were six countries which together absorbed 88 per cent of the credits authorized ($2.6 billion) as of December 31, 1958. Of these countries, Brazil accounted for $1 billion, or 38 per cent; Argentina $420 million, or 16 per cent; and Mexico $325 million, or 12 per cent. The principal purposes of Exim Bank operations in the period 1950-57 were as follows:

Balance of Payments	31%
Transportation	24%
Steel Mills	12%
Electric Power and Water	12%
Other Industries	9%
Mining	6%
Agricultural Equipment	5%
Other	1%
	100%

The fact that balance of payments loans are the largest single item in Exim Bank lending in recent years corroborates the hypothesis noted in an earlier section that the United States government, while refusing to be a partner to commodity stabilization schemes, apparently stands ready to provide the resources and to compensate in some sizable fraction for the short-fall in exchange earnings occasioned by drastic swings in the prices of principal exports. To be sure, the earlier balance of payments lending to Argentina, Brazil and Chile had no direct connection with export commodity price fluctuations, but in the last year or two, balance of payments loans to Brazil, Colombia, and Chile, for example, are directly associated with the decline in exchange earnings in those countries as a result of declining coffee and copper prices.

In connection with these balance of payments credits, the Exim Bank endeavors to use its lending capacity as leverage to induce monetary and fiscal reforms that will correct the fundamental problem and, hopefully, prevent a repetition. The borrowing countries, however, tend to resist proposed corrective measures and the record of the last few years is not an impressive one. In the last year or so this leverage function has been delegated to the International Monetary Fund as will be discussed presently.

The World Bank

The operations of the International Bank for Reconstruction and Development (World Bank) in Latin America represent total loans of $893

136

million at the end of 1958, of which Brazil alone received $255 million, or 29 per cent of the total; Mexico received $186 million, or 21 per cent; Colombia $111 million, or 12 per cent. The rate of disbursement over the last five years is set forth in the table below:

The World Bank
(Millions of Dollars)

	1953	1954	1955	1956	1957	1958
Balance Outstanding Year's End	244	309	368	445	506	547
Loans Disbursed		69	77	95	82	72
Repayments		4	18	18	21	31
Net Investment		65	59	77	61	41

The purposes for which World Bank loans were made in Latin America were as follows:

Electric Power	52%
Transportation	34%
Agriculture	6%
Industry	5%
Communications	3%
	100%

The role of the World Bank in financing economic overhead capital is conspicuous in comparison with the Exim Bank. Thus, electric power and transportation account for 86 per cent of loans for Latin America as against 36 per cent for the Exim Bank. Moreover, the World Bank does not lend for balance of payments purposes, which is a second reason for the difference in loan composition of the two institutions. Although the World Bank does not engage in balance of payments lending as such, it endeavors to use its lending capacity, like the Exim Bank, as leverage to induce borrowing governments to adopt monetary and fiscal policies which will promote development and, particularly, to create the conditions under which private enterprise may take up its role in the development process. In comparing the aggregate lending of the Export-Import Bank and the World Bank in Latin America, it appears that the two institutions are not far apart. In the five-year period 1954-58 the World Bank made a net investment of $303 million; this compares with the figure noted earlier of $457 million for the Exim Bank in the same period. As usual these comparisons are based on net investment, that is actual disbursements less amortizations.

137

International Monetary Fund

The resources of the International Monetary Fund are to be distinguished from the Exim Bank and the World Bank, because they are not drawn directly for development purposes or specific projects but rather to assist countries having balance of payments difficulties. Nevertheless, the use of Fund resources through the mechanism of drawings or through standby arrangements, does provide foreign exchange exactly like the balance of payments loans of the Exim Bank. Drawings from the Fund may be repaid over a period of three to five years. Since the Latin American countries have been experiencing chronic difficulties over the last five to ten years, access to the Fund is an additional source of capital and drawings may be "rolled over" if the need can be demonstrated.

The volume of Fund resources being used by the Latin American countries is substantial. In the five years 1954-58 the amount was $240 million in net drawings plus $93 million under standby arrangements or a total of $333 million outstanding at the end of 1958. The principal recipients were Brazil with $85 million, Chile with $55 million, and Argentina with $75 million. These substantial drawings are an important supplement to lending from the two banks, and they play an important role in the growth rates of these countries. Having access to Fund resources of this magnitude, the borrowing countries are able to maintain a level of imports, including capital goods, higher than they could otherwise afford. Moreover, development programs need not be discarded or sharply cut back for lack of foreign exchange. Thus, the Fund resources permit some continuity in development plans and avoid costly interruptions in the construction of development projects into which considerable capital may already have been committed.

The Fund has come to occupy a position of increasing importance in the last year or so by virtue of the leverage which it employs upon would-be borrowers to take the fiscal and monetary measures needed to correct the conditions causing chronic balance of payments deficits. In recent years this leverage has not been very effective, because the would-be borrower could go to the United States government and get financial aid from the Exim Bank for balance of payments purposes. Now, however, a significant change may be noted. Both the United States government and the World Bank have increasingly adopted the line that a borrower must first make his peace with the Fund before he can hope to qualify for loans from either of the Banks. This position enormously increases the leverage which the Fund now exercises. At the same time it suits the purpose of the United States to delegate the bargaining function to the Fund, because, as an international organization, it is perhaps in a better political position to mobilize a consensus of world financial opinion and to bring the weight of such pressures upon a country reluctant to undertake the necessary reforms. The United States is always limited by political considerations in the amount of pressure which it can bring to bear upon Latin American countries, but the Fund, as an international organization with sixty-eight members does not necessarily suffer from the same inhibitions. In short, therefore, the significance of the Fund in Latin American economic development is much greater than the resources which it can supply for relatively short periods of time.

Development Loan Fund

Yet another institution providing capital for development purposes in Latin America is the Development Loan Fund. During the first year or two of its operations, however, the loans to Latin America were very small. As of January 31, 1959, Latin America had received only $50 million, or about seven per cent of total loans. Latin American proposals then under consideration still aggregated only seven per cent of the total proposals under review. Evidently, the bulk of the Development Loan resources are being committed to other areas of the world, especially to the Middle East, South Asia, and the Far East for reasons that are more or less self-evident.

Public Law No. 480 agreements

The final source from which Latin American countries are able to get resources for economic development comes from the sale of United States surplus agricultural commodities under Public Law No. 480 agreements. As of December 31, 1958, Latin America had absorbed $350 million of surplus agricultural commodities since the program started in 1954. One country, Brazil, accounts for 50 per cent of the total, with Chile and Colombia each getting 11 per cent, and Argentina, Mexico and Peru each getting 7 to 8 per cent. The local currency generated by the sale of these surplus agricultural commodities is the property of the United States; but for the region as a whole, 75 per cent of these local currency funds have been lent to the respective governments. In the case of Brazil this is obviously a sizable amount, the equivalent of $149 million. These funds are being used to finance the local currency cost of various development projects since both the Exim Bank and the World Bank lend only the foreign exchange components. Even in countries such as Chile and Colombia, which have borrowed lesser amounts (the equivalent of $25 to 30 million), these resources make it possible to finance additional projects without creating inflationary pressures on the economy. In the case of Brazil, virtually all of the loan proceeds are allotted to the National Bank for Economic Development, which carefully allocates the amounts to development projects of high priority, principally for the expansion of

139

electric power which the Brazilian government has accepted as a top priority item in its current development program. In Chile, for example, some portion of the loan proceeds were allocated directly to private projects where the foreign exchange components were supplied by the World Bank (coal mining) and the Exim Bank (nitrate mining). Since one of the major limitations on the capacity of a country to absorb foreign loan capital is its ability to mobilize the necessary domestic capital for local expenditures, these P.L. 480 funds may provide the means for accelerating economic growth. The evidence suggests that they are being wisely used in the several countries of Latin America where they are available.

The Inter-American Development Bank

Some mention must be made of the newly organized Inter-American Development Bank. The articles of agreement were signed on April 8, 1959, and they are now pending ratification by the various Latin American governments. The United States ratified the agreement on August 8, 1959. The authorized capital stock is $1 billion; $150 million is destined for the "Fund for Special Operations," which loans are payable in local currency, while the bulk of the capital, $850 million, is intended for hard currency loans. The twenty Latin American governments and the United States government will pay in one-half of their capital subscription quota and the other one-half will remain on call. The paid-in capital will in turn be one-half in dollars and one-half in currency of the member with actual payments spread over three years, 20 per cent by September 1960, another 40 per cent by September 1961, and 40 per cent by September 1962. Total loanable resources will, therefore, be rather modest for the first year or two.

The share of the United States in the total operation is nominally 41 per cent of the Bank and 66 per cent of the Fund for Special Operations. With respect to actual paid-in shares, however, the United States has a quota of $150 million, or 37.5 per cent of paid-in capital; Argentina and Brazil each has 13 per cent; Mexico has 8 per cent, and Venezuela has 7 per cent.

Although the dollar portion of the paid-in capital will be modest, $275 million for the Bank, the founders have hopes that the Bank will be able to borrow funds by the sale of its own securities in the open capital market. The reception which such securities will meet in the capital market will depend, of course, on the strength of the management and the operating record of the Bank itself. It is likely, therefore, that no attempt will be made to go to the market until some years of experience have demonstrated the credit worthiness of the institution. The United States quota of callable capital is $200 million, which perhaps provides one gauge of the amount which the private capital market might be willing to absorb in bank securities. Again, the experience of the World Bank in approaching the private market suggests that dollar borrowings should not greatly exceed the amount of paid-in dollar capital. By this criterion an amount of $275 million might be borrowed in the case of the Inter-American Development Fund.

The Inter-American Development Bank will be a useful institution, and will contribute an additional increment to the capital resources available to Latin America. The increment, however, appears small in relation to existing resources as may be seen below.

The amount of capital, approximately $2.3 billion, currently outstanding at the end of 1958, may be recapitulated as follows:

	(Millions)
Exim Bank	$1,314
IBRD	590
IMF	333
DLF	50
	$2,287

Inter-American Development Bank	
Bank (paid-in dollar capital)	$ 275
Special Operations Fund (paid-in dollar capital)	$ 125

It appears, therefore, that the Inter-American Development Bank, when fully loaned up, could increase by about 17 per cent the dollar resources currently invested in Latin America from official institutions. The non-dollar portion of the paid-in capital, equivalent to approximately $150 million is omitted from the above calculations because it is unlikely that many loans will be made for equipment manufactured in the Latin American countries. Over the years, however, this situation will change, and it is conceivable that countries will eventually be purchasing freight cars made in Brazil, heavy electrical equipment made in Mexico, and so on.

5. Diplomatic relations

HERBERT L. MATTHEWS

We need not be too precise in defining United States diplomatic relations with Latin America. Geography put us in one hemisphere, and history followed as a matter of course. Our destinies have gradually been woven together until there is now an interlocking pattern of politics, trade, strategy and culture. Our relationships today are a mixture of what the past has contributed and forced upon us, what we judge to be the possible and desirable objectives today, and what actions we are taking to achieve these aims.

But it takes two to make a relationship as well as a quarrel. We must not get so involved in United States relations with Latin America as to forget that there is such a thing as Latin American relations with the United States. The two influences work upon each other, sometimes hostile, sometimes friendly, clashing or coinciding, adamant or yielding, and often failing to meet for lack of understanding.

The dominant feature is best realized in the Latin label for the United States: the Colossus of the North. Our power and wealth and their weakness and poverty form the background against which the hemispheric drama has to be played. The adjustment and conciliation of these two inequalities in the midst of the global struggle of democracy and totalitarianism is the major problem.

Underdeveloped agrarian nations demanding industrialization, the great mass of the poor demanding social justice, the emotional thrust of nationalism, the pressure of the greatest population explosion on earth, the

143

paradox of "rising expectations," the wave of anti-dictatorial revolutions—such are the forces working in Latin America and therefore working on us.

Twenty different countries are heaving and thrusting under the compulsive drive of these forces, each at a different stage of progress, each demanding and needing different things or more or less of the same things. We on our part have global responsibilities, domestic needs and our security and way of life to defend.

To fashion an ideal "Latin American policy" out of these diverse and conflicting forces and aims would be a superhuman task. Diplomacy, like politics, is an art not a science. United States relations with Latin America have never been neat or precise and never will be. We muddle along, doing well and badly, rightly and wrongly, all at the same time. History tells us that; so does contemporary study, and so, no doubt, will the story of the future.

The Monroe Doctrine

United States relations with Latin America are generally considered by historians to have begun with the No-Transfer Resolution of 1811. Samuel Flagg Bemis in his "Latin American Policy of the United States" calls this "the first significant landmark in the evolution of United States-Latin American policy." It was a Congressional resolution concerned with Florida, then under the weak control of Spain. The key phrase held that the United States "cannot without serious inquietude see any part of the said territory pass into the hands of any foreign Power."

What we said then, we still say, and the Latin American republics say it with us, although they would confine the "no-transfer" principle to territorial conquest while we (as Guatemala showed) would extend it to ideological subversion by international communism as well. The possibility of a victorious Nazi Germany taking over the French and Dutch possessions in the Caribbean at the time of the Second World War showed that the "no-transfer" policy could still be challenged.

Our attitude toward the Latin American countries as they struggled for and won their independence in the years from 1810 to 1824 has left a generally pleasant legacy. The picture of a young United States stoutly championing the brave efforts of the other American nations to win freedom from Spain, France and Portugal is true enough, especially at the beginning and the end of the period of conflict. In between, we had our war with Britain, starting in 1812, while our successful negotiations to purchase Florida from Spain, which did not end until 1821, made it impolitic to offend the Spaniards.

We were the first outside nation to recognize the new Latin American states, and that was a great service. There were, of course, hard-headed reasons both of trade and strategy to want to see the European powers

144

weakened or driven out of the Western hemisphere. It happened also to be in England's interest to keep the European continental powers out of the hemisphere. England herself, then going through the Industrial Revolution, was interested in trade and investments, not conquest. She wanted a balance of power on the European continent and as part of such a policy "called the New World into existence to redress the balance of the Old" in George Canning's immortal and somewhat exaggerated phrase. Thus it was that American policy was made feasible because of British control of the high seas.

The Monroe Doctrine was part of President James Monroe's message to Congress on December 2, 1823, and in form it was a purely American statement of policy, as Secretary of State John Quincy Adams wanted it to be. The key sentence comes in the middle:

> We owe it, therefore, to candor, and to the amicable relations existing between the United States and those [European] powers, to declare that we should consider any attempt on their part to extend their system to any portion of this hemisphere as dangerous to our peace and safety.

The Doctrine was not, at the time, an incentive to closer relations between the United States and Latin America. Three years before, in his famous conversation with Speaker of the House Henry Clay, Secretary Adams said pessimistically: "I have little expectation of any beneficial result to this country from any future connection with them [the Latin American countries], political or commercial."

At first the Doctrine was little heeded on either side. As Professor Dexter Perkins wrote, "There can be no doubt at all . . . that Monroe's message of 1823 was directed against an illusory danger. There never was any fixed purpose to reconquer the Spanish colonies."

Moreover, when it came to minor infractions of hemispheric territory, the United States did not consider that the Monroe Doctrine obligated us to employ military force. The British and French were especially active— in Mexico, Brazil, Argentina, Uruguay and Chile—with no reaction from the United States. So long as the Latin American states maintained their sovereignty and independence from Spain, France and England, we paid little heed. In any event, Britons ruled the waves, not Americans.

The Doctrine, of course, was never intended to prevent the United States from getting more territory. "Manifest Destiny" was leading us to covet and acquire the land stretching West to the Pacific Ocean.

It was President James K. Polk (1844-1848), with an eye on Texas, who revived the somewhat neglected Doctrine. It also proved useful later in restraining England's activities in Central America, in forcing the Emperor Maximilian and the French out of Mexico, and in blocking Spain's efforts to regain Santo Domingto and Peru.

The greatest mark left on hemispheric relations by the Monroe Doctrine stretches over a period from 1875 to 1921. Our Good Neighbors will never let us forget those years.

In 1875, Great Britain and Venezuela started a controversy over the Venezuelan-Guiana boundary. Venezuela tried in vain for two decades to appeal to the Monroe Doctrine. A good public relations man, former American Minister William L. Scruggs, is credited with finally stirring up United States opinion. Congress passed a resolution urging arbitration, and Secretary of State Richard Olney sent a fiery note to Lord Salisbury, the British Foreign Secretary, on July 20, 1895. Lord Salisbury replied that the Monroe Doctrine had nothing to do with the dispute.

"The Government of the United States," he wrote, "is not entitled to affirm as a universal proposition with reference to a number of independent states for whose conduct it assumes no responsibility, that its interests are necessarily concerned in whatever may befall those States simply because they are situated in the Western Hemisphere."

This was cruelly logical and doubtless right in international law, and it is the interpretation now accepted by the Latin American countries. But in practice it can be argued that we have never accepted it, and in 1895 we were starting our one and only burst of genuine imperialism.

President Grover Cleveland replied vigorously to Lord Salisbury, and the British, no doubt with an eye to their great and lucrative investments in the United States, yielded gracefully. The boundary was settled by arbitration as the United States had asked.

The dispute was interesting in many ways. In reality, as Lord Salisbury unkindly wrote, the Monroe Doctrine had nothing to do with it, but it was invoked by the Americans; it was an example of defending a Latin American republic against a European power, and it did stir up American nationalism to a point that made intervention in Cuba less than three years later a natural sequel. We were, in effect, proclaiming a hemispheric hegemony.

Moreover, the realization that we were threatening to fight with a navy containing one modern battleship against much the greatest naval force in the world, started the United States on a rearmament program that was to make us a world power in reality.

Aside from the natural rejoicing in Venezuela, the Latin American reaction was mixed. Any display of power by the United States was always calculated to arouse fear and jealousy. The specter of intervention was only too visible to Latin American eyes. And as some commentators pointed out, the danger of a European attempt to conquer hemispheric territories had long since passed. The peril, decades later, was to become one of political and ideological subversion by totalitarian powers and their doctrines, not one of forceful conquest.

In the brief imperialistic phase of our history it was natural that the meaning of the Monroe Doctrine should be stretched to include an American exercise of "police power." This was done in the so-called Roosevelt Corollary to the Doctrine. It followed a ruling of the Hague Court in 1904 on a Venezuelan claims controversy of the previous year. This gave Great Britain, Germany and Italy priority over the claims of other foreigners because these three countries had resorted to military operations to force Venezuela to pay the claims of their citizens residing in Venezuela.

This confirmation of accepted international law—that armed force could be used to collect debts—seemingly opened the road to much European intervention. The political instability of Latin American countries often led to defaulted loans or to seizure of alien property so that there was a constant temptation to the European powers to intervene.

For President Theodore Roosevelt this meant that "in the Western Hemisphere the adherence of the United States to the Monroe Doctrine may force the United States, however reluctantly, in flagrant cases of such wrong-doing or impotence, to the exercise of an international police power." This was the "Roosevelt Corollary."

We were at the time imposing an American customs control on Santo Domingto to forestall action by European continental creditors, and Germany, incidentally, was also showing undue interest in Venezuela at the beginning of the century.

To "Teddy" Roosevelt our response was "part of that international duty which is necessarily involved in the assertion of the Monroe Doctrine." Even President Woodrow Wilson, the spiritual father of the Organization of American States as well as of the League of Nations and the United Nations, could argue that "chronic wrong-doing, or an impotence which results in a general loosening of the ties of civilized society, may in America as elsewhere ultimately require intervention by some civilized nation."

The era of imperialism

Roosevelt, as stated, felt this was "part of that international duty which is necessarily involved in the assertion of the Monroe Doctrine." In reality, the Roosevelt Corollary was a complete departure from the spirit of the Doctrine, and it came to be so regarded. The whole system of "protective imperialism," as Bemis called it, had to go—control of customs, Marines, the right to intervene, "dollar diplomacy."

The focus of our brief imperialist fling was not unreasonable—the Isthmus of Panama and its role in the defense of our continental Republic. By any concept of strategy, the United States either had control of the Isthmus (and the Canal when it was built) or our Atlantic and Pacific coasts were going to be endangered. As a corollary, the approaches to the Canal had to be ours or in friendly hands. This principle was appealed to in the case of Guatemala in 1954, and earlier it was a factor that led us to fight Spain over Cuba and Puerto Rico.

147

The value of the Panama Canal today is greatly reduced, especially militarily. The fact that we now have navies on both the Atlantic and Pacific, the growth and importance of air power and the vulnerability to atomic or nuclear bombs, all reduce the Canal essentially to its commercial value. In a limited war, in which nuclear weapons were not used, it would still be of great value. And the convenience of getting the strategic raw materials of the West Coast of South America up to the East Coast of the United States by a direct route is also something to consider.

In general, there was one simple, basic factor—which seemed obvious, natural and necessary—behind the Monroe Doctrine, the imperialist fling, and, indeed, every aspect of our Latin American policies. This was the security of continental United States.

Our five Caribbean interventions (Cuba, Haiti, Dominican Republic, Nicaragua and Panama) had in each case a two-fold objective—to restore order to the finances of the country involved and to build up or train military forces in each case in order to maintain political stability. In all five cases the immediate results were beneficial, and in all five the long-range results were nil, or worse. We put political power in the hands of the military and made them invincible. Since the bases on which to build democracies were still not present in these countries, and since the traditional concept of politics as a spoils system still prevailed, our well-meant efforts led inevitably to results like Trujillo in the Dominican Republic and Somoza in Nicaragua.

Every one of our interventions—Mexico included—left a legacy whose effects are still operative. The most obvious is the case of Panama, for the very creation of that country was a result of American intervention.

The French, it will be recalled, began digging a canal under a concession from Colombia, to whom the territory then belonged. The activities of the Panama Canal Company, organized by Ferdinand de Lesseps, aroused fears in the United States and much talk of the Monroe Doctrine, but the venture failed before anything could or had to be done about it.

Our manipulation of the diplomatic, legal and financial aspects is something that most Americans wish they could forget—without losing the Canal. Nicaragua was the better site, but some shady lobbying by the clever Frenchman, Philippe Bunau-Varilla, and tricky legal work, switched the locality to Panama. Then some more highly dubious machinations by President Theodore Roosevelt, and the men who were financially concerned, led to the desired solution. Bunau-Varilla managed and financed the revolution of the States of Panama, then part of Colombia, but Teddy Roosevelt could rightly boast later: "I took the Isthmus." Morally speaking, it was one of the most shameless incidents in United States history; practically and strategically it was a valuable thing to have done.

The first intervention in Santo Domingo (1904) was to force that country to meet its debt obligations to all foreign nationals, including Americans. The alternative would have been European intervention. The reason was justifiable, especially as Santo Domingo was in a state of anarchy and chaos. There was no thought of annexation.

This was the occasion when Roosevelt put forward his novel thesis (the "Corollary") that the Monroe Doctrine not only forbade intervention from Europe but sanctioned intervention from the United States in order to prevent such intervention. It was also called the policy of the "Big Stick," and we have spent generations trying to live it down. Actually, the Roosevelt interventions were missionary in intent, not aggressions, and there was never any idea of endangering the liberty or sovereignty of these nations.

The "dollar diplomacy" of his successor, William Howard Taft, was more directly intervention by and for the United States, not deliberately for private business interests. It led to outright military interventions.

In 1909 we landed Marines in Nicaragua to protect American nationals and mining property at Bluefields during a revolution against the dictator, General José Santos Zelaya. Zelaya was overthrown. Again in 1912 we intervened to bolster the regime of Adolfo Díaz. The Marines stayed until 1933, preventing revolutions, not uprisings, supervising elections, training the Nicaraguan police force. However, we were ineffective in other respects and earned much criticism in Latin America. Nicaragua is generally considered as the classic type of military intervention to protect American investments—or "Wall Street"—which is an exaggeration, for the intent was basically neither mercenary nor aggressive. Actually, we had few investments in Nicaragua, Santo Domingo, Panama and Haiti, and it was not business interests who favored intervention in Cuba and Mexico.

The worst result of the Nicaraguan interventions was to turn the country over to a Marine-trained officer named Anastasio Somoza, who maintained a tight dictatorship until his assassination in 1956, when his power and wealth were assumed by his two sons.

There was another revolution followed by chaos in Santo Domingo in 1912, and Taft intervened with 750 Marines to restore order and supervise the collection of customs duties. The disorder continued, and the next time it was Wilson who intervened. American troops occupied the capital in 1916 and remained until 1924.

Haiti fell into a state of anarchy that became complete in 1915. The next year Wilson felt impelled to land Marines. The alternative, as in other cases, would have been to see Britain, France or Germany—or all three—intervene. American financial advisers, customs officials, health experts and officers to train a native constabulary were sent in, and the United States was given the same powers of intervention as in Cuba.

These interventions are still used as sticks by Latin Americans to beat "Tío Sam," but it has to be said in their favor that the policies followed did protect these countries from an intervention that might have been permanent by European powers, and also that the United States certainly proved it had no desire of its own to establish permanent protectorates in Latin America.

The best example of this was Cuba, which many influential Americans in the nineteenth century thought we should annex, and which we could have annexed after the Spanish American War.

True, the Cubans have nothing to thank us for in their long decades of agony, or when they fought a cruel war against the Spanish in 1868-1878, or when horrors were heaped upon them in the years that followed while Grant and Cleveland thought in feeble terms of mediation or worried about the rights of American citizens in Cuba and did their best to prevent hostile expeditions of exiles from the United States to Cuba. Meanwhile, Spain was able to acquire what arms it needed in the United States to supress the Cuban rebels. This was the pattern that recently repeated itself under General Batista, although in the latter case we had the excuse of the non-intervention policy. In 1898 we did intervene, and one of the ironies of history is that it seemed probable that Cuba could have had her independence at the time, and the United States whatever we demanded, without armed intervention. Certainly, the Cubans think so.

At least the joint Congressional resolution of April 20, 1898, for intervention in Cuba did contain a self-denying amendment:

That the United States hereby disclaims any disposition or intention to exercise sovereignty, jurisdiction, or control over the said island except for the pacification thereof, and asserts its determination, when that is accomplished, to leave the government and control of the island to its people.

We were not entirely self-denying because we insisted on adding the so-called Platt Amendment to the Cuban Constitution. Its main purpose was not intervention, although it led to a number of interventions; it was to keep any foreign power out of Cuba by being sure it had no excuse to intervene. It was not exploitation, either, as the generous 1903 treaty of commercial reciprocity proved.

The Platt Amendment dates from July 2, 1904 to May 31, 1934. Article III was the decisive one:

The Government of Cuba consents that the United States may exercise the right to intervene for the preservation of Cuban independence, the maintenance of a government adequate for the protection of life, property and individual liberty, and for discharging the obligations with respect to Cuba imposed by the Treaty of Paris on the United States, now to be assumed and undertaken by the Government of Cuba.

The best expression of American policy—and it was a genuine one—came in a letter from Secretary of State Elihu Root to "Marse" Henry Watterson on March 5, 1908, quoted by Philip Jessup in his biography of the Secretary.

"We don't want Cuba to ourselves," Mr. Root declared; "we cannot permit any other power to get possession of her and, to prevent the necessity of one and the possibility of the other of these results, we want her to govern herself decently and in order."

These hopes were not to be fulfilled, but Cubans would do well to consider who is really to blame—they or we.

This is getting ahead of the story. The Mexicans were the ones who had the best causes for complaint, and they long antedate our turn-of-the-century burst of imperialism.

From the point of view of relations, our early Mexican policy was not conducive to friendliness. "Manifest Destiny," even before it was called that, made it evident enough that the United States was going to covet Texas and all the territory up to the West Coast. That history needs no recounting, nor the dramatic episode of the Emperor Maximilian and the machinations of France, Spain and Britain while we were fighting a civil war.

We had French troops just below our border from 1861 to 1867, and a threat that went deeply into South America. It was the most open and perilous challenge to the principles of the Monroe Doctrine and to republicanism in the New World since the beginning of the century. One might say that the Monroe Doctrine came of age at that time. It was recognized in the United States as a major national policy; it was enforced; it won respect in Latin America and acknowledgment in Europe.

Even Mexico and all of South America appreciated that the United States and Latin America would have to stand together if European intervention was to be blocked. European statesmen could go on scoffing at the Monroe Doctrine, but they knew they could not challenge it with impunity.

Then—in 1910—came the revolution, which Mexicans proudly point out preceded the Russian Revolution by seven years. There also came the violence and anarchy that a profound social upheaval brings, unless or until a strong leader takes over to keep order. The United States being a neighbor, with investments and land holdings worth a billion dollars and more than 40,000 nationals in Mexico, and the American President from 1913 on being an idealist determined to bring the gospel of democracy and morality to all concerned, whether they wanted it or not, it was inevitable that there should be trouble.

The activities of President Wilson from 1913 to 1917 were the most blatant, inexcusable and futile examples of interventionism in the history of our relations with Latin America. He encouraged and armed Carranza and Villa against Huerta in 1913 and occupied the port of Vera Cruz. The mediation of the ABC powers (Argentina, Brazil and Chile) at the time was intended to end with the elimination of Huerta, as it did.

Instead of internal peace and constitutional government, there was anarchy. Pancho Villa deliberately provoked armed intervention by a series of murderous outrages in Mexico and even across the border. Gen-

151

eral Pershing's forays were as futile as Wilson's policies. Meanwhile, war with Germany was imminent.

To be fair to ourselves, Mexico was, indeed, a difficult neighbor in the post-revolutionary period, and as great power politics go, the United States was patient and forbearing. The turbulent period eased up in 1920 with the election of General Álvaro Obregón, but it was another fourteen years before internal peace was really established under Lázaro Cárdenas, and he provoked the United States, not to say Great Britain, by national-izing the oil industry in 1938.

Despite all earlier provocations and pressures, the United States Senate unanimously passed a resolution on January 25, 1927, calling for the arbitration of all outstanding issues and thus rejecting intervention.

That was when President Calvin Coolidge had the wisdom to send Dwight D. Morrow, the Morgan firm partner, to Mexico as Ambassador. His diplomacy has ever since been a model of understanding, fairness and practical accomplishment. For most historians, the Good Neighbor policy really began with him.

Imperialism fades away

With victory in the First World War leaving us so strong and Europe so weak, security was achieved—at least we thought it was. Instead of im-perialism there was isolation, disarmament, the liquidation of commit-ments. The stage was set for the Good Neighbor policy. The Kellogg-Briand Pact of Paris in 1928, which outlawed war as an instrument of national policy, was based on the assurance that no European nation was again going to intervene in a physical, territorial sense in Latin America. Even in this respect it was unrealistic, but the sense of security was what dictated policy.

From the Latin American viewpoint, the problem was to get the United States to give up its right to intervention. A denial of the right to inter-vene on behalf of the nationals of a foreign country was brought up at the very first International American Conference in Washington in 1889. The United States did not agree at the time.

The perennial drive for the codification of "American International Law" which is still a goal of the inter-American system, had at its heart the sovereign equality of all states before the law. This principle was unani-mously accepted as early as 1916 in a "Declaration of the Rights and Duties of Nations." Article IV states: "Every nation has the right to terri-tory within defined boundaries and to exercise exclusive jurisdiction over its territory, and all persons whether native or foreign found therein."

It was inevitable that the Roosevelt Corollary of "police power" had to be abandoned. "The Monroe Doctrine," as Secretary Kellogg put it, "is simply a doctrine of self-defense."

152

The pronouncement which is taken as signifying the end of the Roosevelt Corollary never got beyond the stage of a memorandum, but it was published as an official document by the State Department in December 1928. This was the restudy of the Monroe Doctrine by J. Reuben Clark, Jr., then Under Secretary of State to Secretary Kellogg. It restored the Doctrine to its original purpose of defending the hemisphere against European interventions and in the process discarded the Roosevelt Corollary. However, the right of intervention by the United States was not yet abandoned.

During the Hoover Administration the principle of using non-recognition to condemn governments installed by violent revolutions was dropped, at least in theory. Yet a delay by the United States in recognizing the government of Ramón Grau San Martín in Cuba (Sept. 1933-Jan. 1934) resulted in his collapse by what he aptly called "intervention by inertia." In the same way swift recognition by the United States and the European powers, followed by Latin American recognition, confirmed the Mendieta government in power in January, 1934. The result was to bolster the real ruler of Cuba, the then Colonel Fulgencio Batista, with the idea that he could and would restore order. This, in effect, installed a dictatorship in Cuba. It was a clear example of intervention by manipulating the diplomatic instrument of recognition. There is yet to be an accepted policy on the principle of recognition, as Dr. Fenwick's study in the appendix to these papers demonstrates.

Meanwhile, the Good Neighbor policy had got under way. The famous phrase appeared with apparent casualness and without even a particular reference to Latin America, in President Franklin D. Roosevelt's first inaugural address on March 4, 1933.

"In the field of policy," he said, "I would dedicate this nation to the policy of the good neighbor—the neighbor who resolutely respects himself and because he does so, respects the rights of others—the neighbor who respects his obligations and respects the sanctity of agreements in and with a world of neighbors."

Professor Bemis in his "Latin American Policy of the United States" interprets the Good Neighbor policy as being made possible by the disappearance of any danger from Europe after the First World War. This was no doubt a great consideration, but the development of nationalism, the pervading atmosphere of sovereign dignity with its outlet in the League of Nations, the natural reaction to dollar diplomacy and Marine intervention, the growth of industrialism and self-sufficiency, the wave of liberalism—the whole historic conjuncture—would have made something like the Good Neighbor policy obvious and necessary.

If, now, "international communism" were to provide a serious new danger from Europe (or conceivably China) it would not destroy the Good Neighbor policy. We would try (as we did, however clumsily, in

153

the case of Guatemala) to work within and through instruments of good neighborliness like the Organization of American States.

The doctrine of nonintervention

In expatiating on the Good Neighbor concept and putting it into practice, F.D.R. was, with one vital exception, essentially carrying on the policies of Coolidge, Hoover, Hughes, Kellogg and Stimson. President Roosevelt's Assistant Secretary for Inter-American Affairs was Sumner Welles, to whom the United States and Latin America owe so much in the formulation of policy in this happy period.

The feature that President Roosevelt, his Secretary of State Cordell Hull and Mr. Welles added was acceptance at last of the principle of nonintervention. Only then did Pan-Americanism become a complete doctrine. It could not have come sooner because the United States was still in occupation in Haiti and Nicaragua and still utilized the Platt Amendment giving us the right to intervene in Cuba. Moreover, the consistent hostility and rivalry of Argentina, which felt herself to be the legitimate leader of South America, made a true Pan-American policy all but impossible.

By the time of the Seventh Inter-American Conference at Montevideo, in December, 1933, both the United States and Argentina were vying for the laurel of champion of nonintervention. At the meeting, Secretary Hull let the Argentine Foreign Minister Carlos Saavedra Lamas, take the limelight.

Article VIII of the Montevideo agreement declared: "No state has the right to intervene in the internal or external affairs of another."

Secretary Hull still reserved American rights under "the law of nations as generally recognized," but even this last, weak barrier was to be swept away at the Special Inter-American Conference for the Maintenance of Peace at Buenos Aires in December, 1936, at President Roosevelt's orders. This could be done because at this meeting the American governments accepted the principle of consultation and collaboration in disturbances of the peace.

Meanwhile, American intervention or the right to intervene was ended in Cuba, Panama, Haiti and the Dominican Republic. The Platt Amendment not only led us into a number of interventions, but we used the right to control Cuba's fiscal policies. This, at least, had encouraged American capital to a total of about one billion dollars, half or more in the sugar industry, and since sugar was the mainstay of Cuba, control of the industry in effect was control of Cuba's economy, as the regime of Fidel Castro is now reminding us. However, in practice American treaty rights were not abused, either to win unusual favor for our nationals or to abuse Cuban rights. The antagonism aroused by the Platt Amendment in Cuba was in general nationalistic and, in particular cases, the result of the desire of Cuban individuals to manipulate their own financial polices for their private benefit, and on the part of some politicians who were trying to get in and divide the spoils of office. It would nevertheless be wrong to underestimate the genuine patriotism and sense of national dignity that impelled most Cubans to demand untrammeled freedom.

In these days it may seem strange for Americans to claim credit for not doing what should not have been done, but it is a fact that the opportunities to annex Cuba were frequent over more than a century, the pressure to do so was rarely absent, and as the world went in those days, it would have been a not unnatural thing to do. United States citizens are therefore entitled to feel some pain when caustic historians, like the Cuban, Herminio Portell Vilá, or young leaders like Fidel Castro who have read only the Cuban historians, talk of the Platt Amendment as if it were an instrument of Yankee imperialism at its worst.

After a last intervention in Cuba (in 1933 to get Machado out, and in January 1934 to install a government run by Batista) the United States Senate (May 31, 1934) abrogated the Perpetual Treaty of Relations of 1903, including the hated Platt Amendment. We retained the lease on the naval base at Guatánamo Bay.

This was an impressive demonstration of the acceptance by the United States of the principle of nonintervention. Cuba was strategically of enormous importance, and it was the Latin American country where our investments were then the heaviest.

The mistake made by the Cubans after Machado (and the United States has its share of the blame) was not to have a genuine social revolution. The price paid for this weakness and folly was a quarter of a century of corruption and misgovernment, ending in a period of terrible brutality and civil war.

In 1933, the United States sought to avoid a drastic solution of Cuba's ills. In a sense it was as if a doctor forbade an operation and allowed his patient's illness to get desperate. President Roosevelt sent Sumner Welles to Havana as Ambassador with express instructions to get the murderous and predatory dictator, President Gerardo Machado out, but to ease him out by suggesting he take a leave of absence of the Presidency. Mr. Welles succeeded in August, 1933—and the drastic operation on the body politic which was so necessary was postponed until 1959.

A year later—in 1934—the United States abandoned its last treaty rights to intervene in Central America, and the last Marines were withdrawn from Haiti. The treaty giving us rights to intervene in Haiti was allowed to expire in May, 1936. Then, in July, 1939, the United States Senate ratified the treaty with Panama that abolished our protectorate. Finally, our treaty rights in the Dominican Republic were ended in March, 1941.

155

The way was prepared to liquidate these last interventions at the Buenos Aires Conference in December, 1936. There were a "Convention for the Maintenance, Preservation and Re-establishment of Peace" providing for consultation, and a "Special Protocol Relative to Non-intervention." The latter—a key document in the relations of the United States with Latin America read:

> Article I. The High Contracting Parties declare inadmissible the intervention of any one of them, directly or indirectly, and for whatever reason, in the internal or external affairs of any other of the Parties.
> The violation of the provisions of this Article shall give rise to mutual consultation, with the object of exchanging views and seeking methods of peaceful adjustment.
> Article II. It is agreed that every question concerning the interpretation of the present additional Protocol, which it has not been possible to settle through diplomatic channels, shall be submitted to the procedure of conciliation provided for in the agreements in force, or to arbitration, or to judicial settlement.

From then on the problem was to be: What is intervention within the terms as understood by us and the Latin American countries? The military power and economic supremacy of the United States were such that whatever we did or did not do influenced the internal affairs of every one of the twenty nations below the Rio Grande. This meant that in a practical sense we were always going to "intervene."

The questions, in these practical, although not necessarily legal terms, therefore became: "What was deliberate and what unavoidable intervention?" "What was acceptable and what unacceptable?" "When were trade and fiscal policies a means of intervention?" "When did the sale of arms keep a government in power against the will of the people?" "Was recognition—or non-recognition—of new governments being used as an instrument of policy?" And so forth.

This is not to argue that the principle of nonintervention was not of supreme importance. It did put an end to direct, open intervention by American Marines, by management of customs, by fiscal controls of national indebtedness, by economic sanctions, by unilateral action. It put legitimate "intervention" in the hands of the organized community.

However, it should be noted that when President Eisenhower thought Vice President Richard M. Nixon's life was endangered in Caracas, Venezuela in May, 1958, he ordered Marines to two Caribbean posts to be in readiness to invade Venezuela. Had they been used, the whole carefully built structure of nonintervention might have come crashing down. The mere threat to use them has shaken the faith of many Latin Americans in the principle they value so highly.

Psychologically, formal acceptance of the doctrine of theoretically complete and absolute nonintervention was enormously beneficial. It was the major accomplishment of the Roosevelt Good Neighbor policy.

Pan-Americanism and the United States

By a happy coincidence, the full flowering of the Good Neighbor policy occurred simultaneously with the spectacular rise of German Nazism. It was to prove a valuable countermovement. A dissatisfied and critical Latin America, such as we have had in recent years, could have proved a much more fertile ground for fascism than it was in the Second World War.

As it happened, by the time German Nazism and Italian Fascism had become a serious threat, the Good Neighbor policy, so aptly conceived and so brilliantly carried out, had transformed United States relations with Latin America in a favorable way.

The change, it can be said, was one of spirit. It cost nothing in dollars or material aid. Its essence was to give up rights of intervention, tutelage, and—up to a point—even leadership. The beauty of it, from Washington's point of view, lay in its negative quality. To desist from doing things that we had been doing was relatively easy. There was an element of risk, and specific American interests sometimes suffered, but on balance the policy paid off handsomely.

It was not until this postwar period, when good neighborliness required positive measures of economic and financial aid and a spirit of understanding and sympathy with social and industrial revolutions and with the democratic aspirations that gathered force against the military dictators, that the Good Neighbor policy, as distinct from the policy of continental security, became difficult.

The threat to the Western hemisphere in the 1930's came, of course, from the fascism of Germany, Italy and Japan, and above all, the imperialism of Nazi Germany. We think so much in terms of international communism now that we are inclined to forget even such recent history as the appeasement period, isolation and the enemy we fought in World War II. Had England succumbed and the Axis won the war quickly, the threat to the United States and to democracy in the Western hemisphere would have been appalling.

Many of us believe that our enemy is totalitarianism, whether of the Right or the Left, especially as the two are so much akin to each other. The policy followed by the United States since the war—that we will fight communism at all costs in every country but will not lift a finger to prevent or even oppose right-wing dictatorships—is shortsighted. These dictatorships, strictly speaking, are not fascist, but they are fascistoid, and they do create a climate which opens a way to an upsurge of communism when the dictator is ousted. The only effective defense against communism is democracy, not dictatorship.

At any rate, getting back to the Second World War, the Good Neighbor policy paid dividends. The United States could act with the knowledge that nearly all the Latin American states would work together, first for a neutrality that gave Britain and France a fair break, and after Pearl Harbor, either for benevolent neutrality in our behalf or, in most cases, for active support. Argentina was an ugly exception under her military officers, among whom Colonel Juan Perón was becoming important. Chile was tardy but came along with us in due course.

The "no-transfer" principle that came into being in 1811, when we feared that Florida might go to Britain or France, reasserted itself in declarations against the transfer of the British, French or Dutch colonies to "another non-American State," as the 1940 Act of Havana put it.

American policy went through a confusing and contradictory period after the break between Sumner Welles and Secretary Hull in 1943. Mr. Welles deserves great credit for the success of the Good Neighbor policy. Few American statesmen have had his understanding of Latin American problems. Nelson Rockefeller, Assistant Secretary for American Republics Affairs, after Hull retired in late 1944, was also an excellent and wise influence, but he did not stay long enough to make any permanent mark.

The history of our relations with Argentina then and until the fall of Perón in 1955 could be used as a classic example of how not to conduct Latin American diplomacy. Although the ruling group was pro-Axis in the war, Sumner Welles rightly argued that intervention would only unite Argentines against the United States and behind the military. Secretary Hull nevertheless got tough, with results that Welles had foreseen.

After a brief period of calm while Nelson Rockefeller was in charge of Latin American policy, there was another setback when Spruille Braden went to Buenos Aires in mid-1945 as President Truman's Ambassador and reopened hostilities. His activities in the presidential election of February, 1946, gave Perón a most effective slogan: "O Perón o Braden" (i.e., "Your choice is either Perón or Braden").

To make matters worse, Washington published a "Blue Book" on pro-Nazi activities in Argentina which was accurate but which should have been published after, not just before, the elections.

The results of our policies were so obviously bad that a change was necessary. However, we went to the other extreme and appointed one friendly Ambassador after another with the single exception of Ellsworth Bunker who, before Vice President Nixon invented the phrase, gave a mere handshake to the dictator. We ended up with a notably friendly Ambassador, the later Albert F. Nufer, whom General Perón had asked be kept at his post and not transferred.

Argentina ought to have taught the United States that Latin American dictators should neither be attacked nor embraced. Unfortunately, although we stopped attacking dictators we did not stop embracing them.

The other Latin American states would not accept the blackballing of Argentina, as they showed when the Foreign Ministers met without Argentine representation in Mexico City in February-March 1945, on the eve

150

is under the control of the government's Yacimientos Petrolíferos Fiscales, and the North American companies cannot set up their usual large staffs and towns and all that goes with them.

In broad outline, what needs to be done and what should be done are obvious enough. In the report that Dr. Milton Eisenhower made to the President after his trip to Central America in July, 1958, he wrote:

Neither the people nor their leaders seek financial grants, save in a few isolated and emergency situations. Rather, they want public and private credit in increasing quantities, stable trade relations, greater stability in the prices of raw commodities which they sell, and technical assistance designed to hasten overall development primarily through improvement in education, health and agricultural and industrial productivity.

Secretary Acheson can also be quoted in an equally admirable condensation of the ideal American policy. This was in his speech to the Pan-American Society on September 19, 1949, already cited.

"These then are our three major objectives," he said, "the security of our nation and of the hemisphere; the encouragement of democratic representative institutions; and positive cooperation in the economic field to help in the attainment of our first two objectives."

But the real problem, of course, is implementation—how to put these policies into effect.

Walking along the razor's edge between intervention and nonintervention, leadership and partnership, is always going to be supremely difficult. The influence of the United States, because of our wealth, power and Latin America's need of aid, must in any circumstances constitute a form of "intervention." The problem is to make it an influence that Latin Americans desire. Leadership is necessary since we have the money, the goods, the know-how, the nuclear weapons, the world power, the prestige, the democratic traditions and practices that Latin American countries either lack or do not possess as a whole or in large measure. The goal of this leadership is to win trust, loyalty and support, and to set an example that will make all men of good will and democratic ideals in Latin America want freely to follow us.

In many respects we have been going counter to the stream of Latin American history. We have gone astray since the great days of the "Good Neighbor" policy when we and they were surging forward together. That the wave of democracy sweeping over Latin America in the last four years should have overwhelmed us as well as the dictators—and the resentments against the United States in all the affected countries proves this—shows how badly conceived our policies have been.

American policy makers will forget to their peril that the great, if vague, clumsy and blundering trend toward democracy which has swept over Latin America, and the concurrent demands for social justice, are led by the youth. The boys and girls who fought and survived in Argentina, Colombia, Venezuela and Cuba are the ones who will direct the futures of their countries. Even where older and more experienced democratic laders have taken over, they must satisfy the aspirations of the younger generations.

Youth is constitutionally impatient, over-sure of itself, imbued with high ideals that are not always practical in our imperfect world, courageous to the point of rashness, indifferent to the sufferings and discomforts of maturity and age. In Latin America the young are extremely nationalistic, and that means either outright anti-Yankeeism or a willingness to disregard the consequences of plucking feathers from the American Eagle's tail.

A wise policy will recognize what Dr. Arturo Morales-Carrión, Puerto Rican Under Secretary of State, described as

> . . . the strength and intensity of their purpose, and their high and passionate devotion to a new way of democratic life, to good and honest government and to an emerging sense of unity with other liberal groups across national boundaries. . . . The United States should begin to attune its ears to the democratic clamor in Latin America. It should not expect the upcoming generations to behave like British parliamentarians. It is a tough generation. They will not be easy to deal with. No profit-making philosophy will persuade them. No rosy propaganda will win them over. Only the conviction that freedom is something to be shared by all, that democracy is not a word but an active, living faith, that one must always look beyond a government to the people, will provide a true basis for heart to heart understanding.

For many Latin Americans this problem of understanding on the part of North Americans deserves first priority. They see the need for a new spirit that will revolutionize our mutual relations as the Good Neighbor policy did in the 1930's. Understanding can only come with knowledge, and it would bring sympathy and patience.

There has been a gap between us which does not exist with Europe. These are, in truth, our neighbors and yet they are more remote from our feelings and thoughts than the nations separated by the Atlantic Ocean.

Our press and news magazines give much less space to Latin American than to European news. As a result when a big story breaks like the Cuban Revolution, there is such widespread ignorance and misunderstanding that the whole picture is distorted almost beyond recognition. This could not happen if a revolution occurred in Europe.

Where is the new spirit to be found? In sharing and helping the democratic resurgence; in accepting and even encouraging the social revolution, which is a wave now engulfing the area; in "Good Partnership" as President Eisenhower put it.

These are neither precise nor dramatic policies, nor would they be entirely new. We do not need to search for a phrase, for something to catch the imagination. In any event, we could not by ourselves transform the hemispheric scene. New policies and a new spirit are just as necessary below the Rio Grande as above.

There are no panaceas, no easy solutions, no dogmas, no formulas, no all-wise, omniscient conferences to settle the problems of our relations with Latin America. It is a field that embraces twenty-one countries at different stages of progress and maturity, different in size, population, wealth, race, history, traditions.

Humility might almost be a first requisite for the student, the diplomat or the man-in-the-street. There are no "experts" on Latin America; there are only degrees of ignorance. Yet those who work with open and friendly minds in this vast field will not, in Bolívar's sad phrase, be "ploughing the water." The reward for the North American and for the United States government could be a rich one.

Perhaps the wisest progression would be thus: sympathy, knowledge, understanding, patience, patience, patience. . . .

A note on recognition policy:

Latin American governments and the United States

CHARLES G. FENWICK

No more controversial question can be found in the whole field of international law than that of the recognition of the new governments which come into power from time to time in violation of the procedures fixed in the constitution of the state. Some general principles are accepted, and to that extent it is a legal problem. But inasmuch as the other members of the international community are free to use their own individual judgment as to whether the conditions of recognition have been met, the problem is a political one, with divergent national policies.

We are dealing here with the recognition of new governments, not of new states such as are from time to time admitted as members of the international community. Obviously when a new state is admitted into the

CHARLES G. FENWICK is Director of the Department of Legal Affairs, Pan-American Union. He was Professor of Political Science at Bryn Mawr College from 1920 to 1940. In 1936 he was United States delegate to the Conference on the Maintenance of Peace, and in 1938 to the Eighth International Conference of American States. In 1942-1947 he was United States Member of the Inter-American Juridical Committee. Dr. Fenwick is author of *Neutrality Laws of the United States, International Law, Cases on International Law,* and *The Inter-American Regional System.* In 1952-1959 he was associate editor of the *American Journal of International Law.*

international community the government of the former colony or dependency which applies for recognition is recognized at the same time with the new state. But that is only an incident in the larger issue of statehood; and once recognition of statehood is attained, governments may come and go without in any way affecting the corporate personality of the state.

It is an accepted principle of international law that every sovereign state has the right to organize itself according to what it believes to be its own best interests, and to change at will its form of government. Normally changes in government take place in accordance with constitutional procedures which, in determining the organization of the state, provide for the succession of one government to another. When, therefore, the succession takes place according to these constitutional procedures there is direct continuity between government and government, and no question of a *new* government arises. Recognition is automatic, if it can be called recognition. Under such circumstances we call the government a *de jure* government, that is, a legally constituted government, which, as such, has the right to represent the state, to act in its name, to pledge its good faith, to enter into treaties and to contract other less formal obligations, all of which, being within the constitutional powers of the government, pass from government to government until fulfilled.

But when, in violation of constitutional procedures, a new government comes into power as the result of a revolution the question arises immediately whether it has to be accepted by other states as the lawful government. May the new government claim forthwith the rights of the state in relation to other governments and expect them to treat with it as the lawful representative of the state? Obviously other states will not feel obligated to accept the new revolutionary government as the lawful *de jure* government just because it says it is. They may think it safer to wait and see how stable the new government is; whether it can hold its own against the government which it has dispossessed; whether it appears to have the support of public opinion, so as to give some assurance of permanence; whether in a broad sense it is sufficiently identified with the life of the state to assert its rights and be responsible for its obligations.

These questions may be expected to present themselves to other states as they observe the situation created by the new government; and they are in themselves questions of fact. They are sometimes described as the *objective* conditions of recognition, conditions which have no connection with the policies of the new government, but merely with its representative character. But although questions of fact, they are not always so clear as to lead all other states to arrive at the same conclusion; and it is to be expected that the desire of one government to see the revolution succeed, and of another government to see the revolution fail, will naturally influence on occasion its conclusion as to the facts. Hence the record of history shows

196

that one government may recognize the new revolutionary government and another refuse to do so, in the presence of the same facts of the situation.

Some leading cases

With this background we may proceed to examine some of the leading cases that have arisen in the foreign policy of the United States toward the Latin American states and, then, later, draw conclusions from them. Thirty years before the Latin American states made their entrance into the international community, Thomas Jefferson as Secretary of State, when presented in 1792 with the question of recognizing the government of the French Revolution, laid down the broad rule, to which the Department of State frequently asserts it has held ever since: "It accords with our principles to acknowledge any government to be rightful, which is formed by the will of the nation, substantially declared." Apparently Jefferson took it for granted that the National Convention represented the will of the French people; but here perhaps his sympathies may have influenced his thought; in any case he did not ask for other evidence than what appeared to him to be the case. Any suggestion of a practical test would have been out of the question. The leaders of the French Revolution were in no mood for a plebiscite.

For the next half century the policy of the United States followed fairly consistently along Jefferson's lines, Secretary Martin Van Buren declaring in 1829, with reference to the new government in Colombia: "So far as we are concerned, that which is the government *de facto* is equally so *de jure*." Secretary James Buchanan went so far in 1849 as to say that it was sufficient for us to know "that a government exists capable of maintaining itself; and then its recognition on our part inevitably follows"; but in this case he was referring to a change in the government of France, which, being a charter member of the international community, might well command greater respect for its changes of government. In neither case, however, was there any reference to the will of the nation, even as it might be assumed under the circumstances.

The question next arose as to what constituted a *de facto* government. In 1856 President Franklin Pierce elaborated the designation by referring to a "government *de facto* accepted by the people of the country," adding that their determination might be "by positive action or by ascertained acquiescence." A *de facto* government clearly meant more than a mere temporary group in control of the offices of state. It implied some degree of stability, and in implying stability implied sufficient acquiescence of the people to insure stability. Decisions with respect to the approval or the acquiescence of the people might naturally be influenced by the political development of the country. What might be expected of France could

197

hardly be expected of countries, like many of the Latin American states, less compactly organized. In 1855 the United States found the government of Rivas-Walker in Nicaragua not to be *de facto,* because it appeared to be "no more than a violent usurpation of power, brought about by an irregular self-organized military force, as yet unsanctioned by the will or acquiescence of the people of Nicaragua."

But as the years went by new subjective tests were added to the objective test of the *de facto* character of the government. Was the new government coming into power by revolution ready to carry out the obligations of the state? That could, of course, be assumed from the mere fact that it set itself up as the government of the state. Conditions might exist, however, which would throw doubt upon the succession of the new government to the obligations of the old. Suppose the former government had entered into a treaty believed by the leaders of the revolution to be so detrimental to the welfare of the state as to justify them in repudiating its obligations. So also for other obligations of a less formal character. Perhaps it would be safer in such a case for the state with which the treaty had been made to require of the new government a pledge that it would carry out the obligations of the treaty. An example had been set in Europe when the Great Powers had proclaimed in the London Protocol of 1831 that "treaties do not lose their binding force whatever changes take place in the international organization of peoples."

Thus it was that the United States began to insist that the recognition of a new government should call for a statement from it that it would respect the obligations of treaties and in general abide by the obligations of international law. Revolutions in Latin America had become so numerous and the tenure of certain governments so insecure that recognition by the United States carried weight, with the result that the United States could use recognition for bargaining purposes; and one of the objectives sought was naturally a pledge that treaties and other international obligations would be carried out. In 1876 the United States decided to wait before recognizing General Porfirio Díaz as President of Mexico until assured that his election was approved by the Mexican people and that his administration was "possessed of a stability to endure and of disposition to comply with the rules of international comity and with the obligations of treaties." By contrast, however, the new Government of the Republic in Brazil, established in 1889 following the deposition of the Emperor, was recognized without any requirement of acceptance of international obligations, although respect for contracts and engagements was voluntarily proclaimed by the new government; and pending the delay in formal recognition, provision was made for the maintenance of friendly diplomatic relations with the provisional government.

It was to be expected that insistence upon a declaration as to the obligations of international law would be an opening wedge to exactions of a broader character on the outer fringes of international law. Suppose an earlier government had made concessions to foreign investors for the development of natural resources, or contracts for the construction of public improvements which the revolutionary government might consider to have been unwisely made, or made under conditions which suggested that concessions or contracts were no more than personal obligations of the deposed government. Might a pledge on the part of the new government to respect such agreements be made a condition of recognition? If so, recognition would have departed far from its original purpose of accepting the new government as the legal representative of a sovereign state. On its part the United States, seeking on occasion to protect important economic interests of its citizens, felt justified in taking advantage of the opportunity to exact promises of fulfillment, while the Latin American governments looked with suspicion upon what they considered the abuses of recognition and denounced the procedure in strong terms as unwarranted "intervention."

There were clearly two sides to the problem, largely due to the rapid succession of revolutionary governments, which made it difficult for the United States to apply merely the general principle of stability and the acquiescence of the people, and which encouraged the exaction of special pledges from military leaders whose background did not suggest that they could be counted upon to carry out the normal obligations of a government. An extreme instance of the demand of the United States for an agreement upon the settlement of outstanding questions as a condition antecedent to recognition is to be seen in the list of questions set forth by the Department of State in 1913 in the case of General Adolfo de la Huerta of Mexico, a few weeks before the assassination of President Francisco I. Madero led to denial of recognition on other grounds. Included in the list were the settlement of a boundary question and a prompt agreement upon the distribution of the waters of the Colorado River.

With the turn of the century a new phase of the problem was presented. Could the procedure of recognition be used as a means of discouraging the numerous revolutions which had come to be a grave disturbance of the general peace? Perhaps an agreement beforehand by a number of states to refuse to recognize governments coming into power not as the result of a popular revolution seeking to depose a dictator, but merely as the outcome of a barracks conspiracy having as its primary objective the seizure of the offices of government for the promotion of the fortunes of the individuals concerned. The five Central American States set an example in 1907, signing a treaty by which they pledged themselves not to recognize governments coming into power by revolution against a constitutional government until such time as freely elected representatives of the people had constitutionally reorganized the country. Revolutionary governments might thus in due time be recognized, but not until the will of the people had been concretely demonstrated.

In the same year, 1907, the Foreign Minister of Ecuador, Carlos R. Tobar, proposed that the American Republics collectively should, for their own good name as well as for humanitarian considerations, intervene in the internal dissensions of the hemisphere by refusing to recognize *de facto* governments coming into power by revolutions contrary to the constitution of the country.

The United States, although not directly involved in the Central American project, gave its support to it, as it did to the Central American treaty of 1923 which went even further than the treaty of 1907, providing that even subsequent constitutional reorganization would not be sufficient to justify recognition of new governments if connection should be indicated between the new government and the leaders of the revolution, described as a "dynastic succession of dictators." But in the meantime President Woodrow Wilson had attempted a more or less similar experiment in discouraging revolutions which, undertaken unilaterally, had unfortunate results.

President Madero, who had been duly elected President of Mexico, was overthrown by a barracks revolution in 1913 and subsequently killed while being taken into custody. Should the United States recognize his successor and thus appear to accept the new government as representing the Mexican people and competent to speak in their name? Wilson, the idealist, taking office at the time, refused to do so, declaring that the United States could have "no sympathy with those who seek to seize the power of government to advance their own personal interests or ambition." The policy was interpreted by other states as implying the right of the United States to inquire into the constitutional legitimacy of the new government, and it met with widespread criticism in Latin America. Two full years elapsed between the *de facto* recognition of President Venustiano Carranza in 1915 and his *de jure* recognition in 1917; and again two years between the election of President Álvaro Obregón and his formal recognition in 1923. The long controversies attending the effect of the new Mexican constitution of 1917 upon the interests of American citizens in Mexico led the government of that state to reject the whole doctrine of recognition as an unwarranted intervention in its domestic affairs.

Was it possible to get a general agreement on the question of recognition? Clearly there was need of one, for each state was following its own policies, and conditions which were approved by one state to justify recognition did not so appear at times to another. In 1925 the American Institute of International Law drafted a convention proclaiming that "Every abnormally constituted government may be recognized if it is capable of maintaining order and tranquility and is disposed to fulfill the international obligations of the nation." It may be observed that there was no suggestion of the principle of constitutional legitimism that President Wilson had proposed in 1913 and that had figured in the Central American treaty of 1923. Two years later the draft of the Institute was accepted in substance by the International Commission of Jurists meeting in Rio de Janeiro in 1927, emphasis being put upon effective authority with a probability of stability and upon the capacity to discharge preexisting international obligations and to respect the obligations of international law. But the conference that met in Havana the following year failed to take action upon the draft.

Two years later, influenced doubtless by the recent controversies with the United States, the Foreign Minister of Mexico, Genaro Estrada, proposed the outright repudiation of the practice of recognition, designating it as an "insulting practice," offending the sovereignty of the state and implying the right of other states to pass upon the internal affairs of the state. The maintenance or withdrawal of ambassadors was proposed as an alternative; but no test was proposed for determining whether a revolutionary group calling itself the government of the country was actually in sufficient control to justify the maintenance or the withdrawal of diplomatic representatives. In contrast with the Estrada Doctrine, the leading Latin American writers, while recognizing the abuses frequently attending the practice of recognition, accept the practice as a necessity of international intercourse, due to the necessity of determining whether the new government can properly create obligations for the state and claim the rights pertaining to it.

World War II and after

New issues in respect to recognition arose with the entrance of the United States into the Second World War following the attack upon Pearl Harbor. The danger that an organized group in sympathy with the Axis Powers might take over the government of a Latin American state led the Meeting of Consultation at Rio de Janeiro in 1942 to create an Advisory Committee for Political Defense, as it was called, for the purpose of studying means of preventing subversive activities; and ten months later the Committee adopted a resolution recommending that the American governments refrain from recognizing a new government established by force until consultation had taken place to determine whether it was complying with inter-American commitments for the defense of the continent, and under what circumstances it had come into power. While the resolution met with a favorable response from the American governments as a whole, including the United States, a number of them were careful to point out the danger of intervention if the procedure of consultation and common action were to be carried beyond the existing circumstances of the war.

201

As the war drew to a close the problem came up again before the conference at Mexico City in 1945, where two distinct and opposing tendencies were manifested. Guatemala took the lead with a proposal to deny recognition to "anti-democratic" governments in general, on the ground that by denial of the fundamental rights of the people they constituted a menace to the peace, emphasis being put upon governments resulting from a *coup d'état* against legitimately established governments. Ecuador, reversing the position taken by Señor Tobar in 1907, insisted that the right to change governments belonged to the class of domestic questions, and that any attempt on the part of foreign states to exercise moral coercion in such cases was a violation of the principle of non-intervention.

Both projects were referred to the Inter-American Juridical Committee for study and report; but here also there was diversity of opinion, a majority of the Juridical Committee agreeing that it was not possible to abolish the procedure of recognition; but within this majority one formula based recognition upon effectiveness of control and the other formula upon the "will of the people, freely expressed."

Again at the Conference at Bogotá in 1948 the same conflicting points of view appeared, but this time it proved possible to agree upon a resolution which at least laid down a practical rule for the first stages of the problem. As between the extreme position of eliminating altogether the procedure of recognition and that of the delegation of Uruguay withholding recognition in cases of the grave violation of human rights, the United States proposed a general statement that continuity of diplomatic relations was desirable, and that the establishment or maintenance of diplomatic relations with a government did not involve any judgment upon the internal policies of that government. A Mexican amendment clarified the proposal by the provision that the right of maintaining, suspending or renewing diplomatic relations should not be exercised as a means of individually obtaining advantages under international law.

Thus amended the United States proposal was adopted as Resolution XXXV of the Bogotá Conference, and in spite of its limitations it marked a significant step forward. There still remained, however, the problem of agreeing upon the tests to be applied to determine whether a particular government should be accepted as representing the state and authorized to claim its rights and assume its obligations. The adoption of the multilateral Treaty of Reciprocal Assistance a year earlier, imposing specific obligations upon all the parties in the event of a two-thirds decision in a case of alleged aggression, had given a new importance to the procedure of recognition; so that the Conference found it desirable to adopt a supplementary resolution calling upon the newly created Inter-American Council of Jurists to prepare a report on the subject to be submitted to the next conference.

In anticipation of the meeting of the Council of Jurists, the Inter-American Juridical Committee, representing the American Republics as a body, prepared a draft convention which was duly submitted to the first meeting of the Council at Rio de Janeiro in 1950. The draft followed the traditional lines of the American Institute of International Law in 1925 and of the International Law Commission of 1927, Article 1 declaring that a *de facto* government had the right to be recognized whenever it fulfilled the two conditions of effective authority over the national territory, based on the acquiescence of the people manifested in an adequate manner, and of ability and willingness to discharge the international obligations of the state. In addition the draft followed the resolution of 1948 in rejecting the procedure of recognition as a means of obtaining special advantages from the *de facto* government; and it introduced additional provisions condemning the withholding of recognition as a sanction, fixing the accountability for future acts of the government so recognized, and proposing an exchange of information among the American governments upon request of any one of them for the purpose of clarifying the *de facto* situation. Two strong dissenting opinions were entered.

When, however, the draft prepared by the Juridical Committee was presented to the Council of Jurists, twenty-one in number and each expressing the policy of his own country, the traditional differences reappeared. The United States delegation took the position that recognition was not a "right," that the tests governing recognition were not juridical in nature, and that it could not subscribe to the effort of certain of the delegations to give them that character. The same position was taken when an attempt was made to prescribe the observance of fundamental rights as a condition of recognition. The result was that the Council of Jurists got no further than a resolution to continue the study of the problem at its next meeting.

But once more, the second meeting of the Council of Jurists in 1953 failed to come to an agreement, and Resolution III of the Final Act of the meeting recited that as a result of the discussions that had taken place it was the "almost unanimous opinion" of the delegates that it was as yet premature to conclude a convention on the subject, and that it was not even advisable to formulate the principles governing the practice of recognition as set forth from time to time by writers. The Bogotá rules, it was declared, were sufficient. Two of the delegates protested, on the ground that the mandate of the Bogotá Conference called for something more than such a summary dismissal of the subject, the rules laid down at Bogotá still having left other problems unsolved.

While the resolution of the Second Meeting of the Council of Jurists called for the transmission of the drafts and documents to the Tenth Inter-American Conference, the subject failed to appear on the agenda of the Conference, indicating, as clearly as need be, that the governments saw no hope of reaching an agreement.

No new problems have arisen of recent years to lead the United States to modify the policy set forth in the resolution adopted at Bogotá in 1948. On January 1, 1959, the Government of President Fulgencio Batista in Cuba was overthrown by a revolution under the leadership of Fidel Castro, and on January 7, within six days of the advent of the new government to power, the United States gave full *de jure* recognition to it. The promptness with which *de jure* recognition was given was questioned as a matter of expediency, but it in no way marked a departure from traditional policy.

The principles of recognition

What now, in summary, are the principles of recognition accepted by the United States, and what the unsolved problems in respect to which each individual state has reserved the right to arrive at its own decision in the presence of specific cases?

1. As late as 1931 Secretary Henry L. Stimson, in an address before the Council on Foreign Relations, stated that the practice of the United States in the matter of the recognition of new governments had been "substantially uniform" from the days of Secretary Jefferson in 1792 to the days of Secretary William Jennings Bryan in 1913, and he quoted with approval a statement of Assistant Secretary Alvey A. Adee in 1913, as follows:

> Ever since the American Revolution, entrance upon diplomatic intercourse with foreign states has been *de facto,* dependent upon the existence of three conditions of fact: the control of the administrative machinery of the state; the general acquiescence of its people; and the ability and willingness of their government to discharge international and conventional obligations. The form of government has not been a conditional factor in such recognition; in other words, the *de jure* element of legitimacy of title has been left aside.[1]

The statement is as authoritative as any that might be cited. Perhaps it was going too far to say that there had been substantial uniformity in the policy during the years mentioned; but the decision on that point would depend upon a recognition of the fact that the circumstances presented to the United States in its relations with the Latin American States during the nineteenth century varied greatly on occasion from those contemplated by Jefferson, and account must be taken of them in passing upon the subsequent development of the simple condition laid down by Jefferson of acknowledging "any government to be rightful, which is formed by the will of the nation, substantially declared."

2. The United States reserves to itself the decision as to what constitutes a *de facto* government, as distinct from a merely transient government which, by a military *coup d'état,* might take over the administrative machinery of the state for a time without assurance of permanence. The con-

---

[1] *Foreign Relations of the United States,* 1913, p. 100.

dition that the new government must be in control of the administrative machinery of the state would appear to imply something more than a temporary assumption of the offices of government; so that in a particular case it would be a matter of judgment on the part of the Department of State whether the new government was sufficiently integrated into the juridical order of the state to be accepted as a *de facto* government.

In like manner the United States interprets for itself what constitutes "the general acquiescence of the people," a modern form of stating Jefferson's "will of the nation, substantially declared." Popular elections are not considered necessary as evidence of the "will of the nation"; but they have been regarded as the best indication of it when held without fraud or intimidation; and the pledge of popular elections has rightly been regarded by the United States as evidence of the probable stability of the government.

3. The United States still considers it desirable on occasion to require that new governments give assurance of their intention to observe the obligations of treaties and the rules of international law.

The more general practice, as illustrated in the recognition of Fidel Castro in January, 1959, is that the new government, upon assuming power, proclaims its intention of complying with its international obligations and agreements, and then, in conferring recognition, the United States notes with satisfaction the assurances given. On the other hand the practice, followed on occasion in the past, of requiring, as a condition of recognition, a pledge of certain conduct or the adoption of certain policies not within the scope of the obligations of international law, has now been abandoned in Latin American relations. A resolution (XXXV) of the Bogotá Conference, approved by the United States, declares "That the right of maintaining, suspending or renewing diplomatic relations with another government shall not be exercised as a means of individually obtaining unjustified advantages under international law." The scope of the word "unjustified" was not defined, but it would appear to include special concessions and other favored treatment which the recognized government is not under a legal obligation to grant.

4. The United States has, in general, opposed collective action as a procedure of recognition, on the ground, it would appear, that there is not as yet general agreement upon the conditions of recognition, so that any attempt to adopt a collective policy would create a confusion of counsels. In one case, however, the United States accepted as a war measure the proposal of the Committee of Political Defense in 1943 that a new government established by force should not be recognized during the duration of the war until consultation had taken place to determine whether it was complying with inter-American commitments for defense, and information had been exchanged relative to the circumstances under which it had come

205

into power. The need of a collective decision in the matter of recognition might arise, on occasion, if a case were presented under the Rio de Janeiro Treaty of Reciprocal Assistance in which a two-thirds decision would determine the action to be taken; and the vote of the particular country would or would not count, depending upon the recognition or non-recognition of a new government by as many of the states as were necessary to the decision.

5. The United States now follows the practice of maintaining continuity of diplomatic relations with new Latin American governments, as provided by the Bogotá resolution of 1948; that is, normal contacts are maintained pending the decision whether the new government can meet the conditions calling for recognition. The advantages of this policy are that it gives time for a more careful study of the situation without in the meantime creating an atmosphere of doubt and perhaps antagonizing the new government and making difficult the establishment of more formal relations. The maintenance of informal diplomatic relations has also the advantage of enabling a government to avoid being hurried into *de jure* recognition by the fact that other states are recognizing the new government more promptly, thus suggesting that the country which delays recognition may not be as friendly to the new government as others are.

6. The distinction between *de facto* recognition and *de jure* recognition, that is, between recognition of a government as *de facto* in control and recognition of the same government as the legal representative of the state is still maintained, but not always clearly expressed. Normally the procedure marking the transition from the one to the other is by means of a formal statement by the diplomatic representative of the United States in the particular country expressing the pleasure of the United States in continuing friendly relations with the country through the new government. As observed above, the earlier policy of basing recognition upon the *de facto* character of the new government and nothing more is not the practice of today, unless the words *de facto* are taken in the broadest sense of a government meeting the three conditions of recognition.

7. It is not to be expected that the policy of the United States in the matter of recognition should at all times have proved to be rigidly consistent. The difficulty of judging the stability of a government and its ability to perform the international obligations of the state has led on occasion to decisions which proved to be mistakes of judgment as to the circumstances rather than mistakes of policy. The wide variations in the constitutional traditions of different states have led to corresponding differences in the treatment of individual cases, in some instances recognition being practically automatic and in other instances being delayed for varying periods. Naturally the policies declared by the Department of State would thus vary in the different cases; and general principles have been

declared which, while correct under the circumstances, were not applicable to other cases. The transition of the government of France from republic to monarchy and back again could be recognized with little more delay than a mere succession of constitutional governments, as in 1830, 1848, 1853, and 1870; and no attention whatever has been paid to the transition from one Republic to the other, the latest, under General Charles de Gaulle, being the Fifth.

8. Consistency has also been lacking in the use of terms, due largely to the variety of circumstances under which the conditions of recognition have been applied. As noted above, the term *de facto* was frequently used at an earlier period to indicate a government which was stable and which had the apparent support of the people; and in such cases it was correct for the Secretary of State to declare in 1848 that the United States had always followed the policy of recognizing *de facto* governments. On other occasions the term *de facto* has meant nothing more than a government that is in actual control for the time, but which has not yet met the conditions of recognition. Perhaps the criticism of President Wilson's policy in respect to General Huerta in 1913 would have been less severe if, instead of proclaiming a doctrine of "constitutional legitimacy," which Latin America interpreted as intervention, the President had withheld recognition on the ground that a government coming into power under the circumstances could hardly expect to have the support of public opinion behind it, followed by a declaration that subsequent approval by the Mexican people would have led to reconsideration of the situation.

9. While the policy accepted by the United States at Bogotá in 1948 of continuity in the maintenance of diplomatic relations would suggest that some less formal relations might be established with a new government, pending decision as to its stability, the Department of State actually recognized the new government of Fidel Castro in Cuba at the end of six days. Doubtless the reason for such prompt action was to manifest to the people of Cuba the sympathy of the United States with the change of government— a sympathy which, because of the principle of non-intervention, the United States was not able to express at an earlier stage.

10. The United States has always looked upon the procedure of recognition as a necessary condition of the relations of states and, therefore, as not being open normally to the criticism of unwarranted intervention in the domestic affairs of the state whose government is recognized. The fact that a new government, when recognized, becomes, in respect to the government recognizing it, the legal representative of the state, with the corresponding competence to claim the rights of the state and to assume its obligations, makes the act of recognition one of supreme importance, not to be lightly undertaken. The inquiry which is occasionally necessary into the conditions under which the new government has come into power and

the methods by which it is maintaining itself is, therefore, not an unjustified attempt to pass upon the constitutional legitimacy or illegitimacy of the regime existing in the particular country, but rather a right on the part of other states to assure themselves that those who have set aside the procedures of constitutional government and who proclaim themselves to be the legal representatives of their country are actually in control of the government and have behind them sufficient support of public opinion to justify the claim they are making both to assert the rights of the state and to create obligations binding future governments of their country. Looked at in that light, the procedure of recognition, kept within its proper limits, is a highly democratic act, protecting the people of the state against acts of an irresponsible government which a succeeding government might be tempted to disclaim as not having been within its lawful powers.

Final report of the
Sixteenth American Assembly

At the close of their discussions the participants in the Sixteenth Assembly at Arden House, Harriman, New York, October 15-18, 1959, on THE UNITED STATES AND LATIN AMERICA, reviewed as a group the following statement. Although there was general agreement on the Final Report, it is not the practice of The American Assembly for participants to affix their signatures, and it should not be assumed that every participant necessarily subscribes to every recommendation included in the statement.

Introduction

The importance of Latin America to the United States needs public emphasis and heightened awareness of what the area means to us politically, economically and culturally. We are bound to each other by geographical and historical ties and by many commonly held ideas and aspirations.

In its relations with Latin America, the United States must set an example of democracy, using its influence and resources for the good of all countries in the hemisphere, for basic moral values as well as other reasons of long-range self-interest.

Unless we participate wholeheartedly in determined attacks on continued widespread poverty among Latin American peoples, our own relatively advanced standards of living and our democratic way of life will be threatened. We must identify ourselves with the aspirations of the Latin American peoples for social reforms, higher standards of living and greater educational opportunities. We are in favor of genuine movements of social change which are consonant with representative democracy.

Latin America is our most important investment and trading area. The two-way trade of some $8,000,000,000 a year makes each of us the other's

209

largest trading partner. United States private investments of over $9,000,-000,000 and United States government investments exceeding $2,000,000,-000 are playing a significant part in Latin American economic development.

Part of our trade comprises some thirty strategic materials. In any but a swift and completely destructive nuclear war, inter-American cooperation is vital to the survival of Western civilization. The denial of its products to our industry, the hostile control of any Latin-American country, however remote that eventuality seems today, would point up the necessity for cooperation between Latin America and the United States.

North Americans must realize that Latin Americans differ from the United States in a number of respects—social, economic and political. Latin America is an area of considerable diversity, though there are certain features in common. It is marked by great population increase and is undergoing the early phases of an industrial revolution. The people of the region come from mixed racial strains of European, African and Indo-American origin. There is a sharp contrast between the cultural, social and economic conditions in the cities and the countryside.

There is a necessity to learn about and understand Latin America and its beliefs, ideas, emotional reactions and way of life. It was agreed that such knowledge is generally lacking, that the leaders in the mass communications field should provide, and the readers of newspapers, the listeners and viewers of radio and television should demand, more information and skilled interpretation.

The consensus in the Assembly was that there is a large public which would be interested in more Latin American news and comment if the material were provided. It was also felt that in many cases where such interest is absent an intelligent public demand can be aroused.

The Assembly made various suggestions for remedying these difficulties, United States editors should go to Latin America to learn about the area at firsthand. Latin American affairs and languages should be taught more widely in our schools, colleges and universities. Increased travel by United States citizens in Latin America is desirable.

The exchange-of-persons programs should be extended for university students, teachers, journalists, trade union leaders and others, without neglecting the arts and humanities. For the same reasons, funds should be provided to expand the activities of private and public educational agencies working in Latin America.

Economic policy

An important objective of United States economic policies toward Latin America should be to cooperate with Latin Americans in helping to raise their standards of living. In this process the industrial development and diversification of their economies, the improvement of their agriculture and the modernization of communications are basic.

Since many Latin American nations are dependent on exports of raw materials, the need for greater price stability and more dependable markets in the United States and elsewhere was recognized. There was a consensus that the United States should participate in cooperative efforts by Latin American countries to stabilize the prices of major primary products.

Fifteen Latin American countries are exporters of coffee. The recent agreement of the Latin American, African and European countries to regulate the sales of coffee in world markets was recognized as an achievement of great potential value in which United States government support played an important role. However, without effective control of coffee production, the long-range benefits of price stabilization cannot be maintained.

Considerable concern was expressed at the rising tide of protectionist sentiment in this country and of narrow economic nationalism in some parts of Latn America. If these trends continue they will not only impede trade between the United States and Latin America, but may also seriously reduce the effectiveness of United States cooperation in Latin American development.

It was emphasized that the United States should provide reliable access to its markets for goods sold by Latin America. It was also noted that domestic policies that involve the subsidizing of United States production, and particularly United States exports, should be continuously reviewed in the light of their disrupting effects on Latin American agricultural and mining programs.

Economic progress to improve standards of living in Latin America will require massive amounts of capital for investment which will have to be drawn from all possible sources, private and public, domestic and foreign. Private investment in large and small industries will have to play the greatest role in such development.

The encouragement of such investment requires the creation and maintenance of equitable conditions and fair safeguards, including prompt and adequate compensation in the event of expropriation, on which responsible private investors, both existing and prospective, can rely. In addition, these nations should continue to be able to borrow from public and international agencies for sound projects for which private capital is not available.

There was agreement that the movement toward regional economic arrangements such as common markets and educational cooperation in Latin America should receive the support of the people and the government of the United States. In this way these nations will be able to expand their production and markets.

211

Communism

The danger of communism in Latin America was noted. The best answer to communism is to help raise the standards of living and encourage social justice, democratic governments and free trade-union structures. At the same time, we are opposed to dictatorial movements of every kind. The enemy is totalitarianism at both extremes of Left and Right.

On both sides of the Rio Grande a better understanding of each other's attitude toward communism is desirable. The world position of the United States compels us to treat communism as a primary threat to the security of the free world. To some Latin Americans this danger does not always seem to have the same priority. Yet we all face the same ultimate peril from communism.

Awareness of the different approaches toward meeting Communist threats will make it easier to achieve a united front against the common enemy's efforts to communize the world. A greater effort should be made to stimulate a keener understanding of the immediate and long-term tactics and dangers of communism in Latin America.

The nations of the Western hemisphere share the same strategic aim of opposing communism, but the tactical means of achieving this aim may differ from country to country. Organizations which are developing positive programs against Communist infiltration were endorsed by the Assembly.

The full scope of Communist effort to influence Latin America through cultural methods has not been realized in the United States or Latin America. Communist China and the Soviet Union are believed to be spending more than $100,000,000 annually in Latin America in furthering propaganda campaigns.

It was recognized that the Communist argument that the rapid industrialization of the U.S.S.R. and China should be models for Latin American countries is proving effective as propaganda. The destruction of human values inherent in Communist methods must be exposed. At the same time, it must be demonstrated that higher standards of living can better be achieved through the maintenance of free institutions and the economic procedures of the free world.

It is believed that international communism is attempting to prepare the ground for an eventually decisive bid for control in Latin America. In the near future, international communism is likely to intensify its efforts to create discord between Latin America and the United States.

Military relations

We consider that our military programs should place even greater emphasis on training, technical aid and education of military personnel and

212

that the United States should encourage the use of Latin American military resources for support of economic and social objectives in so far as can be done, while carrying out their security missions. We believe the United States should press more effectively against maintenance of excessive or inappropriate armed forces in Latin American countries and should administer its assistance programs accordingly.

Political and diplomatic relations

Consistent with the traditional American opposition to tyranny, the United States supports the strengthening of democratic institutions, including periodic free elections as well as freedom of the press, assembly, religion and the development of governments which respect basic civil liberties and the rule of law, which are representative in form and which fulfil the principles of the Organization of American States.

We should avoid helping regimes which fail to observe these principles but should support policies which will help raise the levels of education and health and standards of living of people under these tyrannies.

Government officials and private organizations should avoid giving decorations, honors and unnecessary hospitality and praise to dictators or their military or civilian representatives.

The principles of the United States are clear, but it was recognized that in our efforts to encourage democracy we will be faced with a variety of particular situations requiring a choice and timing of methods. The problem in each country may be different, and therefore no precise policy in this regard could be formulated.

The Assembly strongly supported the collective security system of the Organization of American States and its effective use to prevent and resolve international controversies and threats to peace. It was felt that this regional body could be strengthened in other fields to achieve even better results in the future.

In order to meet the extraordinary and complex problems of the Latin American nations, we need the best people available to represent us in important positions in our embassies and other government agencies. For the majority of the diplomatic posts, career diplomats should be appointed, but other qualified groups should not be excluded. Appointments should not be made as political rewards. The Latin American countries being not only so important to but so different from our nation also requires that all representatives of the United States, official and unofficial, should be especially qualified.

At all times our policy and our actions should make manifest that we want for Latin Americans what they want for themselves—democracy, a

213

higher standard of living, industrialization, social reforms. In seeking these goals the cooperation of all nations of the Organization of American States is required.

Participants in the
Sixteenth American Assembly

MILDRED ADAMS
New York

ROBERT J. ALEXANDER
Professor of Economics
Rutgers University

GEORGE V. ALLEN
Director
United States Information Agency

HENRY W. BALGOOYEN
Executive Vice President
American & Foreign Power
Company
New York

ARTHUR BALLANTINE, JR.
Publisher
Durango Herald-News
Colorado

EDWARD W. BARRETT
Dean
Graduate School of Journalism
Columbia University

ROBERT D. BARTON
Director
Inter-American Department
Institute of International Education
New York

JAIME BENITEZ
Chancellor
University of Puerto Rico

WILLIAM BENTON
Publisher
Encyclopaedia Britannica
New York

WILLIAM McC. BLAIR, JR.
Stevenson, Rifkind & Wirtz
Chicago

During the Assembly participants heard formal addresses by Dr. Milton S. Eisenhower, president of The Johns Hopkins University, and Dr. José Figueres, former president of Costa Rica.

ROY BLOUGH
Professor of International Affairs
Columbia University

DUDLEY B. BONSAL
Curtis, Mallet-Prevost, Colt &
  Mosle
New York

ROBERT R. BOWIE
Director
Center for International Affairs
Harvard University

FRANK H. BOWLES
President
College Entrance Examination
  Board
New York

SEYMOUR BRANDWEIN
Economist
AFL-CIO
Washington

HAROLD M. BRIGGS
Rear Admiral, U. S. N.
Director, Pan-American Affairs
  and United States Naval Missions
Washington

COURTNEY C. BROWN
Dean
Graduate School of Business
Columbia University

FREDERICK BURKHARDT
President
American Council of Learned
  Societies
New York

REYNOLD E. CARLSON
Professor of Economics
Vanderbilt University

JOHN COWLES
President
Minneapolis Star & Tribune
Minnesota

JOHN C. DREIER
U. S. Representative on the Council
  of the Organization of American
  States
Washington

ANGIER BIDDLE DUKE
New York

WILBUR EDWARDS
Harriman Scholar
Columbia University

MILTON S. EISENHOWER
President
The Johns Hopkins University

RUSSELL C. EWING
Head, Department of History
The University of Arizona

M. H. FARNSWORTH
The Coca-Cola Export Corporation
New York

JOSÉ FIGUERES
San Jose, Costa Rica

GEORGE P. GARDNER, Jr.
Chairman
United Fruit Company
Boston

LINCOLN GORDON
Professor of International
  Economic Relations
Harvard University

FRANCES GRANT
Secretary General
Inter-American Association for
  Democracy and Freedom
New York

216

LEWIS HANKE
Professor of Latin American History
University of Texas

W. AVERELL HARRIMAN
New York

H. J. HEINZ, II
Chairman
H. J. Heinz Company
Pittsburgh

DAVID HELLYER
Latin America Editor
The San Diego Union
California

T. F. X. HIGGINS
Executive Director
The Foreign Policy Association of
Pittsburgh

HENRY FINCH HOLLAND
Roberts & Holland
New York

KENNETH HOLLAND
President
Institute of International Education
New York

JOSEPH L. JONES
Vice President
United Press Associations
New York

ROBERT J. KLEBERG, JR.
King Ranch, Texas

ALLAN B. KLINE
Western Springs, Illinois

JOHN KONVALINKA
Harriman Scholar
Columbia University

G. A. LINCOLN
Colonel, U.S.A.
Head, Department of Social
Sciences
United States Military Academy
West Point

ROSS L. MALONE
Roswell, New Mexico

HERBERT L. MATTHEWS
The New York Times

L. F. McCOLLUM
President
Continental Oil Company
Houston

ADDISON PARRIS
Committee for Economic
Development
Washington

MOREHEAD PATTERSON
Chairman, American Machine and
Foundry Company
New York

JAMES A. PERKINS
Vice President
Carnegie Corporation of New York

JEAN B. PERKINS
Princeton

JOSHUA B. POWERS
Editors Press Service
New York

THE REV. DAVID B. REED
The National Council of the
Protestant Episcopal Church
New York

SERAFINO ROMUALDI
Inter-American Representative
AFL-CIO
Washington

217

ROY R. RUBOTTOM, JR.
Assistant Secretary of State
Washington

DAVID A. SHEPARD
Executive Vice President
Standard Oil Company (N. J.)
New York

K. H. SILVERT
American Universities Field Staff
New Orleans

WILLIAM K. SKAER
Brigadier General, U.S.A.F.
Director of Staff
Inter-American Defense Board
Washington

JOSEPH E. SLATER
International Affairs Program
The Ford Foundation
New York

JAMES H. STEBBINS
Executive Vice President
W. R. Grace & Company
New York

ADLAI E. STEVENSON
Chicago

FRANK TANNENBAUM
Professor of Latin American History
Columbia University

A. THOMAS TAYLOR
Chairman
International Packers Ltd.
Chicago

W. HOMER TURNER
Executive Director
United States Steel Foundation
New York

ROBERT WAUCHOPE
Director
Middle American Research Institute
Tulane University

SAMUEL C. WAUGH
President
Export-Import Bank of
Washington, D. C.

ALFRED C. WOLF
Director
Overseas Development Program
(Latin America)
The Ford Foundation
New York

PHILIP YOUNG
Harriman Scholar
Columbia University

ARNOLD J. ZURCHER
Executive Director
Alfred P. Sloan Foundation
New York

The American Assembly

219

Since its establishment by Dwight D. Eisenhower at Columbia University in 1950, the American Assembly has held assemblies of national leaders and has published books to illuminate issues of United States policy.

The Assembly is a national, non-partisan, educational institution, incorporated under the State of New York.

The Trustees of the Assembly approve a topic for presentation in a background book, authoritatively designed and written to aid deliberations at national Assembly sessions at Arden House, the Harriman Campus of Columbia University. These books are also used to support discussion at regional Assembly sessions and to evoke consideration by the general public.

All sessions of the Assembly, whether national or local, issue and publicize independent reports of conclusions and recommendations on the topic at hand. Participants in these sessions constitute a wide range of experience and competence. The following institutions have cooperated or are scheduled to cooperate with the Assembly in sponsoring regional, state or municipal sessions across the country:

Stanford University
University of California (Berkeley)
University of California (Los Angeles)
University of Wyoming
University of Denver
University of New Mexico
University of Oklahoma
Dallas Council on World Affairs
The Rice Institute
Tulane University
Southwestern at Memphis
Duke University
University of Florida
Emory University
University of Illinois
Minnesota World Affairs Center
University of Washington
University of Puerto Rico
Lawrence College

Cleveland Council of World Affairs
University of Missouri
Washington University
Drake University
Indiana University
University of Vermont
Tufts University
Foreign Policy Association of Pittsburgh
Southern Methodist University
University of Texas
Town Hall of Los Angeles
North Central Association
United States Air Force Academy
University of Arkansas
Michigan State University
Kansas City International Relations Council
Vanderbilt University
University of Arizona

220

American Assembly books are purchased and put to use by thousands of individuals, libraries, businesses, public agencies, non-governmental organizations, educational institutions, discussion meetings and service groups. The subjects of Assembly studies to date are:

1951 — UNITED STATES-WESTERN EUROPE RELATIONSHIPS

1952 — INFLATION

1953 — ECONOMIC SECURITY FOR AMERICANS

1954 — THE UNITED STATES STAKE IN THE UNITED NATIONS
— THE FEDERAL GOVERNMENT SERVICE ($1.00)

1955 — UNITED STATES AGRICULTURE
— THE FORTY-EIGHT STATES (State Government)

1956 — THE REPRESENTATION OF THE UNITED STATES ABROAD ($1.00)
— THE UNITED STATES AND THE FAR EAST ($1.00)

1957 — INTERNATIONAL STABILITY AND PROGRESS
— ATOMS FOR POWER ($1.00)

1958 — THE UNITED STATES AND AFRICA ($2.00)
— UNITED STATES MONETARY POLICY ($2.00)

1959 — WAGES, PRICES, PROFITS AND PRODUCTIVITY ($2.00)
— THE UNITED STATES AND LATIN AMERICA ($2.00)

Prices indicate available books

Regular readers of the American Assembly receive early copies of each Assembly study and are billed subsequently.

Future Assembly book subjects include The Federal Government and Higher Education and The Secretary of State.

To enroll as a regular reader, or for additional information, please address: The American Assembly, Columbia University, New York 27, New York.

221